12/23

# Imagining America at

In this highly topical, well-written and stimulating book, Cynthia Weber explores the relationship between film and politics, and—more specifically—cinema and war. Using the events of 9/11 as a watershed, she illuminates how ten films released (and re-released) after this date reflect fierce debates about US foreign policy and a more fundamental debate about what it means to be an American. These films include: *Pearl Harbor* (World War II); *We Were Soldiers* and *The Quiet American* (the Vietnam War); *Behind Enemy Lines*, *Black Hawk Down* and *Kandahar* (episodes of humanitarian intervention); *Collateral Damage* and *In the Bedroom* (vengeance in response to loss); *Minority Report* (futurist pre-emptive justice); and *Fahrenheit 9/11* (an explicit critique of Bush's entire war on terror).

This is not just another book about post-9/11 America: it fills a significant gap—as the notion of self-understanding and national identity is rarely discussed in a systematic and scholarly way. *Imagining America at War* will be of great interest to students of American Studies, US Foreign Policy, Contemporary US History, Cultural Studies, Gender and Sexuality Studies, and Film Studies.

**Cynthia Weber,** herself American, is Professor of International Relations at Lancaster University, UK. She is the author of numerous articles on US foreign policy and US hegemony, as well as several books about international relations.

# Imagining America at War

## Morality, politics, and film

Cynthia Weber

LONDON AND NEW YORK

First published 2006
by Routledge
2 Park Square, Milton Park, Abingdon, Oxfordshire OX14 4RN

Simultaneously published in the USA and Canada
by Routledge
270 Madison Ave, New York, NY 10016

*Routledge is an imprint of the Taylor & Francis Group*

© 2006 Cynthia Weber

Typeset in Sabon by
HWA Text and Data Management, Tunbridge Wells
Printed and bound in Great Britain by
TJ International Ltd, Padstow, Cornwall

*British Library Cataloguing in Publication Data*
A catalogue record for this book is available from the British Library

*Library of Congress Cataloging in Publication Data*
Weber, Cynthia.
     Imagining America at war : morality, politics and film
     / Cynthia Weber.
       p. cm.
     1. National characteristics, American, in motion pictures.
     2. War films—United States—History and criticism. I. Title.
PN1995.9.N34W43 2005
791.43'658—dc22                                        2005012064

ISBN10: 0–415–37536–3 (hbk)     ISBN13: 978–0–415–37536–8 (hbk)
ISBN10: 0–415–37537–1 (pbk)     ISBN13: 978–0–415–37537–5 (pbk)

# Contents

# Acknowledgments

This project began on September 11, 2001, when I started to wonder what the US response to the terrorist attacks in New York City, Washington, D.C., and Pennsylvania would be and what that would mean for "America" and "Americans," not just politically but morally. Like most of us, I read the daily papers, listened to radio accounts, and spoke with hundreds of people about the 9/11 attacks. This book has been enriched by all those engagements. In particular, though, as the direction of this project at the intersections of post-9/11 cinema and US foreign policy began to emerge, a number of people had a direct impact on my thinking and writing.

Sasha Roseneil and I had countless discussions about 9/11, morality, America and Americans, and US and British foreign policy in the months after 9/11. At the same time, I engaged in parallel conversations with Annette Davison about 9/11, cinema and politics, and post-9/11 films. Though Sasha, Annette, and I did not always agree, I doubt this book would have taken the form it has without those early conversations.

As I began drafting sections of this project and presenting these ideas publicly, I benefited from comments by staff, students, and visitors at the Australian National University; the University of Copenhagen; York University in Canada; the University of the Americas in Puebla, Mexico; Brown University; the New School University; Hobart and William Smith Colleges; the University of Florida; Cambridge University; the University of Bristol; the University of Leeds; and Birmingham University, as well as participants at the International Studies Association annual meetings in New Orleans in 2002 and in Portland in 2003 and the ESRC-sponsored Critical Boundaries project. In particular, Robert Albritton, Jens Bartelson, Shannon Bell, Thomas Biersteker, Dider Bigo, Ricardo Blaug, Charlie Dannrather, James Der Derian, Julie Dowsett, Kevin Dunn, Ellen Freeberg, Jose Luis Garcia, Larry George, Lena Hanson, David Hesmondhalfh, Derek Hyrnshyn, Marianne Marchand,

Isidro Morales, Ruth Pearson, Jindy Pettman, Jo Shaw, Elizabeth Silva, and Ole Weaver made key intellectual interventions during these presentations. I thank them all.

I taught much of this material in a graduate course called "Moral Grammars of War" at the New School University in the Spring of 2003. My students there (Alana Chazan, Maya Joseph, Anne Kirkham, Evan Rowe, Amy Sodaro, Masha Spaic, and Roberto Trad) worked through this material with me. In so doing, each made an important contribution to this project. Additionally, I thank David Plotke of the New School University and Duncan McCargo of the University of Leeds for making it possible for me to spend my 2003 sabbatical at the New School University, and I thank Lily Ling for her support intellectually and personally, particularly while I was at the New School but also with the project generally. Lily, like John Howard, reviewed the prospectus for this book. Lily, John, and an anonymous reviewer all offered invaluable comments at that stage, and Lily and John continued to do so as I taught and wrote this book. Finally, I owe a debt to Patricia Molloy, not only for suggesting materials to teach on the Moral Grammars of War course but for her input into the project as it was developing at that stage, something I appreciated enormously given our shared interest in international politics and cinema.

When I moved from Leeds University to Lancaster University, where I finished this book, I had the opportunity to present the nearly finished work publicly to a large number of colleagues and students and to circulate drafts of the manuscript to several more. Thanks to Ngai-Ling Sum for organizing that presentation and to Mick Dillon, Mark Lacy, and Jackie Stacey for their critical feedback on drafts. My greatest debt in Lancaster is to Anne-Marie Fortier, who not only read and commented on the final manuscript but provided me with support and encouragement as I brought this project to a close and began to think about the next one.

Beyond Lancaster, my two most persistent readers—Francois Debrix and my father, Charles Weber—also read and commented on the manuscript in its final stages. As always, thank you.

An earlier version of Chapter 2 appeared in *Millennium* as "Flying Planes Can Be Dangerous" [31(1):129–47, 2002] and appears here with permission. The journal's editors at the time, Elisabetta Brigeri and Harry Bauer, caught my early missteps and challenged me to clarify key concepts in the project. Thank you. A portion of Chapter 4 appeared in *International Feminist Journal of Politics* as "Not without my Sister(s): Imagining a Moral America in *Kandahar*" and portions of Chapter 6 appeared in *Geopolitics* as "Securitizing the Unconscious: The Bush doctrine of Pre-emption and *Minority Report*" and in *Journal of American Studies* as "*Fahrenheit 9/11*: the temperature where morality burns." All appear here with permission.

Finally, I thank Nicola Carr, who offered unwavering support for and critical input on the project as it developed, as did Jeremy Valentine and Benjamin Arditi. Last, I thank Heidi Bagtazo for seeing this project through to publication.

The publishers thank the following for permission to reprint their material:

*Geopolitics* & Routledge/Taylor and Francis for permission to reprint "Securitizing the Unconscious: The Bush Doctrine of Pre-Emption and *Minority Report*," *Geopolitics,* Vol. 10, 2005.

*Millennium* for permission to reprint "Flying Planes Can Be Dangerous," *Millennium*, Vol. 31, No. 1, 2002, pp. 129–47.

Routledge/Taylor and Francis for permission to reprint "Not Without My Sister(s): Imagining a Moral America in *Kandahar*," *International Feminist Journal of Politics*.

Cambridge University Press for permission to reprint "Fahrenheit 9/11: The Temperature Where Morality Burns," *Journal of American Studies*, © Cambridge University Press, with permission.

# 1   Introduction

On a Saturday after that Tuesday, September 11, 2001, I extracted myself from my cocoon of newspaper, television, and radio reports long enough to go to the cinema. I was not alone. Record numbers of people in the West flocked to cinemas in the weeks after the terrorist tragedies. I (a US citizen living in Britain) went to my neighborhood cinema because I sought an escape from catastrophe and a return to calm. There I lost myself in an extravagant production in which—for a full two and a half hours—no one died. My sense of normalcy was temporarily restored, at least until I was exiting the cinema. Lulled as I was back into my old routines, I did what I usually do on leaving: I turned to the rack of advertisements masquerading as free postcards targeted at teens and 20-somethings. Among the images of the hip and the cool that Saturday was a photograph of a landing craft filled with Royal Marine Commandos outfitted in camouflage, their fingers on the triggers of their automatic weapons, their boat speeding through the open seas toward what one suspects is a foreign shoreline. The caption read, "Please take your seats. The show is about to start."

I could not have found this post-September 11 mixing of military recruiting and cinematic troping more chilling. Instantly, the postcard ruptured my sense of having accomplished a momentary escape from reality, reminding me that I was merely awaiting the next reel/real to roll in what would become known as the "war on terror'" and that the cinema was as much a battlefield in this war as were the ruins in New York, Pennsylvania, and Washington, D.C. and the cities and countrysides of the soon-to-be bombed Afghanistan and, later, Iraq.

Alerted as I was by this advertised fusion of cinema and war, from that day forward I began paying a lot more attention to films. I was especially interested in films that were playing in US cinemas between 9/11 (a moment when US foreign policy was being rethought) and the following summer (by which time the new Bush Doctrine of Preemption had cemented itself as a cornerstone of US foreign policy).

What I found was that it was not only the unfolding of official US foreign policy options that could be traced in these post-9/11 films (all of which were produced prior to 9/11 but released or re-released thereafter). More interesting, to me at least, was that a selection of these films was linked to an ongoing public debate in the United States that took on grander proportions after 9/11. That debate revolved around what is arguably a foundational question of US-ness—what does it mean to be a moral America(n)?—with the hemispheric term *America(n)* euphemistically (and some might say imperially) standing for the United States of America and its citizens.

September 11, 2001 arguably rendered another rethinking of US morality possible, for the events of that day shook US self-understandings to their very core: about who "Americans" are, about what "America" represents to the rest of the world, and about what Americans and America might be in this new, new world order. Yes, US citizens were traumatized by the events of 9/11, unable to put into words what September 11 meant for them and to them (Edkins, 2001, 2003), but even more striking than what US citizens could not articulate immediately after 9/11 was what many of them repeatedly posed as the simple question: Why do they hate us?

This question, like all us–them questions, has the power to fix who "we" are in relation to "them," something the Bush administration's official response—"we're the brightest beacon for freedom and opportunity in the world" (Bush, 2001a) and "they" are "the axis of evil" (Bush, 2002a)—certainly tried to do. However, in the moment of September 11, this question also offered the possibility for rethinking who we are, who they are, and what the relationships between us and them might be, as the glut of unofficial commentaries and political protests by many US citizens evidenced. Understood in this way, September 11 is a liminal moment in US history, not so much as a trauma that requires a national therapeutic response but rather as a "confrontation" (Lowenstein, 2001) or an "encounter" (McAlister, 2001) with questions that haunt US relationships both between self and other *and* with(in) the self (Weber, 1999). As such, these questions have the capacity to place America and Americans at the threshold of a "moral remaking" (Roseneil, 2001), culminating in the question, Who might we become?

As indicated by my own encounter with that fateful postcard, one important site in which this debate is staged is in cinemas, where the theaters of wars and the theaters of film are sometimes startlingly conjoined. Indeed, thinking about September 11 is almost impossible without thinking about film, whether one saw the events of that day in person or on television. A New York City resident who watched from the streets as planes flew into the twin towers told me her first thought was, "Someone is making a movie."[1] This blurring of reality and film— of real time and reel time—was endlessly repeated on CNN Headline News. Below its images of the twin towers collapsing, it ran a ticker tape that included not only the names of those known to have died in New York, Washington, and Pennsylvania but of Hollywood movies past and (then) future that depict similar events, films such as *Executive Decision*, *The Siege*, *The Peacemaker*, and *Collateral Damage* (Bhabha, 2001). Because Hollywood appeared to have foretold the future of terrorism better than the US government, the Pentagon formed the 9/11 Group. This Group was composed of Hollywood filmmakers and directed to brainstorm about future terrorist scenarios to better aid the Pentagon in securing the US homeland (*Panorama*, 2001). And commentators as diverse as such intellectuals as Slavoj Žižek (2002) and such scriptwriters as Michael Tolkin (2001) crowded onto the editorial pages with their testimonies of how the events of September 11 confirmed the postmodern collapsing of the real and the hyperreal, of reality and film. In all these ways, film functioned as a metanarrative for experiencing September 11.

Alongside its metanarrative function, film served other important functions in relation to 9/11 and its aftermath. In the weeks after the terrorist attacks, US movie-goers who may (like me) have been craving an escape from the realities of war and a return to normalcy all too often found themselves caught up in national debates about the status of the war on terror merely by going to the cinema. Was the war on terror "another Pearl Harbor," as governmental officials from the President on down declared? As 9/11 morphed into Pearl Harbor in US discourse, what did it mean to see the re-released film *Pearl Harbor* in the cinema just after 9/11? Was this a patriotic act? Was it a search for a strategic response to 9/11 (Zakaria, 2001)? Was it an act of mourning for the loss of US innocence, again (Crepeau, 2001)? Was it a moment of rekindling and reclaiming of historical moral outrage (Morrow, 2001)? Whatever it was, viewing *Pearl Harbor* in September 2001 was rarely (if ever) an escape from reality.

*Pearl Harbor* is a clear example of how a film circulating in post-9/11 America provided not a metanarrative for September 11 (9/11 is like film) but a specific historical and moral narrative about September 11 (9/11 is like *this film* and the historical events and moral codes it depicts). It might seem that *Pearl Harbor* is an exceptional case, for it is a film that happens to portray a specific historical event that was explicitly linked by many US citizens in and out of government to the war on terror. Yet, interestingly, so too were many other films that were produced prior to, but released or re-released, after 9/11. The re-release of the film *Kandahar* in November 2001 coincided with the Bush administration's claim that the plight of Afghan women was among its justifications for overthrowing the Taliban regime. Just about any film depicting military conflict or terrorism resonated with US audiences, regardless of its historical setting, from the Vietnam War film *We Were Soldiers* to the humanitarian intervention disaster *Black Hawk Down* to the revaluing of America's humanitarian mission in *Behind Enemy Lines* to the postponed Arnold Schwarzenegger vehicle about terrorism, *Collateral Damage*. And, of course, the tale of preemptive justice in *Minority Report*—released less than one month after the Bush Doctrine of Preemption became official US policy—was first linked to homeland security and later linked to the removal of Saddam Hussein (Lithwick, 2002; Lott, 2002; Edelstein, 2002a).

This selection of post-9/11 films marks a site in which official US foreign policy converged with popular symbolic and narrative resources to confront the "United States" with questions about its individual, national, and international subjectivities, especially in relation to the war on terror. Sometimes (as in the official rendition), traditional US moralities are confirmed in this cinematic space; at other times, they are confounded there. Either way, popular and official discourses of September 11 converge in this space to enable the production, reproduction, and transformation of everemerging US individual, national, and international subjectivities.[2]

*Imagining America at War* traces the unfolding of this encounter and the subjectivities it produces. It argues that between 9/11 and the following summer (when the United States and a very few of its allies made the decision to invade Iraq in what became known as Gulf War II), who Americans were as citizens and what America was as a national and international space was not only in flux (which it always is) but in crisis. The shock many US citizens felt by the events of 9/11 led to a national debate about what it means to be American individually, nationally, and internationally, and the terms of this debate were primarily moral. For US citizens, this debate wasn't just about what we ought to *do* in response to 9/11; it was about who we *are*—about how our responses to 9/11 morally configure us (a collective form of inclusion in the US nation) as individual, national, and international subjects and spaces.

A number of different *we's* compete for star billing in this debate as it is screened in post-9/11 cinema. These *we's* differ not only in terms of whether they describe individual or collective Americans or Americas. More interestingly, these *we's* vary in how each articulates a different inflection of US morality. Are *we* or should *we* be heroic, hurt, humble? Films from *Pearl Harbor* to *Collateral Damage* to *Minority Report* all offer different answers to this question by constructing distinct US *we's*. Indeed, there are as many *we's* in post-9/11 cinema as there are post-9/11 films. What these different *we's* do is anchor distinctive "moral grammars of war"— codes or contexts (or both) about the good and the bad that structure narratives of interpretation about war.[3] So, for example, in every case, the *we's* of post-9/11 cinema stand for a US-ness that is being constructed at the intersections of cinema, national trauma, and US foreign policy decision making but are portrayed as if US citizens and US-ness itself were already fixed, firm identities. Yet who *we* are or should be and how this *we* should guide our morality in a post-9/11 world—toward humanitarianism or toward vengeance, for example—is expressed differently in each film and in official and popular discourses about each.

*Imagining America at War* explores how these various US *we's* were mobilized in post-9/11 cinema to construct US individual, national, and international subjectivities as well as diverse historical trajectories for "becoming a moral American" and a "moral America." It traces the "official story" of US moralities by reading post-9/11 films not in order of their release dates but in order of the historical situations they portray. It argues that, read together, *Pearl Harbor, We Were Soldiers, Behind Enemy Lines, Black Hawk Down, Kandahar, Collateral Damage,* and *Minority Report* constitute a specific trajectory of US morality from past to present to future. This official morality tale unfolds in four parts, which might be subtitled as follows: who we think we were/are; who we wish we'd never been; who we really are; and who we might become.

Who we think we were/are recounts past US-ness through the World War II film *Pearl Harbor*, slipping into *who we think we are* with the post-9/11 morphing of the events of Pearl Harbor with those of 9/11. Who we wish we'd never been is the story of US involvement in Vietnam, patriotically renarrated through a mixture of traditional and contemporary US moralities in *We Were Soldiers*. Who we really are is a two-part morality tale: on the one hand, it is the story of US humanitarianism, whether expressed in episodes of humanitarian intervention in the 1990s (such as it is in *Behind Enemy Lines* or *Black Hawk Down*) or in the new millennium through the Bush administration's reading of

*Kandahar*. On the other hand, it is the celebration of justified vengeance in response to the tragic loss of home and family, as depicted in *Collateral Damage*. Finally, who we might become is an open-ended tale about making moral choices in our policy decisions and in our personal lives, as seen in the more critical futuristic film *Minority Report*.

What this four-part "official" rendering of becoming a moral America(n) clearly shows is how dependent moral understandings are on historical codes and contexts, on how the "grammar" of the story is as important as its narrativity. What is missing from this story so far are the specific characters who enact this US morality. Who are these *we's*, and where do they come from?

*Imagining America at War* argues that to understand the character(s) of US morality, one must investigate the character(s) of and in the US family. Fathers, mothers, sons, and daughters all figure predominately in cinema, and post-9/11 cinema is no exception. By examining precisely how these family characters are drawn in post-9/11 cinema, it is possible to get indications of how the official moral character of the United States is drawn, individually, nationally, and internationally. For, if the nation is a narration (or, in this case, a screening of various visual and narrative forms; Bhabha, 1990), it is always also a narration of the family (Sommer, 1991; Berlant, 1997; Hunt, 1992). In other words, [the desire for] the domestic of state and of nation is always already [the desire for] the domestic of home(life).

What this means for the trajectory in post-9/11 cinema for becoming a moral America(n) is that official public history alone does not tell this story. For what the moral history of the US is about is the moral movement within and between the imagined character(s) of the family and the nation. So, for example, *Pearl Harbor* is not only about World War II; it is about the gendered and sexualized codes required to produce the US imaginary of "the traditional family." *We Were Soldiers* is about how the patriarchal promises of WWII could not be translated into US foreign policy outcomes in Vietnam. *Behind Enemy Lines*, *Black Hawk Down*, and *Kandahar* are about the roles of post-Vietnam era sons and daughters in (re)making new moral orders. *Collateral Damage* is as much about vigilantism as it is about meddling mothers, one of the classic stereotypes of the feminine capacity to disrupt order. And *Minority Report* is a glimpse into what future US moralities based in future US families might be and become.

This official cinematic story of becoming a moral America(n) is, of course, deeply flawed. It is rife with lapses, contradictions, and imperfections, all of which are too easily skimmed over to present a seemingly coherent tale of a moral America(n) in the making. It relates neither a complete public history, a complete post-9/11 cinematic history, nor anything approaching real representations of the US family.

Missing from this particular public history, for example, are any discussions of the Korean conflict or Gulf War I, both of which arguably left unfinished business in their wakes (as attested to by the post-9/11 disputes about North Korean nuclear programs or two of the justifications for Gulf War II: finally "liberating" the Iraqi people and capturing Saddam Hussein). These historical omissions from the official US story are attributable to the fact that no films released in US cinemas between 9/11 and the summer of 2002 covered these conflicts (an interesting point in and of itself).

But what about the vast array of films that more critically engaged with various US *we's*, various US moral grammars of war, and various trajectories for becoming a moral America(n)? What about, for example, *The Quiet American*, which raises questions about US motives and actions in the build up to the Vietnam War? Or *In the Bedroom*, a quiet, complex morality tale that explores how unbearable grief leading to vengeance does not provide moral closure because it is not based on moral certainty? Unlike the film *Kandahar*, which was intended to be critical of US foreign policy but was couped by the Bush administration, neither of these films figures in the official story of becoming a moral America(n). Because these films did not fit—and could not be made to fit—the official story of post-9/11 US morality and did not support— and could be made to support—Bush administration foreign policy decisions from 9/11 to Gulf War II, they were ignored by the administration.

They are not ignored in *Imagining America at War*. *The Quiet American* is read alongside *We Were Soldiers* to challenge its patriotic reconstruction of the American soldier and the American family. *In the Bedroom* is paired with *Collateral Damage* to dislodge the moral certainty of vengeance. And *Kandahar's* "unofficial story" is read against the official stories of humanitarian intervention presented by the Bush administration and in such films as *Behind Enemy Lines* and *Black Hawk Down*. And to carry concerns about preemptive justice in *Minority Report* further, one film that was produced after 9/11 and released well after the Bush Doctrine of Preemption played itself out in Iraq—Michael Moore's *Fahrenheit 9/11*—is paired with it because of its explicit critique of Bush's entire war on terror.

What was also ignored in the official US story is how US families "actually" are configured in the contemporary US. Whether depicting the white, heterosexual nuclear family that is America's legacy and foundation from WWII in *Pearl Harbor*, the decline of the patriarchal family in *We Were Soldiers*, or even the contemporary multicultural family of *Collateral Damage*, this selection of post-9/11 cinema always pictures the American family wrongly. Far from reflecting anything like "real" representations of the family, these films project an idealized, desired account of the US family and US family life, best described through the title of Stephanie Coontz's book on US families, *The Way We Never Were* (2000). Like the forgotten moments of US public history and forgotten post-9/11 films, forgotten constructions of US families are insistently recalled in *Imagining America at War*.

By reading all these lapses in official US memory together, alternative US *we's*, US moral grammars of war, and historical trajectories for becoming a moral America(n) can be turned back onto the official story as a way of reopening debate about what it means to be a moral America(n) in light of 9/11. This move is applied to each specific story about the US *we* in individual chapters in this book and to the composite official US story about the US *we* in the conclusion of this book.

Theoretically, *Imagining America at War* is not claiming to be a unique project. Its arguments about morality, family, nation, and culture are nothing new. They are indebted to, for example, Lauren Berlant's work on US national fantasy and its relationship to the heterosexual nuclear family (1991, 1997); Sasha Roseneil's argument that yearnings for a new moral order may be found in spontaneous, collective (cultural) responses to national (political) tragedies because "the political" is thoroughly imbricated in "the cultural" (2001); Camilla Grigger's notion of becoming a subject in a mass-mediated American culture (1997); Homi Bhabha's claim that the nation must be understood through narrative practices (1990); Michael Shapiro's mapping of global politics through his notion of moral geographies (1997); and Charles Taylor's conceptualization of modern social imaginaries (such as the family) as what enable the practices of society by being the very concepts used to make sense of these social practices (2002).

What *is* unique about this project is the blending of these diverse theoretical strands to trace the telling—and retelling—of a specific tale about becoming a moral America(n) after 9/11. In this way, *Imagining America at War* takes on the political in a variety of ways. It challenges the separation of theaters of culture from theaters of war. Film and family, it suggests, have much to tell us about how "moral America" casts its character and constructs its interpretative codes for under-standing itself—what I call moral grammars of war—in relation to its new war on terror. By reconsidering film and family, it suggests, one may also reconsider the official stories of US foreign policy and the morality tales that provide them with their specific grammars of war.

In the process, *Imagining America at War* rejects fixed notions of morality in favor of a genealogy of their specific constructions under specific historical, political, cultural, and domestic (national and familial) circumstances. And it rejects a totalizing and finished notion of US-ness as much as it rejects the equation of US-ness with some broader hemispheric notion of American-ness (even though in its telling of the official US story it often employs the term *America* for *United States* because this is how *we* appear in the official story).

Where *Imagining America at War* leaves us is not with a definitive reading of reconfigured moral US subjectivities and US spaces. Instead, it leaves us with complex, fragmented, and therefore uncertain moral Americans and moral Americas posed (if they so choose) to take ethical responsibility for who they think they were/are; who they wish they'd never been; who they really are; and, most important, who they might become.

# 2 Who we think we were/are

In his book, *Aspects of the Theory of Syntax* (1965), Noam Chomsky argues that the same sequence of words can have what he calls different deep structures. He offers the sentence "Flying planes can be dangerous" as his example. Flying planes, he explains, can refer to the act of flying planes, in which case the word *flying* functions as a verb. Alternatively, flying planes can refer to planes that are flying, in which case the word *flying* modifies the noun *planes*. What's more, Chomsky explains, "If a sentence such as 'Flying planes can be dangerous' is presented in an appropriately constructed context, listeners will fail to detect the ambiguity. In fact, they may reject the second interpretation, when this is pointed out to them, as forced or unnatural ..." (Chomsky, 1965: 21).[1] What Chomsky's analysis suggests is that the danger of flying planes is not only literal but figurative because the same sequence of words produces multiple meanings, the validity of which depends on how grammatical structures are interpreted and ignored, which in turn depends on contexts.

Informed by Chomsky's analytical observations about this provocative, now timely illustration, I analyze two occasions when flying planes literally was/were dangerous. One is the events of September 11, 2001, to which I refer by their mediatic name: *Attack on America*. The other is the events of December 7, 1941, the Japanese attack on Pearl Harbor. These two events are twinned in US commentary about September 11 in the first instance because, like Chomsky's illustrative sentence, they abide by a similar "sequencing." Though some distinctions are routinely noted between them—mainland attack versus off-shore attack; targeting symbols and civilians versus targeting a military base and military personnel; terrorist attack versus state attack—it is the similarities between the two events that dominate discussion. These events are described as two dates that will live in infamy and on which the United States lost its innocence (again) thanks to a surprise attack at a moment of US history when the rhetoric of isolationism was in play (Crepeau, 2001). Similar historical sequencing gives rise to arguments for a similar sequence of planning and processing, with Pearl Harbor conjured up in US discourse as a foreign policy response model (Zakaria, 2001) and as an emotionally parallel time that justifies "rage and retribution"— what one commentator called "a unified, unifying, Pearl Harbor sort of purple American fury" (Morrow, 2001).

What interests me about these two events is not the figurative danger of reading them differently (which is the risk Chomsky implores us to take) but the danger of reading them as the same, of reducing similar sequencing to similar meaning. As in Chomsky's example, such a reduction is possible only if one ignores grammatical structures and interpretative contexts.

This, I suggest, is precisely what many US citizens did in the immediate aftermath of 9/11. By allowing their desire for their perceived moral clarity of the past to overwrite their concerns about the moral uncertainty of the present, who we think we were during WWII was equated with who we think we are in the post-9/11 war on terror.

I want to recover one grammatical structure and interpretative context that has so far been missing in the Attack on America/Pearl Harbor discourse: a grammar of morality that is rendered meaningful through an interpretative context dependent on a specific rendering of relations of gender and sexuality. I focus on the moral grammar of these events because it is on the axis of morality that they are most firmly twinned. As one US commentator speaking on November 5, 2001 put it, "…Certainly in the States right now I don't think you have any sense of moral ambiguity about the rightness of this particular cause that America's engaged in. September 11 has an almost December 7 kind of clarifying impact for Americans. So I don't think that the war on terrorism is going to be fraught with ambivalence and ambiguity, at least in the American imagination" (Doherty, 2001).

I would suggest that this apparent lack of moral ambivalence and ambiguity results as much from what actually took place on these two infamous dates as it does from American's imagination and imaginary about them.[2] It is in part for this reason that I turn to the 2001 Hollywood blockbuster *Pearl Harbor* (Touchstone Pictures) as my initial point of departure and interpretive guide to investigate the US moral grammar of war (i.e., US moral codes that structure narratives of interpretation about war).[3] To be clear, I am not arguing that the historical events that took place at Pearl Harbor are identical with their filmic representation.[4] Rather, I am suggesting that *interpretations* of historical narratives and their popular signifying forms are so crossed and confused with one another that attempting to police fact from fiction is not only likely to fail. More important, such attempts turn a blind eye to what popular representations can tell us about the politics and the politics of desire bound up in *interpretations* of historical events and their resulting constructions of a US *we*.[5]

Rather than discuss *Pearl Harbor* as others have—by debating its historical authenticity or raving about the graphics of its battle scenes— I focus on the film's love story. In contrast to the view that the film is "betraying to a nation" because of its "sugar-coating...fictional love story that has nothing to do with the event" (Tin Man-5, 2001), I suggest that *Pearl Harbor's* love story is essential to an appreciation of the twinning of Attack on America with Pearl Harbor. For what this love story reveals is the gendered and sexualized grammatical structure of morality that 2001 Hollywood attributes to a United States suddenly and surprisingly at war.

Analyzing this grammatical structure and the gender and sexuality codes that render it meaningful provides insights into a nagging question raised by the Attack on America/Pearl Harbor discourse: if Attack on America and Pearl Harbor abide by different grammatical structures that depend on different interpretive contexts (which I argue they do), why have US commentators on the events of September 11 so consistently and deliberately substituted the moral grammar of Pearl Harbor for that of Attack on America? Why have they read them as if they had the same meaning? These questions take us to the issue of how desire functions in the Attack on America/Pearl Harbor discourse, for, as Freud's work demonstrates, desire speaks its name only through substitution.

The chapter is organized into three sections. The first section examines how a specific grammatical structure of morality popularly attributed to a 1940s United States by Hollywood is enacted in the film *Pearl Harbor*. Section two, Attack on America, compares and contrasts a 1940s moral grammar of war against a state with a twenty-first-century moral grammar of a war against a terrorist network. The chapter concludes by asking, "What desires are expressed in a US rhetoric about September 11 that twins it with Pearl Harbor?" Or, to employ a Freudian turn of phrase, it asks, "What does America want?"

Overall, my analysis suggests that whatever America may want by twinning Attack on America with Pearl Harbor is foiled because the events are inflected differently, owing to their differing moral structures that rely on distinct interpretations of gender and sexuality. Specifically, the rhetoric of Pearl Harbor abides by the gendered and sexualized WWII formula for understanding and rehabilitating an enemy: a hypermasculine/hypersexual enemy requires emasculation so that in a postwar world its moral maturation is possible at the knee of a fatherly America. What I suggest is that this WWII formula fails to make sense of and make sense in the US war against terror, primarily because of the different ways in which the feminine functions in the discourses of Pearl Harbor and Attack on America.[6] And what that means is that it is militarily, politically, and morally dangerous to morph who we think we were with who we think we are.

## Pearl Harbor

In the genre of *Titanic* (1997, Paramount Pictures), *Pearl Harbor* is a romantic drama that uses a larger-than-life Hollywood version of history as an emotional backdrop and narrative device. This is rendered clearly in the film's opening sequence. Rather than introduce us to the history of the events surrounding the Japanese attack, the film presents us with the history of the relationship between the two male leads: Rafe (Ben Affleck) and Danny (Josh Hartnett). We first encounter friends Rafe and Danny as boys learning the lesson that flying planes can be dangerous. This is a lesson Danny already knows too well. Danny's father, a WWI veteran flyer turned crop duster, emerged from that war an emotional cripple and an abusive drunk. Flying planes was/were dangerous to Daddy and, as a result, are to Danny. While Danny is consistently portrayed as the less emotionally mature of the two similarly aged boys (Danny is a boy in need of a properly functioning parent), it is Rafe who is slower to grasp the dangers of flying planes.

The film's opening shot is of the two boys in a make-shift "plane" in their Tennessee barn. The boys pretend to be fighter pilots, with Rafe first in command. As the boys play, Danny's father lands his crop duster on the airstrip outside the barn, then begins to make his way home through the fields. The boys take this opportunity to upgrade their plane, abandoning their toy for the real thing. Their game of fighter pilots continues in the crop duster. And then things turn dangerous. They mistakenly start the plane's engine, resulting in the plane careening around the runway, momentarily leaving the ground before it crash-lands. Excited by their adventure, Rafe decrees the boys real flyers. Danny's father, who observes the boys' escapades, violently scolds Danny as he warns him of the misadventures of war. Rafe intervenes to protect his friend, declaring to Danny that he will always look out for him. The scene ends with Danny grateful to Rafe but apologetic to his father.

This sequence establishes not only the terms of the relationship between the two boys but each boy's relationship to the dangers of flying planes. The film's promotional literature suggests that Rafe and Danny grow up like brothers. What the film's opening sequence does is explicitly spell out the terms of this brotherly relationship. Rafe is established as the leader and decision maker who fancies himself as Danny's protector, even though his attempt to protect Danny from his abusive father is inadequate. Foreshadowed in this sequence is Rafe's function as a substitute father for Danny as well as Rafe's initial failure in that role. Rafe fails as a substitute father for Danny not only because Rafe's desire to father his less mature friend is itself premature but because Rafe's prematurity is expressed both in his relationship with Danny and in his relationship to the dangers of flying planes. Though Danny respects the dangers of flying planes, presumably because he recognizes how these dangers can rupture the father–son relationship, Rafe enjoys these dangers. Rafe's untimely courting of the dangers of flying planes is his character flaw, a flaw that drives the film's action. Only when Rafe learns to respect the dangers of flying planes—a respect learned through his triangulated relationship with love Evelyn (Kate Beckinsale) and friend/son Danny, a relationship that temporally resituates Rafe as father and pilot—does the film arrive at its happy ending.

*Pearl Harbor* follows the friendship of Rafe and Danny and their mutual love for Evelyn across three historical terrains: Rafe's and Danny's pilot training that leads to Rafe's involvement in the Battle of Britain; the threesome's stationing at Pearl Harbor prior to and during the Japanese attack; and the post-Pearl Harbor US bombing mission over Japan, known as the Doolittle Raid, in which Rafe and Danny both participate.[7]

Against these three historical backgrounds, love blossoms and friendship is tested. While in pilot training, Rafe meets and falls in love with Air Force nurse Evelyn. This does not, however, prevent him from volunteering for bombing missions in the Battle of Britain (as many US pilots did while the US followed an official policy of neutrality during WWII). Rafe's plane is shot down, and Evelyn and Danny—who have now been stationed at Pearl Harbor—receive word of Rafe's death. The devastated pair take comfort in one another, quickly becoming lovers. Just as Evelyn realizes she is pregnant with Danny's child, Rafe returns from the dead. He was stuck in war-torn France for months, unable to get word to Evelyn that he was alive. Because of her pregnancy, Evelyn tells Rafe she will stay with Danny. Rafe and Danny fall out but, of course, put aside their differences to fight the Japanese, first during the attack on Pearl Harbor and later as volunteers on the Doolittle

Raid. On that raid, Danny is critically wounded. Rafe implores him to live by telling him, "Danny, you can't die. You know why? 'Cause you're gonna be a daddy. I wasn't supposed to tell you, but you're gonna be a daddy!" Danny's dying reply to Rafe is, "No, Rafe. You are." With Danny's death, Evelyn and Rafe are romantically reunited. In the film's final scene, Evelyn watches adoringly while Rafe shows their son Danny the crop duster he flies in the post-WWII South.

*Pearl Harbor* tells its story of love, loss, and rebirth by developing a moral order the various aspects of which are characterized by the three leads. In this moral order, Rafe symbolizes a consistent (if often premature) moral clarity, Danny stands for lapses in moral judgment, and Evelyn marks the location in which struggles to reconcile questions of morality take place.

Deciphering the film's moral grammar requires a consideration of its reliance on strategies of doubling and codes of gender and sexuality. That the film functions through doubling has already been established. The film presents us with two male leads whose lives, loves, deaths, and rebirths pass through twin histories. Rafe and Danny grow up together. They fall in love with the same women. They both die in the course of the film (Rafe symbolically in the Battle of Britain; Danny literally in the Doolittle Raid). And they are both reborn (Rafe returns from the dead to join his friend and girlfriend at Pearl Harbor while Danny is reborn as Rafe and Evelyn's son). The motif of rebirth also doubles the film's father–son relationship, with Danny as symbolic son to Rafe becoming his literal son, thus allowing Rafe to pass from Danny's inadequate father substitute to his proper father.

The terms of this moral grammar become meaningful only when read through the film's relationships of gender and sexuality, relationships that find their focus in the pivotal character of Evelyn, herself a double for the feminized Pearl Harbor.[8] It is through their relationships with Evelyn that Rafe and Danny represent a double-sided morality of moral certainty (Rafe) and moral uncertainty (Danny).

Rafe's moral certainty is presented to us from the start, when Rafe offers himself up as a substitute father and defender of young Danny. This early scene establishes that Rafe has a clear sense of what is right and wrong, even if he is not always able to execute his moral code. Rafe's inability to defend Danny from his abusive father by becoming his fatherly substitute is a theme returned to throughout the film, in adult Rafe's literal doubling of Danny's father by becoming "a rotten drunk" and in Rafe's failure to save his friend from death.

In contrast to Rafe's difficulties in executing his moral code in relation to Danny, Rafe has no such problems in his relationships with his country and his girlfriend. Rafe's clear sense of duty coupled with his excitement at the dangers of flying planes means that he always finds it easier to defend and protect the United States than to defend and protect his friend Danny. This is because Rafe's moral code—and indeed Rafe's entire character—doubles as that of a United States emerging from isolationism. Rafe is the film's heroic "Captain America," overly eager to seek opportunities to project US actions and values into the wider world. As Rafe tells his commanding officer when he volunteers for the Battle of Britain, he is not eager to die, "just eager to matter." But Rafe/outwardly looking America finds it difficult to matter before the United States officially joins the war and before the postwar United States reorders global affairs. This is because he, like the United States, as yet lacks a proper platform from which to project American values, interests, and power internationally. This is something the United States gains by being forced into the war by events at Pearl Harbor and something Rafe gains through his relationship with Evelyn. Pearl Harbor becomes America's platform to move out of isolationism and to make meaning in the world; Evelyn becomes Rafe's.

Rafe's defense of his country never threatens the moral terms of his relationship with Evelyn, even when Rafe gets ahead of himself and volunteers for service in Europe before the United States is officially at war. This is because Evelyn represents America's symbolic home front, the girl back home needing protection but also propping up the boy abroad. It is in relation to Evelyn that Rafe stages not only his heroism but his morality. The night before leaving for Britain, Rafe does the honorable thing by passing up an opportunity to spend his final night in the United States with Evelyn. When Rafe learns of Evelyn's impregnation by Danny, he does what he can to secure Evelyn and Danny's relationship, even though it leaves him heartbroken. And on Danny's death, Rafe again does the right thing by (we are led to believe) marrying Evelyn and raising her son Danny as his own.

Though Rafe always seems to know the right thing to do, even when he can't (yet) do it, Danny is a figure always caught in the middle. From the start, he is torn between two inadequate fathers and their conflicting relationships to the dangers of flying planes. Danny's father pulls him toward the legacies of WWI, impressing on him the merits of isolationism. Rafe, on the other hand, pulls Danny toward entry into WWII, a war in which Danny does not really belong and which therefore leads to his death. Danny's middle position on the war is articulated in his conversation with Rafe on learning of Rafe's British assignment. Danny explains to Rafe, "It isn't training over there, it's war. Where losers die and there aren't any winners, just guys who turn into broken-down wrecks like my father. Now if trouble awaits me, I'm ready. But why go looking for it?"[9]

Given his familial positioning between two fathers and his historical positioning between two wars, Danny not surprisingly finds himself in the middle again in his love triangle with Rafe and Evelyn. Unlike Rafe, who refuses to consummate his relationship with Evelyn before marriage, Danny does the "wrong" thing by allowing comfort to lead to sex, which leads to pregnancy. Interestingly, neither Evelyn nor Rafe ever give Danny the chance to do the right thing by Evelyn—to marry her—until Danny is on the brink of death. This is consistent with how Danny is cast in the film: as emotionally less mature than either Rafe or Evelyn and lacking the ability to mature, resulting in his moral unreliability. This is also consistent with how Danny, a boy in need of a good parent, takes more comfort from Evelyn than she does from him. Danny's character ruptures the clarity of Rafe's moral order around the axes of gender and sexuality by rejecting Rafe as not (yet) father enough for him, by allowing himself to be mothered by Evelyn when he is supposed to look after her in Rafe's absence and by having what might, therefore, be read as a doubly incestuous relationship with Evelyn, for she is both his "brother's" betrothed and his own mother.

And what of Evelyn? How is the morality of this fallen woman with a bastard son coded? Not at all. The film leaves Evelyn morally uncoded because the film's moral codes are exclusively masculine. Evelyn has a function in *Pearl Harbor's* moral grammar —to secure masculinity— but she has no proper place within it. Like the feminized playground of pleasures she doubles, Evelyn functions as an accessible feminine space in which masculine moral struggles are staged (Irigaray, 1985). Sometimes, masculinity is secured in the twin home fronts of Evelyn and Pearl Harbor. And, sometimes, it is unhinged. But the film's progressive moral narrative ensures that insecurity and moral uncertainty will always be temporary, even in the face of betrayal, incest, and attack. It is the feminine that functions as the basis for this moral recovery, as the only reliable site from which moral progress can occur.

The film explicitly makes this point through Evelyn, for Evelyn is the location from which the story rights the moral missteps of its lead characters. It is Evelyn's misidentification of Danny as a lover rather than a son that enables Danny finally to gain access to his proper father, a mature Rafe.[10] Prior to his rebirth as Evelyn's son, Danny's fathers were temporally out of sync, with his natural father behind the times and his substitute father ahead of his time. It is only when Danny is reborn through Evelyn and when Rafe is again reborn through Pearl Harbor that the Rafe–Danny, father–son relationship works. For Rafe/"outwardly-looking America" is finally in his appropriate historical period, when he can make (more) legitimate claims to fatherhood (of Danny and of a new global order) and can educate Danny/"America caught between isolationism and outward projection" to take his place in the new, wider world. Rafe's/America's moral certainty finally triumphs over Danny's/America's moral uncertainty, thanks to America's refiguration through the feminine figures of Evelyn and Pearl Harbor.

A parallel logic runs through the film's representation of Pearl Harbor. In the film's accounting, Pearl Harbor (itself/herself a fallen woman thanks to the surprise attack) is the location that provides the symbolically feminized flyers who avenge America's moral mistreatment by the hypermasculine Japanese with the Doolittle Raid.[11] By acting on their moral certainty, these US flyers emasculate Japan, thereby symbolically restoring America's and their own security and masculinity. The moral certainty of the US mission over Japan is twinned with the film's depiction of the moral uncertainty of the Japanese about the attack. Though the Americans know they must fight to restore their masculinity, the Japanese first-strike surprise attack is represented as somewhere between cowardly and courageous, thereby denying Japan both moral certainty and mature masculinity. This is rendered clear by the angst conveyed by Admiral Yamamoto, the mission's mastermind. Responding to praise that his attack on Pearl Harbor is brilliant, Yamamoto replies, "A brilliant man would have found a way not to fight a war." The film leaves it up to its viewers to complete the narrative of Japan's moral progress, something that is easily done, given our knowledge of the postwar US occupation of Japan and the film's doubling of Japan and Danny on the axes of moral uncertainty and immature masculinity. From this, we can surmise that Japan's moral uncertainty comes to an end just as Danny's does: when its old character dies, making way for a new character to mature into masculinity when properly fathered by America/Rafe.

Overall, *Pearl Harbor* presents its viewers with a moral grammar open to moments of uncertainty when relationships of gender and sexuality are out of time/place. These moments of moral rupture both occur at and are sutured through the film's use of its twinned feminine figures, Evelyn and Pearl Harbor. It is through Evelyn that Rafe's masculinity is first unhinged (when Evelyn takes Danny as her lover) and then matures into the domesticated masculinity emblematic of the post-WWII United States. With his masculinity ultimately contained within the safe space of the heterosexual nuclear family, Rafe is able to change his relationship not only to Danny but to the dangers of flying planes. In this postwar context, Rafe trades in his fighter plane for a crop duster, a move that symbolizes not only America's postwar security but Rafe's comprehension that flying planes can be dangerous to the father–son relationship.

The moral ruptures and closure experienced by *Pearl Harbor's* three lead characters is, of course, doubled in America's historical relationship with Pearl Harbor. Pearl Harbor is both what made America feel vulnerable and what enabled America to take up its "proper" place in the moral economies of violence and order during and after WWII. Like Rafe, America emerged from the war stronger than when it entered it, because it arrived at what is presumably its proper place in history: global hegemon, father to a new world order. Having secured itself and the wider world, America, like Rafe, can turn inward, enjoying postwar domestic happiness while offering morally certain fatherly guidance to its morally maturing sons, like Japan, thanks to its more nuanced grasp of the dangers of flying planes.

Without the role of the feminine, of Evelyn in the film *Pearl Harbor* and of Pearl Harbor in America's narrative of its own moral certainty and its helping hand in the moral progress of other states, the moral grammar of *Pearl Harbor* and Pearl Harbor does not makes sense. Nor does it make sense without a specific rendering of sexuality. In this rendering, sexuality may momentarily overflow the bounds of good moral practice (through betrayal, incest, or attack) but, because sexuality is grounded in heterosexual relationships, it can (and these narratives promise it will) ultimately be contained by the heterosexual nuclear family, a site that ensures that moral certainty can be passed on from father to son and from the victors in war to those they defeated.

What *Pearl Harbor* and Pearl Harbor offer America is what appears to be a traditionally gendered, closed moral grammar, the movement of which reassures Americans that it is only a matter of time before threats to their moral economy, whether played out in personal, familial relationships or in relations within and among states, are rendered harmless.[12]

## Attack on America

If *Pearl Harbor* presents a moral grammar rendered meaningful by domesticated, heterosexualized codes of gender and sexuality and Pearl Harbor functions as a rhetorical equivalent in American discourse for Attack on America, it begs the question, "Does Attack on America abide by the same gendered and sexualized moral grammar as do *Pearl Harbor* and Pearl Harbor?"

Like the moral grammar of *Pearl Harbor*, the moral grammar of Attack on America functions though the motif of twinning. The twinning motif is not only literally suggested by the first target of the September 11 attacks: the twin towers of New York City's World Trade Center. It is also figuratively suggested in a US discourse that sees the Japanese attack on Pearl Harbor doubled in the events of September 11, through rhetorics of isolationism, surprise attack, loss of innocence, and policy responses. All this suggests that Pearl Harbor and Attack on America bear the same relationship to the dangers of flying planes both literally (flying planes brings/bring war by surprise attack) and figuratively (surprise attacks by flying planes activate the same meaningful responses).

Rather than contradict this impression, the grammatical structures of Attack on America and *Pearl Harbor* seem to abide by the same moral design. In both cases, morality is double-sided. *Pearl Harbor* portrays its double-sided grammar in the run up to the Japanese attack through its two male leads: the outwardly looking, morally certain Rafe and the inward/outward, morally uncertain Danny. Attack on America presents a similar moral grammar prior to the terrorist attack, locating certainty and uncertainty in similar locales. Before September 11, moral certainty was found just where *Pearl Harbor* told us it would be found in a postwar world—in the outward projections of US power. Whether characterized through America's global military superiority or through its neoliberal capitalist policies of globalization, the United States projected a triumphalist moral standpoint. Inwardly, America's moral position was less certain, owing to events both at home and abroad. Though there is much debate about whether the suturing of moral certainty/uncertainty that *Pearl Harbor* depicts was ever realized in the post-WWII United States (Coontz, 2000), there is widespread agreement that whatever its relative success may have been, it was not sustained. Such events as the Vietnam War and Watergate and political concerns expressed in rhetorics as diverse as antiwar, feminism, postmodernism, and antiglobalization meant that from at least the 1960s onward, claims to moral pluralism, moral relativism, and even nihilism were as much in play in the United States as were claims to moral certainty.

All this changed on September 11. The United States initially retained its outwardly directed moral certainty. Combining clash-of-civilizations arguments with cowboy posturing, the United States declared a "war on terror" and its supporting "axis of evil" while its president set the bounty on Osama bin Laden: "Wanted: Dead or Alive." Inwardly, self-assured nationalism and patriotism replaced critical discourses seen as immoral (the left), amoral (postmodernism), or simply in bad taste (humor),[13] thereby substituting moral uncertainty with moral certainty.

In the weeks after September 11, movement along the moral certainty/uncertainty axis increasingly teetered toward one pole but, unlike *Pearl Harbor* in which that pole was moral infallibility, in Attack on America it was a pervasive, contagious moral confusion. Yes, the United States embarked on the dual missions of building a global coalition against terror and bombing Afghanistan. Yet, one could not help but feel that America's missions were morally contradictory. Its global coalition against terror included states with appalling human rights records and other states who some would call terrorist states. As for the bombing of Afghanistan, even though the United States rolled out its traditional foreign policy rhetoric, stating "We have no quarrel with the Afghan people," its mission turned thousands of Afghans into casualties of war either by death or displacement. Trying to blunt any immoral edges to the mission, US forces for the first time dropped bread (idealist humanitarian relief) as well as bombs (realist foreign policy tools) over enemy territory, thereby delivering a morally mixed message. Not surprisingly, America's moral uncertainty spread inwardly, with its public raising questions not primarily about whether or not the United States should take a moral stand against international terrorism generally and who the Bush administration identified as the al Qaeda terrorists specifically, but precisely how—and importantly, *where*—it should do so.[14] As envelops filled with anthrax began to circulate through the US postal system, this question became all the more urgent.[15]

The question of where America's moral activity might be located is the very point at which the parallel between the moral grammars of *Pearl Harbor* and Attack on America breaks down. In *Pearl Harbor*, as in Pearl Harbor, America was able to project its masculine moral certainty into the world when the time was right, when its doubled home front of Evelyn and Pearl Harbor needed protecting. Functioning as symbolic sites of US territory, these two feminine figures provided both the foundation from which US masculinity could be projected into the world and the place in which debates about moral certainty/uncertainty were resolved in favor of moral certainty. Abiding by traditional heterosexual codes of gender and sexuality, what these figures promised is that moral certainty would tame moral uncertainty at home and abroad by first containing uncertainty and then enlightening it.

This is not at all how the moral grammar of Attack on America is rendered meaningful by its codes of gender and sexuality. Unlike in *Pearl Harbor*'s moral grammar, in which the enemy, the home front, and gender and sexuality codes are easily identified, Attack on America's moral grammar locates no clear enemies, no clear home fronts, and no clear traditional codes. And this has important consequences for where and how the battle between the twin sides of morality—certainty and uncertainty—are staged. Grasping how gender and sexuality codes actually do function in the moral grammar of Attack on America and why WWII codes fail requires an appreciation of the identity and strategy of America's new enemy and an appreciation of the new home front America is defending.

No clear, containable enemy can be located in Attack on America's moral grammar. Whereas Pearl Harbor's moral grammar of war successfully identifies enemies as states, Attack on America's moral grammar attempts, but fails, similarly to identify the enemy. One of the first moves of the Bush administration was to equate Osama bin Laden's al Qaeda network with Afghanistan's Taliban government (Bush, 2001a and 2001b), an equation that translated the war on terror into a war among states. Yet, this equation was always a failed one. Yes, it meant that the United States could commence its bombing campaign in Afghanistan; but both rhetorically and strategically, the United States seemed insufficiently respectful of what it surely knew about terrorism: that terrorism is not containable within state borders.

Instead of being at war with territorially based states whose hypermasculinity could be emasculated and whose resulting moral immaturity could be subjected to fatherly correction, America's enemy in the war against terror is more like an international firm that projects its (hyper)masculine influence and power internationally through what neoliberal globalization perspectives regard as amoral capitalist mechanisms of supply and demand, the success of which depends on market research, technological efficiency, and forward thinking. As one commentator put it, this new form of transnational terror attributed to the al Qaeda network functions more like a Kentucky Fried Chicken franchise than a sovereign state.[16] Just as a KFC franchise succeeds by enticing customers through efficient service and with products that their competitors have yet to think of, so too does al Qaeda seem to function by providing a product (an Islamic fundamentalist ideology turned terrorism) to meet customer demand through technological efficiency (training programs that enable "employees" to perform one or more specific tasks in the "production process") and forward thinking (transforming Hollywood-like scripts into actual events).

Like other global corporations, when circumstances sour on the ground, rendering operations from one locale unattractive (e.g., unfavorable terms from host governments), al Qaeda just moves its ground operations to more welcoming sites. These places include not only Afghanistan and parts of the Arab world but Germany, Britain, Canada, and America. And these are just the ground operations. Not only is al Qaeda, this time like a "dot.com" business, located everywhere; it is located nowhere. It exists as a mobile network of connections of cash and carriers accessible from just about anywhere but locatable almost exclusively as mere network nodal points (Cassells, 1998 and Duffield, 2001). Like a stereotypical, elliptical feminine figure, al Qaeda is so fluid that it, like its leader, cannot be pinned down (Irigaray, 1985). Al Qaeda, then, is as changeable as its gender. Today it is one thing, like a free-flowing, feminine dot.com company. Tomorrow it is another, with its terrorist cells/franchises springing into action as hypermasculine (anti)heroes on US domestic airliners.

Not only is al Qaeda's gender doubled; so too is its sexuality. Though internally it seems to follow a strict heterosexual ideology (albeit exercised through a violent homosociality), outwardly it grasps how processes of exchange actually function in today's globalized world, recognizing that penetration goes both ways (Gibson-Graham, 1998). Penetrating foreign markets requires opening yourself up to global flows that might in turn penetrate you. Al Qaeda does this, for example, through a global recruiting strategy that respects religious boundaries but not national ones. This is how British-born Muslims fighting American and British coalition forces in Afghanistan were reported to have become the first "foreign" (whatever that now means) casualties in the war on terror.[17] Al Qaeda's appreciation of the dual nature of penetration is also what enabled it to exploit the open societies of the West and attack the United States.

What all these mean is that al Qaeda is neither masculine nor feminine, straight nor gay. Instead, it is both: masculine and feminine, straight and gay. It is what Roland Barthes would call the *both/and* (1976) and what I would call *metaphorically queer* (Weber, 1999). As such, al Qaeda "*confuses* meaning, the norm, normativity" (Barthes, 1976: 109) of the traditional identity of an enemy target.

Like its identity, al Qaeda's war strategy confounds the traditional codes of war. What rendered its hypermasculine attack possible was the al Qaeda network's ability to capitalize on, while repudiating, a neoliberal economic logic that the United States has long regarded not as morally repugnant or morally immature but as morally neutral, for that is how markets and the "laws" that govern them are understood in this economic ideology.[18]

Al Qaeda's strategy of war that both mirrors and exploits a neoliberal economic strategy confuses the United States. On the one hand, US rhetoric is clear in its view that al Qaeda's anti-Semitic, anti-Christian, misogynist ideology and practices are immoral and that this moral inferiority will not be remedied by moral maturation. This is why the United States is at war with al Qaeda/terror. According to US foreign policy rhetoric, you must make attempts to enlighten the enemy but, if enlightenment is impossible, your enemy must be killed. On the other hand, US rhetoric is confused about how to regard al Qaeda's economic logic in its strategy of war. That, in America's terms, this strategy has effected evil and danger is beyond question, evidenced by al Qaeda's multiplication of the dangers of flying planes by selecting civilian and symbolic targets and by transforming passenger planes into missiles. However, US rhetoric has long reserved a place of respect for neoliberal economic strategy as beyond morality. Recognizing that what US rhetoric regards as amoral neoliberal economic strategies can have immoral global effects is precisely the point to which US economic policy has long turned a deaf ear, most recently when voiced by antiglobalization protestors. Unlike antiglobalization protestors, al Qaeda is not fighting for global economic justice for all. It is exploiting logics that neoliberal ideology places beyond justice or injustice for its own immoral cause. The irony here is that the United States may rethink neoliberal ideologies of economic (and, sadly, political, social, and intellectual) openness and the moral enlightenment that neoliberals argue naturally spills over from this economic openness more as a result of al Qaeda's activities than of those by the antiglobalization movement.

Like al Qaeda's identity, its strategy also confounds the gendered and sexualized terms and the moral application of America's WWII formula for defeating and rehabilitating an enemy. The function of America's WWII formula of emasculation and moral progress of its enemy depends, as we saw in the discussion of *Pearl Harbor*, on a pivotal term that is never represented in this formula. That term is *the feminine*. The feminine is what secures America's ideals of moral progress by functioning as the morally neutral stage on which moral struggles are resolved in favor of moral progress. And, as we also saw in *Pearl Harbor*, this morally neutral stage doubles as America's home front. It is what the United States is protecting and defending, for it is from this location that American power is projected into the wider world.

In Attack on America, what the United States is protecting and defending is of course US territory, this time New York and Washington, D.C. But the symbolic function of this territory could not be more different from the symbolic function of Pearl Harbor. Pearl Harbor, the feminized, domesticated colony turned US state, symbolizes America's military might. The Twin Towers of the World Trade Center— the target with which Attack on America's discourse is so preoccupied that the attacks in D.C. are often forgotten—symbolizes America's masculine projection not of military power into the wider world but cultural power made possible by economic power. By targeting the Twin Towers, al Qaeda targeted the symbolic power of United States-led neoliberal globalization.

What all this means is that America's home front in the war on terror is not a domesticated feminine figure, such as Pearl Harbor, the site where America's moral outrage was mobilized. Nor is it a domesticatable feminine figure, such as Evelyn, the girl back home with whom American masculinity will make a home after the war and, from that site, domesticate immoral global forces. The only site in US discourse on Attack on America that properly parallels the feminine sites of Pearl Harbor and Evelyn is the neoliberal economic market. This market functions as a feminine site not only because it was the symbolic target of the first attack (an attack designed to emasculate US power more than feminize it). More important, the market functions as a feminine site because, like the feminine in the rhetoric in *Pearl Harbor* and Pearl Harbor, the market is itself located beyond moral debate in traditional US rhetoric. It is neither morally good nor bad, neither morally certain nor uncertain: it is morally neutral. As such, it is the place in which questions of morality are reconciled. The promise of the neoliberal market is that these struggles will be resolved progressively because the market is itself progressive. According to neoliberalism, amoral market practices lead to moral effects in the global order: such things as peace, democracy, and increased standards of living for all.

The problem for the United States is that its home front—neoliberal economic principles, policies, and institutions—has not just been attacked by al Qaeda. It has been infiltrated by al Qaeda, not (only) because al Qaeda's operators are clever but because the character of neoliberal globalization is that it does not respect international boundaries. This renders it the perfect strategic double through which a transnational terrorist network might operate, and it renders it the nightmarish home front that an America at war with terror finds itself trying to protect.

Furthermore, because the feminine in Attack on America is not itself contained or containable, it harbors no promise that it can morally contain and correct an immoral enemy. Unlike the feminine in *Pearl Harbor* and Pearl Harbor, the feminine in Attack on America is not an amoral stage on which moral conflicts take place and are resolved in favor of an American brand of morality; it is merely the place in which moral conflicts are staged. Like the neoliberal narratives of globalization in which it resides, this feminine space promises an openness that goes both ways but no closure, especially moral closure.

## What does America want?

Finally, we arrive at the question of desire, of what America wants by substituting historic and filmic narratives of Pearl Harbor for those of Attack on America, narratives that cross who we think we were with who we think we are. There is no shortage of answers to this question. Such a substitution would provide a nostalgic, twenty-first-century United States with a clear enemy that is located outside its borders and inside some other borders and against whom the United States could defend itself using its superior military capabilities. President George W. Bush could play F.D.R. (and British Prime Minister Tony Blair could play Churchill). And the United States and its allies could take comfort in the knowledge that it is only a matter of time before they restored global order and security.

What this paired reading of *Pearl Harbor* and Attack on America suggests is that there is something more that America wants by slipping between these twinned discourses and these past and present *we's*. This something more is a grammatical structure and interpretive context that provides the United States with guarantees that is it only a matter of time until America's internal axis of moral certainty/moral uncertainty flattens out into self-assured moral infallibility and that the United States is once again in a position to reorder global politics morally by over-seeing the moral progression of its enemies (be they terrorist states, terrorist cells, or individual terrorists).

Though there are striking similarities in the moral grammars of *Pearl Harbor*/Pearl Harbor and Attack on America, the differences in these moral grammars is clarified only when they are examined through the very differently inflected codes of gender and sexuality that make them meaningful. It is at this point, especially when we recognize the nonplace and nonplacability of the feminine in Attack on America compared to the domesticated and domesticatable place of the feminine in *Pearl Harbor*/Pearl Harbor, that not only the distinctions between the two moral grammars but their different movements become clear. One promises rebirth and redemption; the other promises only repeated penetration and penetrability: not what America seeks for itself at this moment in its history. Is it any wonder that *we* would rather think of ourselves as someone more secure(ly) in the past?

What America wants is a moral grammar that will promise it not security but a United States-led discourse of securitization; not closure but the possibility of enclosure of its enemy and of its resecured domestic space; not a baseless, premature fatherhood for this war-torn world but a domestically grounded, proper fatherly role in a postwar world. All this was promised by the moral grammar of WWII and the *our* story of who we think we were. It is not surprising, then, that American moral outrage at the events of September 11 has led to its willfully substituting these events and this morally uncertain US *we* with the events, understandings, and morally certain US *we* of December 7. These similar historical sequences and the desire to read these similar sequences as if they have the same meaning and produce the same US *we* (the very error against which Chomsky warns us) have so far led America to apply its WWII playbook on how to fight a war against a state to how to fight a war against an enemy without borders, without a home front, and without the promise of moral correction. But because America's success in the war on terror is not a matter of the United States defeating and morally rehabilitating a territorially contained hypermasculine enemy employing a traditional military strategy, the WWII playbook must minimally be revised, if not rewritten altogether.[19]

This does not mean that America's moral outrage over September 11 is unjustified. I think it is justified. It does, however, mean that America has not yet developed a sufficiently nuanced grasp of the literal differences between the moral grammars of WWII and Attack on America and, more important, of the different moral movements within these grammars that rely on differently inflected figurations of gender and sexuality producing very different US *we's*. America does not want to recognize that the dangers of flying planes in Attack on America do/ does more than momentarily rupture moral narratives of progress. It/ they rupture the very foundations on which these narratives are based: domesticated, heterosexual families and domesticated, "heterosexual" states/enemies. This is what makes America's twinning of September 11 with Pearl Harbor desirable. It is also what makes flying planes not only literally but figuratively dangerous.

Of course, we learned this a long time ago. In very different ways, the domesticated, heterosexual nuclear family that expressed who we think we were in WWII was fragmented if not smashed altogether by the events of the Vietnam War. The tragedy for the post-9/11 United States is that this aspect of our Vietnam history is often missing, so much so that, ironically, after 9/11 the Vietnam War became yet another memorialized memory through which to recover a traditional (albeit differently traditional) sense of the all-American US family. In so doing, it suggested a slightly different but equally conservative US moral grammar of war as a way to understand the events of 9/11 and engage in the wider world. It is to competing understandings of the US *we* in Vietnam War films that I now turn.

# 3   Who we wish we'd never been

World War II—whether narrated through the historic imaginary of Pearl Harbor or the filmic re-imaginings of *Pearl Harbor*—portends to tell the United States and its citizens what they can know for certain about the past. Probably more important, it also tells them what they *want* to know for certain about the present. They knew and they want to know that the world is filled with enemies located beyond US borders and that those who cannot be morally rehabilitated (such as Fascists or al Qaeda members) can be killed. They knew and they want to know that the United States has a clearly defined, united homefront that can and must be defended against enemy attacks. They knew and they want to know that the moral promise of progress and of "right" in the United States is firmly grounded in its foundational families, which are traditionally white, heterosexual, and nuclear and which are the cornerstones of the nation. WWII, then, is a rich vein of past moral certainties that the United States mines at moments of its greatest moral uncertainty, which (as we saw in the last chapter) goes some way toward explaining how the WWII story of who we think we were so easily became the 9/11 story of who we think we are, reassuring "us" not only about ourselves but also about our ability to triumph over "them."

However, there are other *we*'s in the US imaginary and other morality tales that they anchor, and not all of them narrate the United States in glowing moral terms. Some of these stories, for example, express not who we think we were/are (moral America[ns]) but who we wish we'd never been (immoral or amoral America[ns]). The paradigmatic public event that these tragic tales recount is inevitably the Vietnam War. For it is the Vietnam War more than any other memorialized US public event that fractures the idyllic images of external enemies, unified homefronts, and rock-solid foundational families that the morally certain tales of WWII endlessly rehearse.

So it was with some initial concern on the part of Hollywood distributors that a couple of Vietnam War films were scheduled for release in US cinemas between 9/11 and Gulf War II, for how could films reminding the United States of its moral failings find audiences in an "America" that sought to narrate 9/11 and WWII as moral equivalents? Could Vietnam War films actually present a moral grammar that could shore up the official government discourse on 9/11? Or would such films inevitably lead to the kind of critical self-reflection about the morality of US foreign policy that the administration hoped to avoid?

Two very different Vietnam War films—*We Were Soldiers* and *The Quiet American*—presented two very different answers to these questions, so different that the first had its release date brought up to March 2002 and the second was postponed more than a year from September 2001 until the following December (Thomson, 2002). In many ways, both films are classic Vietnam War films. Both recognize the mixed moral messages in US self-narratives and how these erode (or should erode) moral certainties, and both offer revisionist histories of the war as a way to reinscribe its moral meanings and morally to resituate the United States and its citizens. But how these moral reinscriptions take place could not be more different. This is because each film employs very different inscriptions of gender, sexuality, and the family in its casting of the US moral character. The moral American of *We Were Soldiers* is the postcolonial professional soldier who is both father and son in post-WWII foundational families. In contrast, the moral American of *The Quiet American* is the lone neocolonial professional policy maker who willfully transmutates good moral conduct to fulfill his desire for the neocolonial subject (be it Vietnam or his Vietnamese fiancé). In so doing, each constructs a very different moral grammar of war that suggests different trajectories for "becoming a moral America(n)" after 9/11.

This chapter examines each film in turn. It begins with a reading of how *We Were Soldiers* constructs a US *we*, a moral grammar of war, and a trajectory for becoming a moral America(n) that supports the official story about moral America after 9/11. It then explores how *The Quiet American* contests the character, grammar, and conclusions on which this official story relies. Finally, it concludes by reading the two films together to reconsider who we wish we'd never been.

## We Were Soldiers

If *Pearl Harbor* is a film about the (re)birth of the traditional US family as the secure foundation of America's proper place in a post-WWII world, *We Were Soldiers* is a film about the death of the US patriarchal family and of what this foundational family so long secured: a sense of moral certainty at home and abroad. In an eerie *The Sixth Sense* sort of way, it is only post-Vietnam era viewers who come to terms with these deaths; the film's major characters remain oblivious to them. What the film depicts are men fighting and dying in the coming absence of a coherent national moral strategy, as if an abiding faith in a Christian God and in post-WWII patriarchal promises were enough to secure family, nation, and America's place in the world. By substituting faith in who we were for self-knowledge about who we are and who we are becoming, *We Were Soldiers* supports the official US narrative about its post-9/11 morality.

The film tells the story of the first major battle between the armies of North Vietnam and the United States, which Lt. Col. Hal Moore (played by Mel Gibson) led and journalist Joseph L. Galloway (Barry Pepper) witnessed. Like many war films, the main action in *We Were Soldiers* unfolds in three acts. Act I depicts Lt. Col. Hal Moore's physical, mental, and spiritual preparation of his young troops for combat in Vietnam. Act II, like the opening sequence of *Saving Private Ryan,* assaults its spectators with the realism of war, as platoons are cut off from their units, as battle lines are broken, and as aerial assaults kill both friend and foe in the battle for the Ia Drang Valley (known in Vietnam as The Valley of Death). Act III reflects on the implications of the action in the aftermath of battle, but *We Were Soldiers* does not begin with Act I; in its pretitle sequence, the film begins by asking about beginnings.

> With its view slightly obscured by leafless trees and tall grasses, the camera focuses on an empty winding dirt road. As we hear clicking on an old-fashion keyboard, white typed letters form words at the bottom of the screen, across this barren landscape. Simultaneously, a narrator (their author) reads the words aloud, eventually replacing these written words with pure narration. These are his words: "These are the events of November 1965, the Ia Drang Valley of Vietnam. A place our country does not remember, and a war it does not understand. This story is a testament to the young Americans who died in the Valley of Death and a tribute to the

young men of the People's Army of Vietnam who died by our hand in that place."

As the narrator pauses, red-bereted French soldiers and their white-capped officers appear on the dirt road. The narrator continues: "To tell this story, I must start at the beginning. But where does it begin? Maybe in June of 1954 when French Group Mobile 100 moved into the same central highlands of Vietnam, where we would go 11 years later."

The narration stops. It is replaced by French dialog, subtitled in English. The French commander speaks to his second-in-command:

CAPTAIN:  See anything?
SECOND-IN-COMMAND:  No, Captain.
CAPTAIN:  Fucking grass. Fucking heat. Fucking country.

The camera focuses on the captain as he wipes his brow, then cuts to his second-in-command standing next to him. As the second-in-command consults his map, a shot rings out and splatters blood across his face. This blood is that of his commander, who has been shot through the head by the Vietnamese troops who have surrounded them.

The translation stops. Bombs assault the French troops, who quickly descend into chaos. The new commander instructs his bugler to sound the alert. As the bugler does, he is shot in the throat, his bugle (the French voice) picked up and claimed by the Vietnamese. A massacre ensues. The translation resumes, this time from Vietnamese to English, as the Vietnamese commander instructs his troops to take no prisoners: "Kill all they send," he tells his soldiers, "and they will stop coming." Of course, we know that they do not stop coming. Though the French eventually ended their military involvement in Vietnam, the Americans stepped in to take their place, to reclaim from the Vietnamese the right to speak for and write themselves into and over this space. This is symbolized not only by the typewritten letters of a US author over the "empty" North Vietnamese landscape in the opening shot but also (as we see later) by US soldiers recovering what appears to be the French bugle from a dead North Vietnamese soldier in the aftermath of the battle for the Ia Drang Valley.

Cut to black.

Cue military drumbeats and mournful brass.

Fade in the opening credits over an oblique red and white background, which we later recognize as the stripes of the US flag.

Slowly dropping in from the top of the screen is the insignia of the Seventh Cavalry, the unit that was commanded by Lt. Col. Hal Moore and would fight in this very place a decade later, the same unit Custer commanded at the massacre of Little Big Horn (a.k.a. Custer's Last Stand). As this insignia is centered on screen, the film's title fades in over it.

Cut to Fort Benning, Georgia, 1964.

The narrator resumes: "Maybe the story beings in America, when the army first realized a new kind of war was coming its way."

Cut to two US military officers discussing US interests in Vietnam.

OFFICER 1 (cynical):  Washington wants a victory over cavemen in dark pajamas.

OFFICER 2:  We wouldn't be there if they hadn't already beaten the French army.

OFFICER 1 (sneering):  French army? What's that?

The officers explain that Washington understands that the problem in Vietnam is the terrain. What is needed is a new cavalry—of helicopters, not horses—that can make quick raids into and escape out of enemy territory. But such a unit will need a strong commander. So they suggest as their man Moore, an experienced paratrooper who served in Korea and who earned a Master's degree in International Relations from Harvard.

Cut to a station wagon filled with young children singing. As the camera pans up the vehicle from back to front, we are finally introduced to one of the film's two heroes. Lt. Col. Hal Moore sings along with his children as he drives the family car, his wife (Madeleine Stowe) lovingly resting her head on his shoulder. The Moores are on their way to take up the lieutenant colonel's post at Fort Benning. As they settle in, Act I begins.

It is not unusual for a film to have an opening sequence that sets its interpretive terms. Indeed, as we saw with *Pearl Harbor*, an opening sequence almost always introduces major characters, establishes the grammar of the film, and sets in motion the trajectory of that grammar. What is unusual about *We Were Soldiers* is that it offers so many contradictory terms of interpretation, from time to space to morality. Even the film's voice is visually and narratively ambiguous.

That *We Were Soldiers* does not know when to begin—with France's failed colonial conquest of Vietnam or with the United States combating Cold War communism in this space—is but one way the film expresses its temporal confusion. Two temporalities inform the moral grammar of *We Were Soldiers*: the eternal time of God and the earthly time of Man (a term I use advisedly to stand for the gendered figure of the Enlightenment who claimed the place of God on His death).

The God of *We Were Soldiers* is a Christian God. Eternal time, God's time, is recorded in the testaments, whether these are biblical (as in Christian theology) or filmic (as in the narrator's description of the film: "This story is a testament"). Eternal time is also signaled by the location of the main action; it takes place in the Ia Drang Valley, The Valley of Death. "Though I walk through the shadow of the valley of death, I will fear no evil, for Thou art with me" (Psalm 23:4). God's time, then, is not only about eternity (the promise of heaven for the repentant and hell for the wicked); it is also about faith. By placing one's faith in God the Father, one need not fear earthly evils (such as enemy soldiers) or even death itself (which is [fore]shadowed by the Ia Drang Valley).

Though God's time offers us the moral certainty that access to the unchanging good, which always already exists in the pure form of God, is merely a matter of faith, earthly time is far less certain. For there are at least two earthly times: progressive time and the time of recurrence and repetition. So while on earth there exists the possibility of progress toward the good, this progress is never guaranteed, and where there is no progress, there is merely recurrence and repetition, usually of (moral) mistakes. It is the earthly time of recurrence and repetition that features in *We Were Soldiers*. This is signaled as much by the action the film depicts (the repetition of brutal battles in the Ia Drang Valley, the twinning of Custer's last stand with the fate of Moore's Seventh Calvary and ultimately with his North Vietnamese rival) as much as it is by the way the story is told (beginning with the massacre of the French and then beginning again with the training of US forces at Fort Benning).

Not knowing *when* to begin is also about not knowing *where* to begin. Does this story begin in Vietnam or does it begin in the United States? Where to locate this story spatially is as problematic as where to locate it temporally. And, of course, space and time here are connected. For the film's first beginning in Vietnam, in the dual temporalities of eternity (the valley of death) and recurrence and repetition (US troops will be here next), also situates the action in colonial time, in the colonial ambitions of the French and the struggle for independence of the Vietnamese. In contrast, the film's second beginning in the United States situates the action in postcolonial time, a time the United States knows itself to occupy. US interests are not colonial interests; they are Cold War interests. US soldiers will not go to Vietnam to lay claim to this country; they will go there to liberate it from communism. However, this second beginning of the film in postcolonial time is necessarily read through the film's first beginning, thereby raising questions: Is the United States really in postcolonial time or is colonialism also an eternal feature of foreign policy, even if its form has changed? If colonialism endures in another form, then how does the Vietnamese struggle against the United States differ from their struggle against the French?

There is no doubt that *We Were Soldiers* marks the dubious nature of Western involvement in Vietnam with its dual beginnings, but it hardly eschews colonialism or neocolonialism for, as we saw, its very first move is to type the words of a US author across the screen of the presumably barren Vietnamese landscape, a gesture that implies not only the masculine power of the West to write on a blank page but also the feminine positioning of Vietnam as the blank page on which Western ambitions will be written (Gubar, 1985). The film never pauses to consider this move, to consider the gendered bases of (neo)colonialism. And the reason for that is that *We Were Soldiers* is not (self-consciously) a story about women; it is a story about men. In case we did not catch this fact from the film's themes and characters, the film's tagline underscores it for us: "We were fathers, brothers, husbands, sons." What the film is interested in is how these familial masculine bodies enact their dramas on the feminine landscape of Vietnam, a feminine entity that Western powers misrecognize as a blank page.

The feminine in *We Were Soldiers*, then, could not be more different from the feminine in *Pearl Harbor*. In *Pearl Harbor*, the feminine is the morally neutral stage on which moral dilemmas are resolved. In *We Were Soldiers*, the feminine is the moral abyss itself, the quagmire that eternally threatens to undo moral certainties (of Catholicism in the Moore household;[1] of capitalism in the wider world). The feminine, in other words, is that "fucking landscape" about which the French commander complained before it killed him, and it is the problem of "terrain" that the US military advisors at Fort Benning worried about as they prepared to commit to US military intervention in Vietnam (see McClintock, 1995). From the film's US masculine familial perspective, it is only by domesticating the feminine under masculine authority—in the home (as seen in the orderly US Army wives) or by creating a unified homeland in Vietnam (a domestic space free of civil war)—that the feminine can play the supporting role that is her traditional calling, as US home front or as capitalist ally in the Cold War. What all this means is that the role of the feminine cannot be critically engaged in *We Were*

*Soldiers* and, as a result, the question of (neo)colonialism can only be marked but can never be interrogated.

The film rushes on from its two beginnings (colonial and problematically "postcolonial") to tell a different story—a story that, despite its fragmented histories, offers a unified morality spoken through a unified masculine voice. Never mind that this voice (as our opening sequence suggests) is sometimes French, sometimes Vietnamese, and sometimes American. Never mind that unclear is whether it is being narrated by a journalist (Galloway) or an army commander (Moore). All we need to know about this voice is what the film's title tells us: it is the voice of the soldier who is witness to history.

The soldier, then, is the unifying figure of the film. He (and it is always "he" in this film) is the character through whom all of the contradictions of the opening sequence—temporal, spatial, narrative, and moral—are resolved *so long as* he remains firmly situated in a moral universe rendered meaningful by a traditional take on patriarchy guaranteed by God the Father. Temporal contradictions between eternal time and earthly time find resolution through the figure of the father: God the Father guides men on earth; human fathers (who are also soldiers) guide wives, children, and young nations on earth. This soldier/father figure also resolves the film's spatial contradictions. For whether the film is set in Vietnam or in the United States or in both, it is a film about soldiering. This means that the seemingly contradictory dedication of the film in the opening narration, as both a testament to US soldiers and a tribute to North Vietnamese soldiers, is not contradictory because both were soldiers. Indeed, even the narrator, who we figure out sometime later is journalist James Galloway, is included in the *we* of *We Were Soldiers*, not because he picked up a machine gun to defend himself in the battle for the Ia Drang Valley but because his fight for hearts and minds was better fought by spreading the Word with his typewriter and camera.

Thanks to the film's specific renditions and fusing of time, space, and morality, even the film's idyllic still-life depictions of 1960s America free of racism, sexism, and religious bigotry make perfect sense. This is best illustrated in a pair of scenes in which first Mrs. Moore and then her husband call their troops to assembly.

> First we see Mrs. Moore gathering the young Army wives at Fort Benning, GA to discuss day-to-day living at their new post. Nearly all the wives are white. The one black wife is seated next to Mrs. Moore. When a young white wife complains that the base washing machines are full of sand, another joins in with a suggestion:

WHITE NORTHERN WIFE: In the meantime, the laundromat in town's okay, but they won't let you wash your colored things in their machines.

WHITE WIFE TWO: In a public laundromat?

WHITE NORTHERN WIFE: It didn't make any sense to me either, but I'm telling you they have a big sign right in the window that says, "Whites Only."

An embarrassed silence prevails.

WHITE NORTHERN WIFE: What?

At this point the black Army wife intervenes.

BLACK WIFE: Honey, they mean white people only.

WHITE NORTHERN WIFE (upset, after a pause): That's awful. Your husband is wearing the uniform of a country that allows a place to say that his laundry's not good enough when he could die...(pause). I'm sorry, I just...

BLACK WIFE (interrupting): That's all right, honey, but I know what my husband's fighting for, and that's why I can smile. My husband would never ask for respect. And he'll give respect to no man who hasn't earned it. The rest of his family's the same way. (Her tone changes from pious to playfully putting on airs.) And anybody who doesn't respect that can keep his God-damn washing machine 'cause my baby's clothes are gonna be clean anyway.

All the wives laugh.

MRS. MOORE (laughing): Well, I guess that takes care of item number two.

These ideas are echoed a short time later in Lt. Col. Moore's speech to his troops and their families in a farewell ceremony the day before they head off into battle: "We're moving into the shadow of the Valley of Death, where you'll watch the back of the man next to you, as he will watch yours. And you won't care what color he is or by what name he calls God. They say we're leaving home. We're going to what home was always supposed to be."

In these two scenes, the heads of the household—Lt. Col. and Mrs. Moore—shepherd their young men and women from the earthly time of the recurrence and repetition of racial and religious prejudice into the eternal time of tolerance and good will, even though this means they all must pass through the shadow of the Valley of Death. What enables this transformation, these scenes suggest, is the Army. Soldiers such as the black wife's husband know why they are fighting (although this why is never explained to viewers), and all soldiers in the field must equally rely on one another. All are merely soldiers of God. By substituting a United States marked by racial, religious, and gender inequality in earthly time (now firmly positioned as "off base") with an eternally tolerant United States (the increasingly feminine/wifely time of Fort Benning and the masculine/soldierly time of foreign battlefields), any critical representation of a 1960s US notion of home is overwritten with "what home ought to be."

However, of course, all this good will flowing from God's will comes at a price. It forecloses on the possibility of critically reconsidering patriarchy. We must accept the goodness of the film's scripting of the traditional US family, just as we must accept that (neo)colonialism is not what US soldiering in Vietnam is about. But because of the film's particular rendering of the relationships between God, father, and soldier, we need accept this reading only so long as two conditions apply. The first is that fathers and soldiers are (of) the same (moral) character. And the second is that the infallibility of God the father can be transferred onto earthly fathers/soldiers.

The film explicitly addresses each of these conditions through the relationship between Lt. Col. Moore and one of his young officers, Jack Geoghegan (Chris Kline). On the birth of Jack's first child, Lt. Col. Moore finds the worried young man in the hospital chapel:

> JACK:  Colonel may I ask you a question?...What do you think about being a soldier and a father?
> MOORE:  I hope that being good at the one makes me better at the other. Why? What about you?
> JACK:  I don't know, sir. Between college and here, Barbara [Jack's wife] and I spent a year in Africa. We helped build a school for orphans. They were orphans because the warlord across the border didn't like their tribe. I know God has a plan for me. I just hope it's to help protect orphans, not make any.
> MOORE:  Well, why don't we ask Him. (Gets up) Come on, let's go ask Him.

The Colonel and Jack walk to the front of the chapel where they kneel at the altar and pray.

MOORE: …I pray that you watch over the young men like Jack Geoghegan that I lead into battle. You use me as Your instrument in this awful hell war to watch over them, especially if they are men like this one beside me deserving of a future in your blessing and good will. Amen.

This scene draws an equivalence between fathering and soldiering not only narratively but also visually, for it is the visual double of an earlier scene in which Moore kneels and prays with his children at bedtime. This visual parallel transposes Jack from just any soldier into "Moore's son," a move that is narratively confirmed in a conversation between Moore and his wife:

MOORE:  The men are so young…I look at' em. I see our boys.
MRS. MOORE:  Well, then you're just the man to lead them.

But is he? He seems to be. The Colonel promises to be the first on the field of battle and the last off, a promise the film shows him keeping. And he promises to leave no man behind, dead or alive, another promise he keeps. But what the film tells us is that even though Lt. Col. Moore is an honorable man from an honorable era, the moral legacy of this holy father is not transferable to the next generation, however much that generation might wish to carry it on.

The first US casualty in the battle for the Ia Drang Valley makes this point. Just before he dies, the soldier announces, "I'm glad I could die for my country," a sentiment very much associated with earlier US wars, such as WWII, rather than a collective US memory of the Vietnam War. We soon learn that this soldier is the husband of the white northern wife who was so naïve about both southern racism and about the lack of racism among US Army wives. By coupling this soldier with this wife, the film begs the question, "Is this soldier as naïve as his wife?" The film's answer is both no and yes. He is not naïve to fight and die for his country; he is naïve not to understand what is dying with him: the moral certainties of a WWII US moral grammar of war that could shield his dying words from sounding corny to a contemporary US audience.

The film offers two answers to this question because it is very much caught between the old era of WWII and some new era. As one reviewer described it, "…*We Were Soldiers* is not your father's Vietnam movie: In the stature of its warriors, it's your grandfather's; in the visceral immediacy of its combat scenes, it's your son's" (Edelstein, 2002b). It is to this visceral immediacy of combat that the film quickly moves, with US battle lines failing to hold and the US body count mounting. The further the film moves away from this first death, the further it moves away from a "grandfatherly" depiction of the Vietnam War, like that of John Wayne in *The Green Berets*. Only one other soldier's death comes close to occupying such a morally certain space: it is Jack's death. Jack's death is less patriotic than patriarchic. For this young father dies while trying to rescue a fellow soldier in battle, trying to fulfill Lt. Col. Moore's promise to leave no man behind. What Jack's death symbolizes is that neither the Colonel's faith in God the Father nor his equation of fathering and soldering are enough to pass the patriarchal promises of a WWII moral order on to his son's, our father's.

*We Were Soldiers* not only bears witness to the death of WWII moral certainties; it situates its action at a time when the old is dying and the new has yet to be born. What would become the "new moral certainty" of this era (at least officially) is the rhetoric of the Cold War. But *We Were Soldiers* barely mentions the Cold War. This term is uttered only once, by President Johnson in a televised speech. None of the soldiers, whether in training or in battle, seem to be aware of the Cold War, much less its moral grammar of us/capitalists versus them/communists that "ensures" the eventual victory of us over them. In this way, the moral time of *We Were Soldiers* parallels the time *between* 9/11 and the Bush administration's articulation of the war on terror in us-versus-them terms: "Either you are with us, or you are with the terrorists" (Bush, 2001b). In *We Were Soldiers* as in the brief period after 9/11, the terms of the new morality had yet to be articulated.

This is not to say that no moral certainty is celebrated in the film. Once the seemingly eternal space of the US patriarchal family and the patriarchal US nation acting in foreign affairs is ruptured by the realities of war, the passing of time, and the coming of death, all that remains is the soldier. And it is his sacrifice that enables a new moral future. This is symbolized in the relationship between Lt. Col. Moore and Jack, for when this godly father loses his only (soldierly) son at the hands of "heathens," what is marked is not only the failures of past patriarchies but the passage from an old moral order (laid down in the Old Testament) to a new one (found in the New Testament). It is this sacrificial soldier who is reclaimed as the foundation of a new moral certainty in an era of post-WWII uncertainties. *We Were Soldiers* celebrates the professionalism of the soldier, whether he wears a North Vietnamese uniform or an American one, whether he carries a gun or a camera.[2] As journalist-photographer James Galloway explains in his closing narration, "We who have seen war never stop seeing it. In the silence of the night, we will always hear the screams. So this is our story, for we were soldiers once, and young."

What makes Galloway as much as Moore or any of his men into a soldier is this seeing, this witnessing of war. And, finally, this is what *We Were Soldiers* is about: not only being a witness/soldier who saw these historical events unfold but being a witness/soldier who spreads the Word about soldierly sacrifices and soldierly professionalism. This last point is made in an almost tearful exchange between journalist Galloway and (his) commander Moore in the aftermath of battle.

GALLOWAY:  Sir, I don't know how to tell this story.
MOORE:  Well, you've got to, Joe. You tell the American people what these men did here. You tell' em how my troopers died.
GALLOWAY:  Yes, sir.
MOORE:  Thank you.

In the end, Galloway and Moore told this story together, as soldiers and as witnesses, in their book *We Were Soldiers Once...and Young*. The film's title is the book's title, minus the markers of the passage of time and the change of subject position. In both, the hero is the professional soldier, an eternal figure—sometimes Christ, sometimes disciple—who is called on to bear witness eternally. Beyond fighting and witnessing, this soldier has but one other duty: to protect the man beside him. As Galloway explains of these soldiers, "Some had families waiting. For others, their only families would be the men they bled beside. There were no bands, no flags, no honor guards to welcome them home. They went to war because their country ordered them to. But in the end, they fought not for their country or their flag. They fought for each other."

What Galloway bears witness to as the story closes is not only the professionalism and heroism of US soldiers in Vietnam and their innocence for the policy mistakes of their government. He also bears witness to the basis of another familial order that sustains men during and after battle: a brotherhood of (Christian) soldiers, a family of soldiers who have shed blood together in war. This is the "family" that truly occupies that place to which Moore refers as "what home was always supposed to be." It does not matter that this home and family happen to be articulated in relation to Vietnam for, as every sacrificial soldier knows, they are transcendent and eternal.

Ultimately, then, *We Were Soldiers* inscribes the US *we* as a soldier who is eternally faithful to the execution of his mission and to his men.

This does not mean that the soldier believes in his mission. Mission briefs are beyond him; he merely does what he is ordered to do. But without a doubt, this soldier believes in his fellow soldiers. This is the foundation of his professionalism, and this is the new foundation of the moral American family. As a moral trajectory for becoming a moral American, the film suggests that attaining the same high levels of professional conduct exemplified by the US soldier in Vietnam ought to be the aim of US policy professionals as well. In this way, bad foreign policy decisions, such as misreading our object (Vietnam/the feminine) and misplacing our objectives (silencing/domesticating this Vietnamese/ feminine voice), can (eternally) become a thing of the past. All *we* need is a little faith.

## The Quiet American

*The Quiet American* is a tale about the darker side of US professionalism in Vietnam. Set in 1952 in colonial Indochina, this film begins before the two beginnings of *We Were Soldiers*, before the French withdrawal and well before US soldiers officially replaced them. This is a far more certain time for US policy makers, but their certainty does not come from God, nor in the family. Their faith is a faith in themselves and in their own beliefs. Rather than foreshadowing coming moral uncertainties, *The Quiet American* is a cautionary tale about misplaced moral certainty, about the dangers of having too much faith in one's self and the treacherous paths down which that faith can lead us.

Based on Graham Greene's novel of the same name, the film follows the triangulated relationships among middle-aged Englishman Thomas Fowler (Michael Caine), American Alden Pyle (Brendan Fraser), and sexually available Vietnamese Phuong (Do Thi Hai Yen). Fowler is a journalist for the *Times of London*, Pyle a medical officer in the US Economic Aid Mission, and Phuong the woman/country over whom this older European and younger American compete.

Unlike the characters in *We Were Soldier*, who are all located in and in relation to the family, none of the three main characters in *The Quiet American* are conventionally situated within the family. Fowler is trapped in a loveless Catholic marriage to a wife back in London but lives with his mistress Phuong. Phuong becomes a pay-for-hire dancer and later Fowler's lover when her father dies. And Pyle is a single man who, a good decade into his marrying years, has no wife. At different times, both Fowler and Pyle promise to marry Phuong. The cynical Fowler, we know, is lying; the overly innocent Pyle we tend to believe, but in this film, no marriage takes place. No children are born, no families are formed. Whether because of too little faith (on Fowler's part) or too much (on Pyle's), Phuong/Vietnam never makes it to the altar with either man. She is merely the place in which their passions burn but where no one's desires are ultimately fulfilled. Far from being a love story, then, *The Quiet American* is a tragic tale staged at the intersections of a stereotypical masculine desire for (colonial) conquest (see, for example, McClintock, 1995 and Ling, 2001) and a stereotypical feminine desire for commitment.

The opening sequence sets the terms of this triangulation, as it foreshadows its deadly consequences. During the opening credits, we hear a mournful Vietnamese woman singing in her native language before we see the first image of the film: something small and delicate is perched on the end of a long stick, roasting over a small pot. This image suggests three of Indochina's precious "fruits": opium, the palm date (also known as a *phoenix*), and woman (a soft fruit penetrated by a firm stick). As the singing continues, cymbals shimmer. Two images simultaneously fade in over the opening image, a close up of an emotionless Phuong (whose Vietnamese name, she later tells us, means Phoenix) and a fiery bomb blast. All images fade out until we see only the naked flame of a glass-covered lantern dancing before a tapestry. Fade again to another transparent head shot of Phuong cross-dissolved over another bomb blast. Fade to an image of Fowler sitting at a desk before a typewriter. His narration begins.

FOWLER:  I can't say what made me fall in love with Vietnam. That a woman's voice can drug you. That everything is so intense— the colors, the taste, even the rain. Nothing like the filthy rain in London.

As Fowler speaks, his image slowly fades to that of the river running through Saigon. When he pauses, the film's title fades in and then out over this river and is replaced by the fade in and out of the words "Saigon, Vietnam, 1952," as Fowler's narration continues.

FOWLER:  They say what you're looking for, you will find here. They say you come to Vietnam, and you understand a lot in a few minutes. The rest has got to be lived. (Pause) The smell, that's the first thing that hits you, promising everything in exchange for your soul. And the heat. Your shirt is straightaway a rag, you can hardly remember your name or what you came to escape from. But at night, there's a breeze. The river is beautiful. You could be forgiven for thinking there was no war, that the gunshots were fireworks, that only pleasure matters— a pipe of opium with the touch of a girl who might tell you she loves you.

Fowler's narration is interrupted by a thud and a splash. The camera abruptly, very quickly pans down from its fixed view of the busy but tranquil river to reveal the body of a man in a white, blood-stained suit lying facedown on a dock.

FOWLER: And then, something happens, as you knew it would. And nothing can ever be the same again.

Fade to a shot of the French Viceroy's office, the camera approaching the Viceroy, doubling Fowler's point of view.

VICEROY: Monsieur Fowler, thank you for coming in. I'm sorry to have to ask you in at this hour.

Fade to a time-lapsed shot of Fowler seated opposite the Viceroy.

FOWLER: Well, I know as much as you do. He's an American, he's about thirty, he works for the Economic Aid Mission, and I like him. He's a very good chap, serious, not like those noisy bastards down at the Continental. He's a quiet American.
VICEROY: Yes, a very quiet American.
FOWLER: He's dead, isn't he?

The Viceroy gives Fowler a suspicious look, to which he stutters defensively.

FOWLER: Not guilty. I, I, I, I...just...put two and two together.

As Fowler then identifies Pyle's body and claims him as a friend, we see that Pyle has been stabbed through the heart.

VICEROY: To tell you the truth, I'm not completely sorry. These Americans are causing a lot of trouble to us. But still, a murder is a murder. Anything to help us?
FOWLER: No.

Fade to Phuong standing in the street outside Fowler's flat. Fowler rushes out to bring her inside and tell her the news of Pyle's murder. As he leaves the flat, the camera tracks his footsteps, rushing down to finally rest on a depression in the freshly poured concrete. A cymbal shimmers, marking this imprint as a clue, raising a doubt in our minds about what we have been told so far about Pyle's death, about what Fowler meant by "And then something happens, as you knew it would."

On hearing the news, Phuong tells Fowler what they both know so well: "Pyle was in love with me." As their conversation ends, the screen fills with white, then fades to a shot of Fowler looking at his watch, thus explaining to the viewers that the rest of the story will be told in flashback, as Fowler begins again on the day he met Pyle. The opening sequence is over.

What is suggested in this opening sequence is what we will soon learn for certain: that Phuong/Vietnam is caught between two suitors, two eras, and two moralities. Her lover at the beginning of the flashback sequence is the morally cynical Fowler, a man who is financially available to her but whose old world commitments (his Catholic marriage) prevent him from marrying Phuong. Her lover at the end of the opening sequence is the morally certain Pyle, the available quiet American who promises to take her back home with him to Boston as his wife.

Even though Fowler himself cannot put his finger on it in his opening narration, he gives clear indications as to why he loves Phuong/Vietnam. Her incantations mesmerize him as much as her opium does. She allows you to lose yourself in her heat. And she promises everything in exchange for your soul.

Throwing himself into this heat, Fowler takes up the promise of Phuong/Vietnam, offering his soul in return. But this moral skeptic lost his soul long ago, by turning his back on his wife and her religion, by turning to the pleasures of opium and women to replace her, by allowing himself to indulge his fantasy about the peacefulness of the war-torn country he occupies. Before Fowler can exchange his soul, he has to recover it. And this is precisely what Fowler does in his relationship with Phuong/Vietnam. His soul is not recovered through love, nor through faith: it is a soul born of torment and, as we will see, the film suggests that a tormented soul is the only kind worth having. What initially torments Fowler is Pyle's love for Phuong. When Pyle declares this love, Fowler lies, telling them that his wife has agreed to a divorce. But when this lie is discovered, Phuong leaves Fowler for Pyle.

Pyle's love of Phuong, like his character, is so utterly naïve that it seems to be transparently honest. He seems to epitomize the pure (of) soul. As Pyle tells Fowler, Pyle came to Vietnam on a medical aid mission to treat eye disease. But Pyle's innocence does not place him beyond politics. Unlike Fowler who, from his amoral journalistic perspective, takes no action and favors neither the French nor the Communists, Pyle resolutely believes a "third force" must be created in Vietnam as a democratic alternative to either French colonialism or to North Vietnamese communism. That he pals around with political figures in the US legation is not the least bit suspicious, given their shared nationality and their shared political views.

Pyle's desire to save Vietnam from herself (the Northern Communists) is paralleled in his desire to save Phuong. As he tells Fowler, his love for Phuong has served only to deepen his political aims in Vietnam. In voice-over, Fowler comments that he should not be surprised that a man like Pyle would conflate a woman and a country, suggesting this is not a mistake he himself would make. But, of course, Fowler, like Pyle, has already made it, albeit differently. Unlike Pyle, Fowler is not looking to rescue Phuong/Vietnam; he is merely hoping to enjoy her. Fowler's and Pyle's different aspirations in relation to woman/country simply repeat the difference between old world colonial instincts (Fowler) and new world (post-)colonial, democratic ones (Pyle).

And what of Phuong/Vietnam herself? Phuong/Vietnam is the space on which the contest between old(er) colonials and young(er) neo-colonials is waged. Phuong/Vietnam never speaks of her own deep feelings. She tells us, "Pyle was in love with me" but never "I was (or wasn't) in love with Pyle." After Pyle's death, Phuong admits that she misses Pyle, but we never know what this missing consists of: a longing for lost youth, lost commitment, lost certainty? As such, Phuong/Vietnam is positioned as the stereotypical feminine figure who reflects masculine desires but who seems to have no desires of her own (Irigaray, 1985). Just as the river running through Saigon reflects distant artillery as if it were fireworks, so too does Phuong reflect back what both Fowler and Pyle wish to see, even though each is only seeing his own illusions.

Like all the feminine figures we have seen so far, Phuong/Vietnam is an amoral staging ground for masculine moral struggles. Her quiet presence and her willingness to be exchanged among men suggest her infinite malleability, but Phuong/Vietnam is never just a placid pool in which masculine desires are reflected. Her very name, not to mention the portrayal of her volatility in the opening sequence, reminds us of her turbulent potential, for Phuong is also a phoenix, a mythical bird who burned away its old self in an intense flame only to be reborn as young. *The Quiet American* takes up Phuong's/Vietnam's story just as she is going up in flames, flickering on the funeral pyre between the old colonial self represented by Fowler and the new (post-)colonial self represented by Pyle. After Pyle's death, Phuong returns to Fowler, to old familiar ways, her explosive potential postponed for a few more years until more Americans finally set her ablaze.

Phuong's/Vietnam's inferno is documented in the film's closing montage of Fowler's newspaper stories that tell the history of Vietnam from 1952 to the French withdrawal in the mid-1950s to the massive US military campaigns of the 1960s. But, more strikingly, it is foreshadowed in the film's depiction of a terrorist attack on the main square in Saigon, the square both Fowler and Phuong visit separately every morning for drinks with friends. As Fowler sits in his street café, awaiting the sight of his lost mistress entering the milk bar across the square, he notices a US journalist positioning himself for an assignment in the lazy atmosphere, then overhears two US women preparing to leave the café (the one explaining to the other that her husband said she had to be home at this precise time for no reason she can understand), and finally seeing a man park a white van across the road, in front of the milk bar, obstructing his view of Phuong's arrival. The film cuts between a slow motion shot of the driver walking away from the van and Fowler's face as he pieces together these three events.

And then the car bomb explodes.

Unhurt, Fowler makes his way through the carnage to the milk bar, desperate to find Phuong, but she is nowhere to be found. As he exits the milk bar, he sees Pyle approaching the scene, looking cool and professional. Fowler helps a dying man while Pyle coldly tries to wipes blood stains from his trousers, then directs the US journalist to take pictures of the dead and wounded. Fowler watches all this in a daze, realizing only later that Pyle—who claims to speak only English and French—commanded a local police officer in fluent Vietnamese not to interfere with the US journalist's work.

And then the penny drops. Fowler realizes that Pyle is not really a medical aid officer: he is a US spy—CIA. His medical cover is what enables him both to travel freely throughout the country and to import diolacton, a chemical used not only in the manufacture of eyeglass frames but in the manufacture of explosives. Pyle is supplying diolacton to General The, whom the Americans are setting up as the "third force," of whom Pyle so passionately speaks, to oppose the French and the North Vietnamese.

On hearing of Pyle's actions in the square, Fowler's assistant (who has ties to the communists) proposes that Fowler work with his forces to assassinate Pyle. But before Fowler agrees, he confronts Pyle in his flat, where Pyle's dog leaves his imprint in the freshly poured concrete. Pyle explains his commitment to a third force under General The and his involvement in the events in the square, another act of violence that will be blamed on the communists.

PYLE: In a war, you use the tools you've got, and, at the moment, he's the tool we've got.
FOWLER: Yes, and in the meantime even more people must die.
PYLE (heatedly): Last year, the US government gave $210 million in military assistance to the French in Indochina. If we are going to stop communism and underwrite a Third Way, we need to give people a leader they admire. Tomorrow morning, when Congress reads the report and sees the photographs of the communist atrocities in the square, they are going to give us that support. The French aren't gonna stop the communists. They haven't got the brains, and they haven't got the guts.

Fowler gives Pyle a chance to recant, to say it was all a mistake, that he was only following order or he was confused, that his love for Phuong had caused him doubts.

PYLE: It is because of Phuong that I am even more determined. Let's just look at Phuong—this beauty, this daughter of a professor, taxi dancer, mistress of an older European man— well, that pretty much describes the whole country, doesn't it? Look, Thomas, we are here to save Vietnam from all that. What happened in the square makes me sick. But in the long run, I'm gonna save lives...I don't think you see the big picture, Thomas.
FOWLER: No, I do not see the big picture.

At that, Fowler turns to the window and opens a book. This is the signal to the lookout below that he will aid in Pyle's murder. Fowler and Pyle agree to disagree and make plans to dine that evening at a restaurant on the river. But, as planned, Pyle never arrives. He is ambushed by the communists, stabbed through his heart by Fowler's assistant, and dumped in the river.

This is the end of the flashback.

The action wraps up. The Viceroy knows of Fowler's involvement in Pyle's murder but does not pursue him. Phuong returns to Fowler, and Fowler tries to apologize to her for Pyle's death without explaining his involvement. And then we return to Fowler's narration, a repeat of much of what opened the film.

FOWLER: They say you come to Vietnam, and you understand a lot in a few minutes. The rest has got to be lived. They say whatever it was you were looking for, you will find here. They say there is a ghost in every house, and if you make peace with him, he will stay quiet.

Cut to the montage of Fowler's newspaper stories. The final shot is of a Fowler article next to a photograph of a wounded US soldier, his head wrapped in a bandage that covers one eye. The camera zooms in on this image, moving from "the big picture" to a minute pixel, until this black pixel fills the entire screen. The closing credits begin.

By the time we reach the end of *The Quiet American*, we are as far away as we could possibly be from the official US big picture about Vietnam as depicted in *We Were Soldiers*. There are no traditional, well-functioning families through which to interpret the film's action. God is nowhere to be found. All we have is a quiet American man whose faith in himself is so great that he seems to have completely usurped the place of God, deciding as he does who will live and how one will live. This is not the sacrificial professional soldier so celebrated by *We Were Soldiers* but more the Kurtz of *Apocalypse Now (Redux)* dressed in a white suit taking such "professionalism" to its logical conclusion. In so doing, *The Quiet American* challenges its viewers to draw their own logical conclusion about its portrayal of the US *we* and of its moral grammar of war.

The US *we* of *The Quiet American* is a US professional who is acting on behalf of the US state and has made terrorism possible while claiming to make democracy possible. And because our official post-9/11 US *we* makes no distinction between terrorists and those who support them, what *The Quiet American* tells its post-9/11 US spectators is that we were terrorists. The film also articulates a US moral grammar of war. This moral grammar is encapsulated in the remarks Fowler's assistant makes to Fowler as he tries to persuade him to help kill Pyle: "Sooner or later…one has to take sides if one is to remain human." This sentence has an almost eerie echo—of President Bush declaring to the world, "Either you are with us, or you are with the terrorists" (Bush, 2001b). Both Fowler's assistant and President Bush would agree that humanity is located on the opposite side of terrorism but, of course, as Fowler's assistant utters this sentence, the terrorist *is* the quiet American. Like the 9/11 terrorists, this quiet American was a man whose misplaced faith in his own vision of morality led him to take extreme and unforgivable actions.

This quiet American (Alden Pyle) dies, then, not for the usual reasons for which men are punished in Vietnam War films: because he made a bad (sexual) object choice (of Phuong and of Vietnam), because the family this pairing would create was out of step with US self-understandings as firmly *not* a colonial power in any relationship. Nor does Pyle die because only with Pyle's death will his sexual, colonial rival regain possession of his, the colonial, prize. These reasons for Pyle's death are too simple for a film such as *The Quiet American*. Though they may be contributing factors to his death, they are not what render it a necessary death. From Fowler's perspective (which is the film's perspective), Pyle's death becomes necessary when the self-assured Pyle proves himself to be incapable of moral *uncertainty*. This is what Fowler pleads with Pyle to express as he weighs whether to aid in his rival's assassination. However, like the one-eyed US soldier in the film's final shot, Pyle can see things only one way: that way is his way, which, in this film, is "the American way."

It is this lack of political perspective caused by a lack of moral uncertainty that proves to be Pyle's undoing. And, the film suggests, it is such a morally self-assured American that "we (ought to) wish we'd never been" and take great pains never to become. We can ensure this by allowing the antiheroic ghost of Alden Pyle to haunt our (national) house, just as Fowler ultimately does. However, unlike Fowler, we should never make peace with him, for then he will go quiet. And we know how dangerous he is when he's quiet.

### Who we wish we'd never been

Though *We Were Soldiers* and *The Quiet American* have strikingly different things to say about a US *we*, a US moral grammar of war, and a trajectory for becoming a moral America(n), both films function in the same way. Both are cautionary tales that remind us of who we wish we'd never been so that these *we*'s will not repeat themselves in future tales about who we might become.[3] The films agree on who one of these US *we*'s is: the US foreign policy official who wrongly chose

Vietnam as an object of US intervention. In different ways, both films remind us that Vietnam is not a barren landscape, a blank page, or a colonial concubine, nor is she necessarily a phoenix. All that we know for certain is that, regardless of whether given the chance to speak, Vietnam has its own voice—and we would have been well advised to listen.

However, this is old news. That Vietnam was a bad object choice is a lesson long ago learned and rehearsed in US cinemas and policy circles at least since the 1970s. What this means is that these two Vietnam films agree only on what we already knew. On just about everything else, they could not be more different. And, not surprisingly, they could not have been put to more different uses in the aftermath of 9/11.

*We Were Soldiers* suggests several lines of criticism toward the United States (especially neocolonialism), but the only line of criticism it sustains has to do with the fracturing of the US home front as a result of this war. After depicting the sacrifices that young American soldiers made in the battlefield, the film ends with a tribute to these men. Its final image is of Lt. Col. Hal Moore visiting the Vietnam War Memorial in Washington, D.C., mourning and honoring his troopers. Before the final credits, the names of each US serviceman killed in the battle for the Ia Drang Valley appears on screen. All this takes place as, in the final sequence, Galloway renarrates blood relations: from the blood you are born with to the blood you spill with others in combat.

What this ending does is to bombard the viewer with reminders that the US public largely shunned Vietnam veterans. And it tells us in no uncertain terms that this is our shame. This, the film declares, is who we wish we'd never been, or at least it ought to be. This was America's moral mistake, and this is why it is appropriate to recover the figure of the US soldier from *any* war, heroize him, and support him. This is exactly what many Americans did in the wake of September 11.

As fate would have it, one of the heroes of the battle for the Ia Drang Valley was also one of the heroes of 9/11. Rick Rescorla, whose photograph graced the original paperback editions of *We Were Soldiers Once...And Young* (before Mel Gibson and his movie replaced him, 1992) not only fought with Lt. Col. Moore and his men; he later became a security officer for Morgan Stanley Dean Whiter and Company, whose headquarters was housed in the Twin Towers of the World Trade Center. When a plane hit his building, Rescorla escorted all of his 2,000 plus employees to safety before reentering the building to rescue others. When he did, the tower collapsed, and he was lost. Rescorla became a figure of public mourning, both (I would argue) for 9/11 and for "our" shame at not having honored Rescorla and others like him for the service they so long ago provided to the nation. This time, it seemed, we were determined to do it right, to honor our fallen soldiers no matter what our personal views might be on the war they were fighting (Grunwald, 2002; Stewart, 2002).

With this renewed celebration of the hero/soldier came calls to support our troops, not only with yellow ribbons and well wishes but with a level of financial backing that went as far as it could to ensure their safety (Fuchs, 2002). All these steps ensured that who we wish we'd never been—a nation ashamed of our soldiers in Vietnam because we were ashamed of ourselves for having fought that war in the first place—was not who we might become in a moral post-9/11 America.

*We Were Soldiers*, then, offers a moral grammar and a moral trajectory to make up for and reconcile with a past that shames us. Arguably so, too, does *The Quiet American*, but its moral demands are much more taxing on us. Unlike *We Were Soldiers*, which exposes and then repairs the crack between soldier and citizen in the disintegrating and then reunified US home front, *The Quiet American* questions the moral character of all of us, especially the (then) new brand of professional US soldier in the battlefield. By dramatically relating the also true story of CIA support for terrorism in 1950s Vietnam to a post-9/11 US audience, the film marks us as terrorists, as the very enemies against whom we claim to be at war.

It is not all that surprising, then, that *The Quiet American* had its release date postponed. The film previewed to an appreciative audience on September 10, 2001. However, in the wake of September 11, Harvey Weinstein, the cochairman of Miramax (which was set to distribute the film), said his studio concluded that "you can't release this film now; it's unpatriotic. America has to be cohesive and band together. We were worried that nobody had the stomach for a movie about bad Americans anymore" (cited in Wiener, 2002). It was not until the film's star, Michael Caine, applied pressure that the film got a limited release in December 2002, showing for two weeks only in New York and Los Angeles so it would qualify for Oscar nominations. When Caine received a Best Actor nomination for his performance, the film was released a bit more widely from January through March of 2003. What this meant was that the film not only created a buzz for Oscar night; it became linked both to 9/11 and to the pending US war in Iraq. As Jon Wiener argued in *The Nation*,

> "The parallels between the plot of the film and plans for war with Iraq today are equally striking. An innocent, energetic young American…is sent to a faraway land of suffering and political

turmoil. He believes in democracy and freedom, and he wants to help, but he doesn't know much about the place. The quiet American finds people who seem to be good guys and gives them money and weapons to support their effort to make their country free. But good intentions lead to bad results, innocent people are killed, and the United States is drawn into a decade of war. Although the film was finished more than a year before George Bush began arguing for unilateral action in Iraq, the arguments have an uncanny similarity" (Wiener, 2002).

However, it is easy to ignore the advice of a film that is critical of the US *we*, especially if it is offered from a point of view other than "our" own. *The Quiet American*, a film rallied around by antiwar protestors as the "war on terror" threatened to become Gulf War II, is told from the point of view of an older, wiser European. At the time of the film's wider circulation in the United States, older, wiser Europeans were again offering their advice to the leaders of the new world. This time it was France and Germany protesting against a second UN declaration that would authorize armed intervention against the government of Saddam Hussein for his failure to comply with US weapons inspections. Hauntingly, from the official US perspective, the Europeans did not get the bigger picture about Iraq and the Middle East region, but the French vetoed the UN resolution against US objections, and the US led a major military offensive in Iraq with a very few of its allies, a war that is officially over but (at the time of this writing in August 2005) is still very much ongoing.

After the ongoing war in Iraq officially ended, questions about the primary justification for war—to shut down Saddam Hussein's weapons of mass destruction programs—came under scrutiny because US and British intelligence seemed to be suspect. In the United States, President Bush's claim in his 2002 State of the Union Address, that Iraq had attempted to acquire weapons-grade plutonium in Africa, and in the United Kingdom, Prime Minister Tony Blair's claim to Parliament that Iraq could launch weapons of mass destruction within forth-five minutes, were both shown to be based on faulty intelligence. Intelligence, it seems, whether provided by such characters as Pyle in 1950s Vietnam or by US and British intelligence offices in the run up to the war in Iraq, seems to be the ghost/spook/spy who has come back to haunt us.

Fowler, speaking of the ghost that haunts his house, tells us that if we make peace with this ghost, it will be quiet—but at what cost? What *The Quiet American* suggests is that such a peace is a false one. This peace is immoral because when our ghosts go too quiet (like Pyle), they may well get up to no good or simply get it wrong. It is our (moral) responsibility to keep track of them and to keep them on track. Becoming a moral America(n), this film suggests, is about facing up to our past—and not just the easy stuff, such as supporting our troops or memorializing our fallen heroes, but the hard stuff as well, the stuff that haunts us. Otherwise, who we wish we'd never been in Vietnam threatens to become who we might become in the war on terror.

# 4 Who we really are (humanitarians)

The Vietnam War film *We Were Soldiers* replaced the WWII foundational family with a new familial foundation for American morality: the brotherhood of Christian soldiers. As long as the professional soldier abided by standards of good moral conduct that (the film suggests) were passed down from God the Father to earthly fathers, soldiers should be celebrated by the nation, even when the nation ceased celebrating the cause for which the soldiers fought. The difficulty with this logic, of course, is that the Vietnam War also gave us failing fathers.[1] And so good moral conduct, whether by the professional soldier or by the professional US foreign policy maker, could not be guaranteed (a point made differently by *The Quiet American*). What we are left with, then, is not (necessarily) a brotherhood of Christian soldiers but merely a band of brothers.

In the post-9/11 era, the moral foundation of this band of brothers was dramatically resecured. Televisually, Steven Spielberg and Tom Hanks coproduced the moral foundation of their *Band of Brothers* by doing what Americans in need of a moral compass usually do: harking back to WWII and mining it for moral certainties. Post-9/11 cinema takes a more difficult historical path, for what some post-9/11 films attempt to do is to reestablish the moral claim of the soldier not by looking back at the morally more certain pre-Vietnam period but by looking ahead to the morally less certain post-Vietnam period. Two films in particular—*Behind Enemy Lines* and *Black Hawk Down*—follow the generation of US soldiers who understand that their familial, national, and international moral inheritance is rooted in the fractured morality of the Vietnam era, not the foundational morality of WWII. These post-Cold War warriors are not enraptured by their "end of history" mission of spreading triumphant liberal capitalism across the globe (Fukuyama, 1993). Instead, they lack aims and ambitions, engaged as they are during the new interwar years (between the end of the Cold War and the beginning of the War on Terror) in morally confounding interventions.

The challenge of such films as *Behind Enemy Lines* and *Black Hawk Down* is to resecure American morality in its post-Vietnam era sons by converting their waywardness into morally meaningful actions; this is precisely what both films do. In very different ways, each film reclaims the moral character of its aimless post-Vietnam era son/soldier by reclaiming the morality of his mission. Each film suggests that, in the 1990s as today, the most moral of missions is not to fight for God and for country; it is to fight for humanity, in whatever country, loyal to whichever God. Humanitarian interventions, then, are the key to morally justified (or at least morally justifiable) interventions. As such, they are also the key to rescuing America from the moral morass that is its post-Vietnam legacy. It should come as little surprise, then, that both the first two battles in the war on terror—in Afghanistan and in Iraq— were justified by the Bush administration in part on humanitarian grounds. It was a third film, *Kandahar*, that the administration explicitly used to buttress this claim.

*Behind Enemy Lines*, *Black Hawk Down*, and *Kandahar* trace the emergence of humanitarianism as a centerpiece of US foreign policy. *Behind Enemy Lines* dramatizes the moment of the US moral conversion; *Black Hawk Down* troubles over the implementation of this new moral agenda in US foreign policy while ultimately embracing it; and *Kandahar* is claimed by the Bush administration to provide the link between 1990s-style US humanitarian interventions and post-9/11 moral aims in the war on terror. Read together, these three films attempt to erase America's Vietnam legacy by providing post-9/11 US viewers with morally meaningful missions and with the proper objects toward which these missions ought to be directed. Collectively, these films not only resituate American morality in its sons; from this new foundation, these sons also collectively construct another US moral grammar of war and another trajectory for "becoming a moral America(n)" in the post-9/11 era.

This chapter recounts the story these films tell when read together. It begins with America's moral awakening through its soldierly son in *Behind Enemy Lines*; the soldierly son's moral quandaries and their resolution in *Black Hawk Down*; finally considering how *Kandahar* (against the intentions of its director and star) was used by the Bush administration to construct the feminized object of rescue this young generation of male humanitarian warriors needed to rescue their own moral sense of self. It concludes by considering what these films tell post-9/11 subjects about who we really are.

## Behind Enemy Lines

In the style of an MTV music video, *Behind Enemy Lines* attempts to instill in interwar-years-America and its disillusioned American hero a sense of moral mission. Vaguely based on the plight of Naval Officer Scott O'Grady (who was rescued from behind enemy lines in 1990s Bosnia), the film follows the moral conversion of US Lieutenant Chris Burnett from a wise-cracking, self-centered twenty-something embarrassed by and for his country's missionlessness into a serious soldier fighting for his life and for the lives of humanity.

> The film renders explicit the urgency of Burnett's humanitarian mission with its opening images, even though the significance of these images is not immediately clear to viewers. To a mournful soundtrack, a man's hands gently pat down a mound of soil around a sapling. The camera cuts to a wider shot. Many men are planting trees. Cut to a close-up of a man walking through this field. He has a gun slung over his shoulder. We realize that all the men in the field are foreign soldiers.
>
> Cut to the film's title. Cue a voice-over by a reporter.
>
> REPORTER: The much criticized Cincinnati accord that brought peace to Bosnia appears to be holding, prompting NATO forces to begin a retreat that should be completed by New Year's Day. Even so, the US military remains at a high state of readiness, eager to answer the call.
>
> As the reporter speaks, cut to an aerial shot of the ocean from the point of view of a speeding plane. As we follow the plane's view of the water, a US aircraft carrier comes into view. A montage of rapid cuts—some only a few frames long—to an up-beat rock and roll soundtrack replaces the slow solemnity of the pretitle sequence. Reminiscent of the television program *Baywatch*, this sequence shows quick-cut slow-motion shots of US Naval pilot Stackhouse (Gabriel Macht) and his navigator Burnett (Owen Wilson) racing to their fighter plane, boarding it, and preparing to intercept an unknown aircraft. These images are spliced together with real-time images of their hi-tech control room support. As pilots and viewers

alike get geared up for takeoff, quite unexpectedly the unknown aircraft is identified as a NATO plane. Mission aborted.

BURNETT:  That's twice today.
STACKHOUSE:  I guess that's the price of peace.

Stackhouse is partly right. From the perspective of a Naval fighter pilot, a ceasefire agreement does result in aborted missions. However, what the film renders clear is that the principle responsibility for aborted US missions is not the peace agreement; it is NATO (here symbolized by the NATO plane). More specifically, it is the NATO chain of command. The NATO Naval Commander is Admiral Juan-Miguel Piquet (Joaquim de Almeida). Though the nationality of Admiral Piquet is never confirmed, what is established is that he is most definitely not American. We first meet Piquet when he briefs US Admiral Leslie Reigart (Gene Hackman), commander of the Adriatic Battle Group and Burnett's commanding officer. Piquet warns Reigart that if his US pilots stray into the no-fly zone on their sorties, they could jeopardize the peace agreement. And this, of course, is precisely what Burnett and Stackhouse end up doing.

Burnett is a problem for Reigart even before he breaches the ceasefire agreement. With only two weeks left on his tour of duty before being discharged from the Navy, Burnett is a pilot off-mission. Not only does he fantasize about flying jets for public figures like Bill Gates or rock stars; worse still is his questioning of the American military mission itself. This is made explicit in two scenes: one in a mess hall conversation between Burnett, Stackhouse, and a US Marine and a second between Burnett and Reigart.

As Burnett and Stackhouse joke around during their meal, a patriotic US Marine tries to set Burnett straight.

MARINE:  Don't you forget what we're doing here.
BURNETT:  What we're doing here? Are you kidding me? Well, I'm eating jello…
MARINE:  You know, everybody has a role to play. See me, I'm a Marine. We take care of the service business. You, you're a Navy pilot, and your role is to eat jello. (serious) You don't get to pick your fight. It comes to you.
BURNETT:  I get it. But at least give me a fight I can understand. Bukavar? Where's the place we flew over the other day? Sreb, Sreb…

STACKHOUSE: Srebrenica.

BURNETT: Good luck trying to explain to someone back home, "Well, today's Tuesday. I think we're helping these people. No, no, now it's switched around. We're helping..." It's like a joke.

MARINE (referring to the peace agreement): Just be glad it's over.

BURNETT: Yeah, I am.

Cut to a bunch of soldiers in the far end of the mess hall having a push-up contest.

BURNETT: Look at these guys. See, that's exactly what I'm talking about. Everybody thinks they're gonna get a chance to punch some Nazi in the face at Normandy. And those days are over. They are long gone. I used to think I was gonna get a chance to do it. Now I realize I'm gonna be eating jello...

In this first scene, Burnett clearly articulates the difference between a WWII moral grammar of war and a 1990s moral grammar of war. In the past, the enemy was identified, his evil was established, people cared about fighting him, and the United States actively fought him. In the 1990s, it is unclear who the enemy is because the enemy keeps changing, and this is difficult to take, not only logically but morally. For how can a soldier morally believe in his cause if the morality of his enemy is constantly shifting: if on Tuesday the United States tries to kill this enemy and on Wednesday it tries to befriend him. What this means is that, for Burnett at least, it makes sense that he redefines his life's mission not in terms of the US public interest (being a Navy pilot) but in his own private interest (securing the lives of rock stars by safely piloting them from gig to gig). Because of the collapse of a clear US public interest (resulting here from the inability of US foreign policy in the 1990s to establish clear lines between friend and foe), being and becoming a moral American is transformed from a public matter into a private one, a sentiment very much in line with interwar-years-America's neoliberal globalization agenda. As such, Burnett is well within his rights to look forward to his release from military service.

This first scene concludes with Burnett being summoned to Reigart's office, where the admiral confronts Burnett about his wasted potential.

REIGART: Just out of curiosity, Lieutenant, what happened to you?

BURNETT: Sir, I signed up to be a fighter pilot. I didn't wanna be a cop. I certainly didn't wanna be a cop walking a beat in a

neighborhood nobody cares about. That and the routine on
the ship kinda wore me out.

REIGART:  The routine...that's what you do to prepare for war.

BURNETT:  We're not at war, sir.

REIGART:  Yes we are. Unless we're parked in San Diego Bay, you're
at war every time you step on this boat. You understand that?

BURNETT:  No, sir. I do not understand. If we're at war, why doesn't
somebody act like we're at war. 'Cause as far as I can tell, we
go out, we fly around, and we come back. Now maybe we're
pretending to be in the middle of a fight, but that's all we're
doing is pretending 'cause we're not fighting. We're watching.

Here Burnett questions not only the category of US military action—
is it a meaningful war or is it a meaningless police action about which
nobody cares—but the authority of his commanding officer to define
the character of US military action for him. Whereas Reigart insists
that "you're at war every time you step on this boat," Burnett insists
that this doesn't make any sense to him. For even when US missions
are not aborted, they aren't "real" missions; they only appear to be
real. This occurs for two reasons. The first reason has to do with the
definition of the enemy. In a war, we know who the enemy is; in a
police action, criminals/enemies emerge all the time. Anyone could be
the enemy (criminal) or could cease being the enemy (cease illegal
activities). In a police action, then, there are no clear enemy lines because
there are no stable enemies. The second reason has to do with what
soldiers do in war (engage the enemy) and what cops do on a beat
(look out for criminals). From Burnett's point of view, US military
missions in the 1990s are all about watching—photo reconnaissance
for peacekeeping—but not about doing. And this keeps them from being
real wars. For Burnett, this is not only frustrating; it is embarrassing, a
point emphasized in a phone conversation between Burnett and his
father.

FATHER:  ...You've got important things to do over there.

BURNETT (uncomfortable):  Dad, I gotta go. I gotta get going.

FATHER:  Well, we're very proud of you.

BURNETT:  Dad, I gotta get going...

What these scenes underscore is something we learned in *We Were
Soldiers*: that there is no guarantee that the patriarchal values that are
the foundations of meaningful moral grammars of war can be transferred
from father to son. The symbolic (Reigart) and real (Mr. Burnett) fathers

of this 1990s son ought to be Vietnam era warriors, but *Behind Enemy Lines* (like so many patriotic US war films) forgets Vietnam altogether, placing its fathers generationally and morally with reference to WWII values, not to those of Vietnam. It is as if these fathers never suffered the disillusions of who we wish we'd never been, believing firmly in who we think we were/who we think we are. Yet the more they insist on the (moral) necessity of their and their son's missions, the more it underscores to navigator Burnett his lack of a moral compass and the meaninglessness of his present (in)actions.

Clearly disgusted by Burnett's attitudes, Reigart refuses Burnett's letter of resignation from the Navy and commands him to behave in a manner befitting a Naval officer until his tour is complete. To emphasize his distain for Burnett and to attempt to toughen him up, Reigart assigns Burnett (with Stackhouse) to a Christmas Day photo reconnaissance mission. This mission, too, is aborted, albeit differently than their last mission, for Burnett and Stackhouse discover they cannot photograph the assigned area thanks to faulty navigational intelligence. Worse still, the faulty coordinates mean that Burnett and Stackhouse find themselves in a no-fly zone. To save the mission from being a complete waste of time and money, Burnett persuades Stackhouse to check out and photograph some activity picked up on the radar screen. It is the Bosnian troops we saw in the opening sequence, massing in what is supposed to be a demilitarized zone.

On seeing the US plane and realizing that it means NATO has evidence of the Bosnian breach of the peace agreement, the Bosnian Serbs shoot down Burnett's and Stackhouse's plane. The two pilots eject from the plane, landing in Serbian-controlled Bosnia. Burnett climbs a nearby mountain to radio for help, leaving the injured Stackhouse behind. Stackhouse is discovered by Bosnian Serb troops and assassinated, and Burnett, who witnesses all this, betrays his position with his reaction. From that moment on, the Bosnian Serbs hunt Burnett down. The tension in the film is about the race to find Burnett: will the Bosnian Serbs find him and kill him or will US troops find him and rescue him?

At first, the US rescue of Burnett seems to be a straightforward affair. Through radio contact with his ship, Burnett is instructed to make his way to a rendezvous point where US marines will pick him up. And so he does but, just as the marines are ready to execute their mission, they are ordered to stand down. NATO Commander Admiral Piquet orders Reigart to cancel the mission and to instruct Burnett to make his way to a safe zone, as he was trained to do. Frustrated but obedient, Reigart respects the chain of command and follows the letter if not the spirit of his orders. As Piquet ordered, Reigart cancels the rescue mission, but then he alerts a reporter on board his ship of the situation, thereby creating public pressure on NATO to allow a rescue to take place. Not surprisingly, Piquet is furious.

> PIQUET:  Do you have any idea how much damage this incident may cause to the peace process?
> REIGART:  All I know is that the American people want their pilot back.
> PIQUET (disgusted):  Exactly. Americans. All you care about is your own damn pilots. What happens when the fighting starts again? Will America recommit its forces to stop a major war? No, you don't have any control over that little detail, do you? You might have helped save your man today, Reigart—and I emphasize might—but you've risked the lives of thousands tomorrow.

Piquet's characterization of Americans as self-interested soldiers who care only about keeping their own safe, even at the cost of thousands of lives of others, is unlikely to be the sort of thing many in a post-9/11 US audience want to hear. Yet it seems to fit perfectly with the film's characterization of its leading man. What is more surprising is that a film such as *Behind Enemy Lines*, which circulates negative stereotypes about Americans, not only was released in mid-November, 2001 but was a box office success.

As it turns out, these facts are not at all surprising because the moral movement of the film is to demonstrate just how wrong this caricature of Americans is. The film does this in two ways. On the one hand, it increasingly establishes Piquet as the film's villain. Yes, there are numerous Bosnian Serb villains in the story, but we expect them to be our enemies. What US citizens watching a film such as this do not expect is for a NATO commander to be against them as well, but Piquet clearly is. For not only does he criticize the American character; he repeatedly orders Reigart not to rescue Burnett. It is by eventually rejecting what the film establishes as this unjust chain of command that Reigart not only saves his man but saves himself as a heroic figure in the film.

On the other hand, the film establishes the injustice of Piquet's stereotyping of Americans by tracing the moral conversion of its hero, the character who (at the moment Piquet utters his critique) appears to best fit this uncharitable description. As our hero Burnett attempts to evade the Bosnian Serbs and make his way into a safe zone where he can be rescued under NATO rules, he literally stumbles on the mass graves of Bosnian Muslims. These dead Muslims save his live, both literally and morally. For not only does Burnett hide himself under these corpses to escape detection by Bosnian troops; he also realizes that these mass graves are the very reasons the Bosnian Serbs want him dead, for the activity he and Stackhouse photographed is both evidence of the massing of Bosnian Serb troops in a safe zone and evidence of the mass graves. Burnett's epiphany might also be the viewers' epiphany, for what we saw in the opening sequence was not a troop of soldiers tending the soil by planting trees. Rather, we saw Bosnian Serb soldiers conceal evidence of their mass killing of Bosnian Muslims.

After a second aborted US rescue attempt (this time because Burnett is presumed dead), (morally) reborn Burnett kills the Bosnian Serb bad guys, recovers the photographic evidence of genocide, and engineers his own rescue by Reigart and his men. The film concludes with Reigart's being relieved of his post because he broke the NATO chain of command. Offered a desk job back in Washington, Reigart instead resigns, with (the film tells us) the respect and admiration of his men. However, Reigart's sacrifice is not for nothing, for Burnett has now matured into a soldier capable of carrying forward America's mission in a meaningful way. And so he does: on being rescued, Burnett asks Reigart to return his letter of resignation from the Navy and, we soon learn, signs up for another tour of duty.

Overall, what *Behind Enemy Lines* tells us is that America's sons do not need to kill Nazis to establish their legitimate claim to the moral inheritance of their (WWII) fathers. Rather, all they need to do is ensure that they fight on the side of right. What is right is to defend humanity by preventing genocide: this was part of what justified US actions in Europe in WWII, and it is what justifies many 1990s US military interventions. According to this logic, if US wars are humanitarian, then US wars are just.

In making these claims, the film not only constructs a clear moral line that (re)connects fathers to sons; it suggests that, enlightened as our soldierly sons are by their conversion to humanitarianism, they now know what their fathers have long known: that they cannot let anyone get in the way of their moral mission. Of course, this means these soldierly sons must oppose the treacherous Bosnian Serbs. It also means that in addition to expected enemies (those who commit genocide), soldierly sons (and soldierly fathers) must be on their guard against unexpected enemies (those who get in the way of the US humanitarian mission).

The unexpected US enemy in *Behind Enemy Lines* is of course NATO Commander Piquet. Though Piquet is supposed to be on "our" side, his bias against Americans in general and his consistent attempts to prevent Burnett's rescue position him on the side of the enemy. Unlike our hero Burnett (who finds himself geographically behind enemy lines because he is in Serbian-controlled Bosnia), Piquet is metaphorically behind enemy lines because, even though he is unaware of it, his actions are complicit with the Bosnian Serb agenda. This is the real "price of peace" about which Stackhouse complained in the opening sequence: the risk of getting things morally wrong by letting genocide go undetected.

The film renders clear that this is the moral morass into which the European Piquet has fallen. In so doing, it not only discredits Piquet and suggests his outburst against Americans is utterly unjustified; more broadly, it declares that this is the sort of moral mistake that Europeans—not Americans—risk making. By converting to a humanitarian agenda, the film suggests, the United States not only rescues itself ("we" have a new/revived moral mission) but rescues Europeans from themselves ("they" are dangerously inactive). Just as in the US telling of the history of WWII, they (inactive Europeans) need us (active Americans) more than they realized. And so it is again up to America to rescue not only those killed at the hand of the enemy (victims of genocide) but those captured by the enemy (Europeans) from behind enemy lines. Needless to say, this story had a powerful resonance in the post-9/11 United States, especially in the build-up to Gulf War II: a war some of America's European allies tried to prevent.

What *Behind Enemy Lines* gives us, then, is both a US moral grammar of war that redefines American morality through humanitarian action and a trajectory for "becoming a moral American." To become a moral American, one must undergo the same moral conversion Burnett does, from a selfish son to a selfless soldier. This conversion is made possible by recognizing that what is in America's private interest (surviving in Serbian-controlled Bosnia; getting our pilot back) is also in America's public interest (recovering evidence of genocide and using this as the foundation of a reborn American moral agenda). Beyond this, it entails recognizing that what is in America's public interest (rescuing its man from behind enemy lines) may well be in the interest of our allies (who might be on the side of the enemy without knowing it).

*Behind Enemy Lines*, then, is not a film that is straightforwardly critical of multilateralism; rather, it is instructive about what it takes for multilateralism to succeed. What it takes, the film suggests, is both a multilateral moral mission and American moral leadership. Never mind that Reigart is relieved of his command at the close of the film; this is a mere gesture of politeness to our NATO allies. For by relinquishing his post altogether, Reigart both rejects the NATO chain of command and insists on proper lines of moral order—not flowing from European to American but from American to American, from father to son, and (at some future date when they again need rescuing) from American to European.

## Black Hawk Down

*Black Hawk Down* seems to be the polar opposite of *Behind Enemy Lines* because each film's hero begins and ends his moral journey on opposite sides of the ideological spectrum. The hero in *Behind Enemy Lines* is a disillusioned, wayward US son (Burnett) who undergoes a moral conversion from pessimistic realism to enlightened (and enlightening) idealism. In contrast, the hero in *Black Hawk Down* (Eversman, played by Josh Hartnet) begins as an American idealist, only to have his ideals questioned in the course of war. *Behind Enemy Lines*, then, moves from moral ambiguity to moral clarity whereas *Black Hawk Down* seems to move from moral clarity to moral ambiguity. This having been said, these two films have a lot in common. Both explore 1990s US humanitarian interventions, both deplore inaction, and both take soldierly sons as their heroes. All these elements are established in the long title sequence of *Black Hawk Down*.

As we listen to what has come to be known as a *world soundtrack* (in this case, African vocals and musical accompaniment), "based on an actual event" appears on the black screen. The pretitle sequence is devoted to explaining the background to this actual event. These words fade away to be replaced by a quote from Plato: "Only the dead have seen the end of war." The background behind the words fades from black to a windswept desert. As the camera pans across the desert, we see mourners preparing bodies for burial. "Somalia—East Africa 1992" appears over the image of a Red Cross vehicle speeding up a dusty road.

> Reminicent of *We Were Soldiers*, the film begins its textual narration of historical events, sometimes over Somali images, sometimes over a black background; yet, unlike *We Were Soldiers*, these words belong to no specific individual or voice. They simply claim to be *the* history of *the actual*: "Years of warfare among rival clans causes famine on a biblical scale. 300,000 civilians die of starvation. Mohamed Farrah Aidid, the most powerful of the warlords, rules the capital, Mogadishu. He seizes international food shipments at the ports. Hunger is his weapon. The world

responds. Behind a force of 20,000 US Marines, food is delivered and order is restored."

The images of dead and dying Somalis continue. "April 1993. Aidid waits until the Marines withdraw, and then declares war on the remaining UN peacekeepers. In June, Aidid's militia ambush and slaughter twent-four Pakistani soldiers, and begin targeting American personnel. In late August, America's elite soldiers, Delta Force, Army Rangers, and the 160th SOAR are sent to Mogadishu to remove Aidid and restore order. The mission was to take three weeks, but six weeks later Washington was growing impatient."

The sound of a chopper joins the world music. As the film's title appears, the music changes: it has more of a beat, reminiscent of both techno-military music and the suspenseful soundtrack of a horror film. The chopper is a US Black Hawk flying over a Red Cross food distribution center. As food shipments arrive, hungry Somalis mob the convoy. Aidid's men guarding the shipment respond by gunning down the crowd with machineguns as one of the guards shouts, "This food belongs to Mohamed Farrah Aidid." All this is witnessed by Sergeant Eversman, our hero on board the Black Hawk helicopter. The crew request permission to defend the unarmed civilians but are told that unless they are taking fire, they cannot engage because the food center is under UN jurisdiction. Close-up of Eversman's bewildered face. Cut to a mocking Somali guard, "shooting" the chopper with his arm while laughing.

US inaction while witnessing the mass killing of civilians goes against everything Eversman believes. Back at base, his fellow soldiers chide him, saying he is an idealist who likes the "skinnies" (what the US troops call the starving Somalis). Eversman explains it is not about liking or disliking them; it is about respecting them.

SOLDIER 1:  See, what you guys fail to realize is the sergeant here is a bit of an idealist. He believes in this mission right down to his very bones, don't you, Sergeant.

EVERSMAN:  Look, these people, they have no jobs, no food, no education, no future. I just figure…we have two things we can do. We can either help or we can sit back and watch the country destroy itself on CNN.

SOLDIER 1:  I don't know about you guys, but I was trained to fight. Were you trained to fight, Sergeant?

EVERSMAN:  Well, I think I was trained to make a difference… (laughter)

SOLDIER 2:  Like the man said, he's an idealist.

As his name implies, Eversman—like everyman—is surely an idealist. Yet what is striking about Eversman's idealism is less his belief in the morality and humanity of all people than his belief in his mission. Eversman's mission is to make a difference. It takes no moral conversion (as it did in *Behind Enemy Lines*) to instill this belief in him. Throughout the film, Eversman is absolutely certain about his mission and about the morality of his mission. What he and the film are less certain of, though, are the content of this mission. The crucial question, then, that *Black Hawk Down* considers through the character of Eversman is, What does it take to make a (moral) difference?

The film explores at least four answers to this question. The first answer, illustrated by Eversman's banter with his fellow soldiers on base, is simply "good intentions." However, because this is where Eversman begins his moral journey, viewers know that this answer alone will prove to be insufficient. Otherwise, there would be no reason for any of the forthcoming action to occur. And they are right. *Black Hawk Down* will test not only the good intentions of Eversman, but the good intentions of the United States.

The broadly stated good US intentions that motivate its actions in Somalia are the very same ones that motivated Burnett in *Behind Enemy Lines*: to stop genocide, and they function in exactly the same way in this film as they did in that one, as the moral purpose of the United States in this battle. Having a moral purpose that can be justified in terms of humanitarianism, then, is a second way to make a (moral) difference. This response comes even earlier in the film, in an exchange between Eversman's commanding officer, General Garrison (Sam Shepard), and one of Aidid's allies, Mr. Atto (George Harris).

MR. ATTO: This isn't the K.O. Corral, General.

GENERAL GARRISON (laughing): That's the O.K. Corral.

MR. ATTO: Don't make the mistake that just because I grew up without running water that I am simple, General. I do know something about history. See all this. It's simply shaping tomorrow—a tomorrow without a lot of Arkansas white boy's ideas in it.

GENERAL GARRISON: Well, I wouldn't know about that. I'm from Texas.

MR. ATTO: Mr. Garrison. I think you shouldn't have come here. This is civil war. This is our war, not yours.

MR. GARRISON:  300,000 dead and counting. That's not a war, Mr. Atto. That's genocide.

Just as in *Behind Enemy Lines*, then, it is the prevention of genocide—the US moral purpose—that justifies US military intervention and provides a second, more specific answer the question of what it takes to make a (moral) difference. And, like Eversman and Burnett, the United States has no moral ambivalence about this justification. However, as this exchange between General Garrison and Mr. Atto evidences, the US view of the prevention of genocide, at least from the outside, only seems to make sense if thought through a white (wild) Western imaginary that refuses to acknowledge local understandings of the situation, as civil war, as power struggles to establish future governmental arrangements. As such, Mr. Atto challenges not only General Garrison's version of events in Somalia but, in so doing, attributes authorship to the nameless narrative of the opening sequence: it is white, it is Western, it is stereotypically United States.

However, the film, like General Garrison, is having none of this and swiftly silences Mr. Atto's objections to the US presence in Somalia. *Black Hawk Down* renders very clear that the prevention of genocide is a humanitarian aim and a just one, and it (through the general) mocks Mr. Atto's self-serving accounts of Somali history. For it suggests that though Mr. Atto indulges in incorrect stereotypes about who America and Americans are, General Garrison is witness to the cold hard facts of life in Somalia that speak for themselves; they are so self-evidently true that they can be presented by a nameless omnipotent narrator. Paradoxically, it is this US general who is able to give the more credible account of events in Somalia, even though he happens to be white, male, and Texan.

However much the film embraces the morality of the US mission to prevent genocide in Somalia, the film does question US tactics to accomplish this aim. As does *Behind Enemy Lines*, the film wonders whether it is possible to make a (moral) difference when the United States is working under the authority of a multinational institution. In *Black Hawk Down*, this institution is the United Nations, and, as we saw in the opening sequence, the UN-to-US chain of command prevented the United States from distributing food to needy Somalis.

However, working under and with the UN was not the primary way the United States chose to prevent genocide in Somalia. Instead, it directed its attention to alleviating what it considered to be the direct cause of genocide: the rule of General Aidid. Unlike its posture in *Behind Enemy Lines*, then, the United States is less under the chain of command of a multinational organization than it is responsible for a parallel military operation that will make the UN's mission of humanitarian food distribution possible. This, then, becomes a third answer to the question of what it takes to make a (moral) difference: the answer is to use US military superiority in the area to secure the humanitarian aid agenda it supports. Put differently, military superiority can make a (moral) difference when it is used for a moral purpose (prevention of genocide). This is certainly a belief Eversman holds, as his statement "I was *trained* to make a difference" suggests.

When three separate intelligence sources report that the long-awaited meeting of Aidid's senior cabinet will take place at 3 PM in an Aidid-controlled area of Mogadishu, the film moves its men from base to battle to test whether the combination of good intentions, moral purpose, and military superiority are enough to make a (moral) difference in the streets of Somalia. The plan is to infiltrate the building, seize all Aidid's men, load the prisoners into armored land vehicles, and drive them out of the city the three miles back to base. Because Washington rejected General Garrison's request for light armored gun ships to provide air cover, four Black Hawk helicopters would be used instead. Estimated mission time: no more than thirty minutes.

These mission conditions are less than ideal—a daylight mission into a hostile area with unarmored air support—and, for Eversman and his men, there are additional difficulties. This mission will be Eversman's first command, and his unit includes a combat-green sixteen-year-old and a replacement soldier whose duties so far have been to type and make coffee. Yet as Eversman's men prepare for their mission, they exhibit a confidence in themselves and their mission that will come back to haunt them. For believing as they do that the mission will be completed in thirty minutes or less in daylight, they leave their night-vision gear, their bullet proof vests, and their canteens behind.

As US troops make their way into Mogadishu, lookouts warn Aidid's forces. They arm themselves and burn tires as signals to their militia that US forces are coming. The Black Hawks drop off the ground troops, who successfully infiltrate the meeting and capture the prisons. As their Black Hawk hovers in the square, Eversman's men begin to disembark on ropes and take up ground positions. All of this is according to plan, but then things go horribly wrong. The sixteen-year-old new recruit Blackburn falls from the chopper into the square. As Eversman's troops come to his aid, Somalis loyal to Aidid surround the square and fire on them. Things go from bad to worse when the Somalis fire a rocket at and hit Eversman's Black Hawk. *Black Hawk down.* The Black Hawk plummets to the ground in another part of the city, killing two pilots and injuring two crew. Eversman's men are ordered to secure the crash site. The plan is for others to join them, and then all will be picked up by the convoy of Humvees on their way out.

However, again things do not go according to plan. Hostile Somalis attack the crash site, rendering the area too hot for a helicopter rescue. As the number of injured US troops mounts, the Somalis set up roadblocks so that the humvees cannot reach the area to collect the men. Then another Black Hawk goes down, creating another crash site in yet another hostile part of the city. This time the pilot survives and is captured by hostile Somalis. Eversman and his men, forced to spend the night in the Aidid stronghold, are never rescued by the humvees. Like Burnett in *Behind Enemy Lines*, they are ordered to hump it out to the safe zone, not because (as in Burnett's case) rescuing them would violate the chain of command but because the United States has no command over their part of Mogadishu, military or moral.

So, as the expected swift, clear military mission becomes protracted and descends into a chaos that mirrors the US view of the failed state of Somala itself, the film passes its judgment on the idea that military superiority linked to good intentions and moral purpose might allow the United States to make a (moral) difference in Somalia. The answer is an unequivocal no. Or is it?

On the one hand, *Black Hawk Down* is utterly clear that the US mission in Somalia is a failure: the United States suffers unexpected casualties. A US pilot is taken hostage (and later released). The bodies of dead US pilots are paraded through the streets of Mogadishu before the cameras of CNN and thus the world, thereby turning Eversman's earlier prediction that US inaction would lead to watching the country self-destruct on CNN on its head, with the US watching itself destruct on CNN. And General Aidid is never captured. At the end of the film, we see the US troops preparing to abandon Somalia, without having changed a thing.

This is how the film ends; on the other hand, this is not at all how the film ends. For as US troops prepare their withdrawal from Somalia, Eversman (now safely back at base) has a heart-to-heart with a fellow soldier in what appears to be an army hospital.

> EVERSMAN:  I go home and people ask me why I do it. Am I a war junkie? And I don't say a thing. They won't understand it's about the man next to you, and that's it. That's all it is. (pause) I was talking to Blackburn the other day, and he asked me what had changed. I said, "Nothing." That's not true, you know. I think everything's changed. I know I've changed. You know

a friend of mine asked me before I got here, just when we were all shipping out. He asked me, "Why are you goin' to fight somebody else's war? What'a you all think, you're heroes?" I didn't know what to say at the time, but if he asked me again I'd say, "No." I'd say, "There's no way in hell. Nobody asks to be a hero. Just sometimes it turns out that way."

As Eversman is speaking, the camera slowly zooms in for a close-up. As he finishes his monolog, it cuts to the dead body of his fellow soldier. Cut to a wide shot of the "hospital." It is an army hanger that has become a makeshift morgue.

In this soliloquy, Eversman establishes a fourth way in which one can make a (moral) difference in Somalia: by becoming a reluctant hero. And how one does that, Eversman explains, is not by fighting for the Somalis but by fighting for the man next to you. As he tells his fallen colleague, "That's it. That's all it is." Eversman's realization could not be more different from Burnett's in *Behind Enemy Lines*. For if Burnett's moral conversion might be expressed as moving from selfishness to selflessness—from the specific to the universal—Eversman's moral movement, in contrast, is from universal to specific, from caring about every man to caring about the men who care for him. And these men, of course, are his fellow soldiers. This changes everything, and this changes Eversman, for what this means is that, ultimately, the humanitarianism of *Black Hawk Down* is not one that joins everyman to everyman; rather, it is one that separates Eversman, as soldier and as American, from civilians and Somalis.

This is utterly consistent with the film's tag line, "Leave no man behind." For, as every viewer knows, the "man" in this statement is not "everyman"; it is the US soldier. As the film closes, no US soldier is left behind, but every Somali is left behind, possibly to face what the United States terms genocide.

What all this means is that *Black Hawk Down*, like *Behind Enemy Lines*, is a rescue film, and just like *Behind Enemy Lines*, what is rescued is the US sense of morality. However, whereas *Behind Enemy Lines* rescues the moral US self by potentially rescuing others (Bosnian Muslims and inactive Europeans), *Black Hawk Down* merely rescues Americans. In other words, *Black Hawk Down* rescues the US self simply by rescuing US soldiers. This action, the film suggests, makes US soldiers into reluctant heroes, but they are heroes nonetheless.

As we saw in such films as *We Were Soldiers* and *Behind Enemy Lines*, celebrating the heroism of US soldiers played well in cinemas after

9/11. *Black Hawk Down* did particularly well, receiving as much attention for its famous director (Ridley Scott) and its star-studded cast as it did for its solemn cinematic style. And the film was no doubt popular because it confirmed that moral Americans are humanitarians. However, because its moral trajectory for "becoming a moral American" is self-referential—to become a moral American, Americans need to rescue themselves whenever they put themselves into danger—the film is ultimately unsatisfying. Like its string of answers to the question of what it takes to make a (moral) difference, with each answer requiring one supplement or another until it ultimately turns back on itself/ ourselves, the film *Black Hawk Down* arguably needs a supplement to make its moral message meaningful. For even while it celebrates the morality of the American soldier, the film proclaims that this morality is based not on a universal humanitarianism but on a myopic Americanism.

As such, the film gives us both moral certainty (we are moral Americans because we are humanitarians) and moral uncertainty (our morality is self-referential). What post-9/11 audiences needed to relate the thoughtful morality of *Black Hawk Down* to the official US post-9/11 narrative was someone else to rescue on the way to rescuing themselves (and, unlike that in *Behind Enemy Lines*, this someone else had to be still alive). What they needed, in other words, was a fifth way to make a (moral) difference in the world: by rescuing a willing and understanding object. The Bush administration "found" such an object in *Kandahar*.

## Kandahar (The Sun Behind the Moon)

*Kandahar*, originally entitled *The Sun Behind the Moon*, is not another Hollywood blockbuster featuring a US band of brothers on a moral rescue mission; it is an art house film by Iranian filmmaker Mohsen Makhmalbaf telling the tale of two separated Afghani sisters. Filmed on location just inside the Iranian--Afghan border and using a largely Afghan cast, *Kandahar* tells the story of Afghan refugee Nafas's journey from Canada back through Afghanistan to find her maimed sister before her sister commits suicide at the last solar eclipse of the millennium. Described as everything from a road movie to a quasidocumentary, *Kandahar* is about unfinished journeys: Afghanistan's incomplete journey out of the legacies of war (landmines, famine, fundamentalism) and Nafas's incomplete journey to rescue her sister.

With this in mind, *Kandahar* is an unlikely film to analyze when looking for articulations of a US *we*, a US moral grammar of war, and a trajectory for becoming a moral America(n), especially as they are expressed in the official US story. Indeed, as a condemnation of what passes as so-called moral encounters by foreign powers (be they capitalist, communist, or Islamic) in and in relation to Afghanistan, *Kandahar* stands as a critique of official US moral foreign policy impulses. It might come as a surprise to learn, then, that President George W. Bush made an urgent plea to see *Kandahar* (Edemarian, 2001) and that, when the film was re-released in US cinemas in November 2001, his administration encouraged Americans to view it.

What accounts for this apparent incongruity between what the film seems to say and how the Bush administration responded to it is the use the administration made of the film. As we will see, *Kandahar* articulates a humanitarian moral grammar of war that competes for the hearts and minds of post-September 11 Americans against conventionally heroic moral grammars of war circulated in the films *Behind Enemy Lines* and *Black Hawk Down*. Yet the allegorical tale in *Kandahar* was easily co-opted by the Bush administration. This was possible not only because the film depicts an incomplete story that the occidental US could step in to complete for an orientalized Afghanistan (which some argue was the first US move in the war on terror). Just as important, the story in *Kandahar* of separated sisters in need of reunion and apparent rescue comports well with one of the traditional ways in which the feminine functions in US national narratives: as a figure in need of physical and moral security, a theme that grounded the official second-wave justifications of the war on terror in both the United States and the United Kingdom and that propelled occidental subjects to "lift the veil" on Afghanistan and Afghan women by viewing *Kandahar*.

What follows are two readings of *Kandahar*: the first suggestive of what its filmmaker Makhmalbaf saw in Afghanistan and the second suggestive of what Bush saw (or hoped to see) in Makhmalbaf's Afghanistan.

## Makhmalbaf's Kandahar

The screen is black, except for a circle of jagged light surrounding a large, dark object. This interplay of light and its obstruction is a total solar eclipse: it is the sun behind the moon. Various views of the eclipse appear and disappear as film credits role and a mournful soundtrack begins. Cut to a burqa-clad woman. She lifts her garment to reveal her face. As she holds her veil overhead, the burqa's mesh casts a grill-like shadow over her eyes. The camera intently holds its focus on this image as dialog ensues. A voice asks in an Afghan language, "What's your name?" The woman answers, "Nafas." The voice asks, "Who are you?" Nafas answers, "I'm the bride's cousin." Nafas's English voice-over joins the mournful music as the camera lingers on Nafas's shadowed face. "I'd always escaped from jails that imprisoned Afghan women. But now I'm a captive in every one of those prisons. Only for you, my sister."

This is the opening sequence of the film *Kandahar*. Set in Afghanistan just before the end of the last millennium, *Kandahar* is a compilation of stories performed by Afghan residents and refugees about a country devastated by decades of war, poverty, and famine. What ties these stories together is the journey of Nafas (Nelofer Pazira), herself an Afghan refugee who escaped to Canada some ten years earlier. Based on Nelofer Pazira's real-life journey to find her childhood friend in Afghanistan before the friend commits suicide, *Kandahar* records Nafas's return to Afghanistan to find the sister that her family left behind when, on their journey out of the country, the sister stepped on a landmine and lost her legs. Alone in the Taliban-held city of Kandahar since the death of their father who stayed behind to care for her, the sister writes to Nafas of her plans to commit suicide at the next solar eclipse. Nafas rushes to the Iranian–Afghan border, determined to infuse her sister with hope, with life, with herself as the breath of life (*Nafas* literally meaning "to breathe"; Onstad, 2001). Arriving just three days before the eclipse, Nafas spends one day in organizing her passage into Afghanistan (for women cannot travel alone in Afghanistan) and two days in traveling. The film is an unflinching record of Nafas's haunted and haunting journey to Kandahar and of the Afghanis and the Afghanistans she encounters along the way.

The film is as much about Nafas's movements through Afghanistan (and the difficulty of such movements, especially for women) as it is about stillness, pauses, impediments, complete stops. We first see Nafas in motion in a Red Cross helicopter taking her to a refugee camp at the Iranian–Afghan border. Speaking into her tape recorder (which she explains to the pilot is her black box "in case I crash and don't return"), she tells her sister and the viewers that this moment of movement was proceeded by nearly a month of waiting in Pakistan. The helicopter passes over Afghan mountains until it reaches a clinic for landmine victims. In a surreal long shot, the difficulty of movement is impressed on us as we watch a pair of legs parachuting toward the ground. The following sequence shows young girls at the refugee camp being prepared for the restricted mobility they will face on their return to Afghanistan, with advice on how to cope with confinement and with a lesson on how to prevent these restrictions from becoming even more severe. Do not pick up dolls, the girls are told, for dolls are wired with bombs. The girls practice walking among clean, new dolls, building up their immunities to temptation. We later learn that it was when Nafas's sister picked up such a doll that she lost her legs, beginning her long pause in Afghanistan that now threatens to become a full stop.

At the refugee camp, Nafas dons a burqa and arranges to accompany an Afghan family on their way to Kandahar by posing as the fourth wife. With only a UN flag as protection, the family board a three-wheeled truck, its flatbed draped with a colorful embroidered canopy. Husband and driver are in the cab; wives and children on the flatbed. When the party stops for lunch, we get our first glimpse of women's defiance in the face of so many restrictions: The wives and girls paint their fingernails, put on brightly colored bracelets, and (later) apply lipstick by slipping makeup and mirror beneath the burqa. As much as Nafas enjoys these activities and what they seem to mean, she is eager to continue her journey. However, once back on the road, the family is robbed; all their money and possessions, including the truck, are carried off by bandits. The family members decide that they are at too much risk in Afghanistan and return to Iran, leaving Nafas stranded in a small village.

Here Nafas encounters Khak, a young boy recently expelled from a madrasah—an Islamic school—because of his failure to memorize the Koran. Khak is trying to earn money by offering to say prayers for women mourning in a cemetery. For $50, Nafas persuades Khak to be her guide. He guides her on foot across the white sand dunes toward Kandahar, stopping to collect saleable treasures and for a drink at a well along the way. When Nafas falls ill, Khak takes her to a village doctor who examines her piece by piece— mouth, ear, eye—through a small hole in a curtain hung between them while Khak negotiates their conversation, as direct conversation between unrelated men and women is forbidden. When the doctor mumbles in English, Nafas replies to him directly in English, confusing Khak. For reasons of safety, the doctor advises Nafas to release Khak as her guide, which she does.

The doctor turns out to be an African-American who long ago came to Afghanistan in search of God, first by fighting the Soviets, then by fighting various tribal factions, and finally by offering his unschooled medical assistance to any needy Afghan. The doctor becomes Nafas's third guide, driving her in his horse-drawn cart to a Red Cross clinic for amputees where he hopes to find someone to take her to Kandahar. Here, the scene of limbs parachuting from the sky is repeated, but this time we see not only the action in the sky but the action on the ground as, in dramatic slow motion, bare-footed one-legged men race on crutches desperate to secure what they are missing, albeit in another form.

Balancing the poignancy of this sequence is its introduction of Nafas's fourth and final guide, a one-handed shyster who regularly returns to the clinic telling tall tales in an attempt to secure legs he can sell.

> Nafas's money and the doctor's chiding convince him to take Nafas to Kandahar. He goes away to make arrangements for their journey, returning in a bright orange burqa and explaining that he and Nafas can travel to Kandahar as members of an all-female wedding party. So Nafas and the shyster join a procession of brightly-colored burqaed women walking through the white sand behind the white-burqaed bride-to-be poised on a donkey. Though some members of the wedding party are suspicious of Nafas and her guide, all goes well until they reach the outskirts of Kandahar. There the group is stopped at a Taliban checkpoint. Each member of the group is searched by two women wearing black burqas. One woman with a book and another with a musical instrument are detained, as is Nafas's guide, his mustached face revealed when he is required to lift his garment. Like every other member of the wedding party, Nafas is also required to show her face and answer questions. The camera focuses on her face as the burqa casts a grill-like shadow over her eyes.

> TALIBAN: What is your name?
> NAFAS: Nafas.
> TALIBAN: Who are you?
> NAFAS: I'm the bride's cousin.

> Nafas lowers her burqa. The camera swaps positions, from looking *at* Nafas to looking *as* Nafas. It sees, and we see, what she sees: the sun obscured through the heavy mesh of the burqa. With all of us—Nafas, camera, audience—fixed on this eclipse of the sun caused not by the moon but by the burqa, Nafas's English voice-over begins. "I'd always escaped from jails that imprisoned Afghan women. But now I'm a captive in every one of those prisons. Only for you, my sister."

> The final credits roll as the solar eclipse replaces the burqa eclipse.

It would be easy to romanticize *Kandahar*, shot as it is in a style reminiscent of David Lean's panoramic cinematography in *Laurence of*

*Arabia.* However, to reduce the film to a romantic moment would be to neglect its quasidocumentary motif, a motif that has little time for heroism, mystery, or adventure. Nafas is the principle character who grounds this motif, both through her vocation and her journey. We are told at the outset that she is a journalist in Canada, a professional identity she enacts by reporting all her encounters into a tape recorder for her sister. As for Nafas's journey itself, it represents less an heroic rescue mission than it does a series of necessary encounters, with her sister certainly but also with other Afghanis and Afghanistans. This is less *Rambo III* and more *Pilgrim's Progress* (French, 2001), albeit with an earthly city in darkness as the destination rather than the celestial gates of heaven.[2]

Yet, no amount of surreal cinematography can transform *Kandahar* into a Hollywood, heavenly, or even hellish dream world. *Kandahar* is insistently of this world. As *Kandahar* director Mohsen Makhmalbaf explains, "The reality of Afghanistan is surreal in itself…When you watch people who've lost their legs in explosions take a shovel and use it as a leg, it seems surreal, but it's reality" (Macnab and Makhmalbaf, 2001). Shot in its surreal reality, the Afghan landscape is presented not as an opportunity for further colonialist conquest and imperialist self-expression (as it is in *Laurence*) but as a glittering wound that demands attention in itself and for itself. Anchored in contrasting cinematic and storytelling styles, *Kandahar* fashions a grammatical structure based on three primary sets of tensions: place and placelessness; progress and nonprogress; lightness and darkness, which it explores spatially, temporally, and morally, respectively.

The place and placelessness of Afghanistan become the symbolic spatial terrain negotiated by the film's characters. Crisscrossing the *Kandahar* landscapes, none of them has a stable place; indeed, all the characters we meet are not only in motion, they are out of place: the Afghan refugees in Iran, Khak in his religious boarding school, the American doctor in Afghanistan, the one-handed man in a burqa, and Nafas herself, who wanders from place to place within and beyond Afghanistan.

It is the one character whom we never meet and yet who dominates the narrative who is firmly in place. This is Nafas's sister, legless and alone in the Taliban stronghold of Kandahar. Crippled in body and spirit, she cannot wander, and ultimately she cannot hope. As an absent presence that drives the film's action, Nafas's sister symbolizes many things: she is Afghan women's fading hope; she is Afghan women's containment within social, cultural, and religious institutions; and she is the absent identity of Afghan women, denied a public image of their own through the burqa. "Perhaps this is why they are called blackheads," Nafas wonders about these women whose individual identities are reduced to a collective category, denied an image of their own making.

And, indeed, as she functions in the storyline, Nafas's sister is herself a collective category. On the one hand, she represents Afghan women as a collective category. As Nelofer Pazira, whose real-life search for her friend was fictionalized into this film, remarked of *Kandahar*, "It is a true story…I play myself in the film, a woman searching for her sister in the prisons of this world. All the women suffering in my country are my sisters" (Makhmalbaf, 2001). The film is as explicit about its critique of the firmly controlled place of Afghan women as is its lead actress. That this control is akin to imprisonment is made clear by the image of Nafas's face shadowed by the burqa's mesh and by her voice-over in both the first and the final narrative scenes.

*Kandahar's* symbolic and narrative concentration on the obscured identity of Afghan women's individuality and image through its focus on Nafas's sister (and other Afghan women) is also a metaphor for Afghanistan as a whole. This is rendered clear by Makhmalbaf, who describes Afghanistan as "a country without an image…Afghanistan is a nation without a picture. Afghan women are faceless: 10 million out of the 20 million population don't get a chance to be seen" (Macnab and Makhmalbaf, 2001). To the outside world, Afghanistan appears to be "a land without a face" (Macnab and Makhmalbaf, 2001). This absence of distinctive images means that there are few points of orientation in or about Afghanistan. As such, getting one's bearings in and about this placeless, half-faceless place is not only difficult; it is dangerous.[3]

By contrasting what appear to be open, faceless landscapes with the daily restrictions on and resistances of distinct individuals who inhabit them, the film depicts how political, cultural, and religious conventions have eroded the individuality and image of Afghanistan, transforming everything, even its people, into minefields. As the doctor tells Nafas, "In Afghanistan, everyone is either a threat or an opportunity." And this, it seems, is precisely how the outside world has viewed Afghanistan.

The tension between Afghanistan's internal images and its external images also finds expression in the film's exploration of opposed temporalities: progressive and nonprogressive. The outside world is forever writing Afghanistan into progressive narratives, be they earthly narratives of capitalism, socialism, or empire, or theological narratives of progress toward a purer form of Islam. The film is a comment on the nonprogressive effects of these Western and Eastern temporal impositions.

Framed as it is through a temporality that demands progress (Nafas has three days by the end of which she must find her sister or risk her sister's suicide), *Kandahar* screens scene after scene that underscore the futility of imposing a progressive temporality onto this premillennial Afghanistan. The film makes this point in three ways: by emphasizing a cyclical temporality over a linear, progressive one; by recording all journeys in Afghanistan as interrupted or incomplete; and by remarking on the effects of the selective incorporation of "progress" into Afghanistan.

It is cyclical time that is emphasized in the film. This is rendered clear in the very first and the very last images of the film: the repetition of a solar eclipse, itself a cyclical event, marking as it does the recurrence of specific orbital alignments. However, even more important are the film's first and final narrative sequences. Both portray Nafas's encounter with the Taliban on the outskirts of Kandahar. Not only do we see the same encounters, we see them through the same shots and hear them through the same dialog. Temporally, the film is a narrative loop, beginning and ending at the very same place. The selection of this particular scene as the opening and closing of the film is important, underscoring as it does how cyclical time—the time of the eclipse—is cheating progressive time, for we never see Nafas progress to her destination.

Indeed, for all the many journeys recounted in the film, not one of them includes a definitive arrival; every journey is in this sense nonprogressive. The Afghan refugee family whom Nafas accompanied on the first leg of her journey meet with too many obstacles to continue with her and decide to return to the refugee camp in Iran, but we do not know whether they make it. Her second guide, Khak, also turns back before the journey's end, leaving Nafas with the doctor; what becomes of Khak we do not know. The doctor leaves Nafas with the one-handed man who, when detained by the Taliban, leaves Nafas alone to face Taliban questions. Not only are the journey's of those closely connected with Nafas nonprogressive; so, too, are those of all characters. The film never depicts a completed journey, whether it is of the one-legged men racing toward prosthetic legs parachuting to the ground or the droves of presumably soon-to-be refugees Nafas passes along the road traveling in the opposite direction.

The dramatic tension created by the film's doubled temporal frame, marked as it is by a necessary arrival and repeated nonarrivals, speaks to the history and historical possibility of Afghanistan. Historically, Afghanistan has experienced "progress" selectively. As the doctor tells Nafas, "Weapons are the only modern things in Afghanistan." *Kandahar* unreservedly critiques this particular form of progress. In so doing, it does not eschew progress itself, whatever that may be; it simply refuses to name it, to decide what it may be for the Afghanistan it portrays. It does this by deliberately holding open a space for progress, by keeping every storyline open, by its refusal to mark an arrival, and by its translation of movement, whether progressive or nonprogressive, into hope. This translation is performed primarily through Nafas. Though she may or may not ever arrive in Kandahar, her journey seems to be as much about collecting encounters that will inspire her sister, her sisters, and herself with hope as it is about ultimately arriving at her destination. *Kandahar* is about the journey, then, not about the journey's end.

This is not to say that *Kandahar* does not articulate a basis for progress: it does so very clearly. The basis for progress, it suggests, is the very same as the basis for hope that Nafas finds on her journey. It is the humanity and humanitarianism of the Afghans she meets.

In the spirit of Kantian idealism, *Kandahar* morally codes humanity according to a simple dualism of light versus dark. What is light is good; what is dark is evil. What is light and good is humanity; what is dark and evil are social, cultural, political, and religious forces within and beyond Afghanistan, such as the Taliban, civil wars, and proxy wars. As with its handling of space and time, the film constructs a tension in its employment of this moral dichotomy. On the one hand, the film is an allegory about the threat of light descending into darkness. In this story, light is personified by Nafas's suicidal sister, who symbolizes Afghan women and Afghan humanity as a whole, while darkness is expressed as the poverty, famine, and political and religious oppression faced by Afghans and symbolized by fundamentalism, the legacies of war, and the pending total solar eclipse. On the other hand, the film chronicles how the light of humanity repeatedly shines through this darkness. It is in humanity's ability to overcome the forces of darkness that *Kandahar* places its hope.

This hope that light will triumph over darkness is made most explicit through the film's symbolic investment in each of its characters. In every case, these characters stand for the goodness of humanity and their struggles against darkness. This is most obviously the case with Nafas, who sacrifices herself to the threat of every form of imprisonment to invest her sister with the hope necessary to avert her suicide. Yet, as in the case of Nafas, we find goodness and its struggle against evil scripted into the core of every character. Just as Nafas's sister's light is being eclipsed by darkness, the young girls in the refugee camp symbolize an innocence/lightness about to be risked on their return to Afghanistan. So, too, does Khak, a young boy we first encounter in the madaris, struggle against darkness as he naively negotiates the religious and economic minefields of Afghanistan. Expelled from school and desperate for money to support his fatherless family, Khak still makes a gift to Nafas's sister of the ring he scavenged from a skeleton, a ring that Nafas refuses to buy.

Goodness is not merely associated with the innocence of youth or with its protection. Characters who long ago lost their innocence are also portrayed as innately good. For example, the refugee family who acts as Nafas's first guide is a metaphor for the wider Afghan community, composed as it is of a husband and wives of different ethnic backgrounds. As refugees, its members are no longer innocent, and still they stand for the possibility of peace among warring Afghan factions. There is also the shyster who is sympathetically drawn, even though he talked the Red Cross out of a pair of legs he intends to sell. He is not a bad man, the film suggests, but just a man in economic need trying to survive like everyone else. Although his agreement to take Nafas to Kandahar is rooted in an economic bargain, on the journey he does this selflessly, all the while putting himself at great risk. An even better example is the American doctor. Having come to Afghanistan in search of God, the doctor begins this search in all the wrong places: in war and violence. Enlightened by the poverty and neglect of the people he encounters, he lays down his weapons to become a doctor, a conversion that represents the possibility for the transformation of the human spirit (see Makhmalbaf, 2001).

Should one ever question the goodness of these characters, one need only recall that though everyone who offered to guide Nafas to Kandahar disappoints her, no one betrays her, even though betrayal is always possible. The refugee family could have taken Nafas's money when they themselves were robbed. Khak could have reported Nafas to the authorities for speaking directly to the doctor. The doctor could have used his gun against Nafas, robbed her, and turned her in. And the shyster could have traded Nafas and her concealed tape recorder to the Taliban for his own freedom when he himself was captured. None of these things happens.

However, just as the film depicts images, journeys, bodies, and histories as incomplete, so too does it stress the incompleteness of an individually based humanist moral grammar. For though part of the point of *Kandahar* is to show how humanity's struggle for goodness and hope often prevails even under the threat of complete darkness, the film's subject is as much "negligent humanity" as it is individual Afghan triumphs (Macnab and Makhmalbaf, 2001). Yes, the human spirit conquers many obstacles, but it should not have to. War and its legacies, such as landmines, poverty, famine, and oppression, persist in wounding Afghanistan and Afghanis. Though there are complex domestic and international origins to these problems (Halliday, 2002), both the West and the East bear responsibility not only for their adventures in Afghanistan but for their neglect of the Afghan people.

Stressing the goodness of humanity and the lack of anything like sufficient humanitarian assistance to Afghanistan, *Kandahar* is not an invitation for West and East to again write their desires onto what they too often regard as an empty landscape. Denied a sense of place in the world's view, Afghanistan is not a faceless, placeless space. It has many images, the film points out, if one will only notice them. Nor is it appropriate for West or East to temporalize Afghanistan according to its grand narratives of progress, which the film notes have participated in rendering the country a battleground. It is not up to either West or East to "complete" Afghanistan through their visions of this space/time.

As a critique of how domestic and international fundamentalist visions of Afghanistan have reduced its people to poverty, hunger, and violence, *Kandahar* is both an illustration of and a call for a re-envisioning of Afghanistan spatially and temporally by those who gaze on it as if their vision were in no way impaired, as if they saw this space/time for what it "is." Subtly yet persistently, *Kandahar* suggests it is not only those within Afghanistan who are suffering from impaired vision. The West and the East, so often seeking to see themselves in their heroic adventures in foreign lands, fail to see this country for itself. Staring at Afghanistan without seeing it, like those who stare at an eclipse, West and East are too often blinded by their own projects and their own desires.

A re-envisioning of Afghanistan, *Kandahar* insists, is the first step toward a moral encounter with Afghanistan. Having focused too much on placing their images of Afghanistan into their scripts of progress, neither West nor East has yet meaningfully embarked on such an encounter. This is why the film is targeted to an English-speaking audience, to whom it reports on how their legacies of heroic encounters with Afghanistan have lacerated its landscape and its people. This is also why the film chooses an outsider (an American doctor) as its symbolic embodiment of the possibility of human spiritual transformation and the humanitarianism such a transformation makes possible (Fraser, 2001). *Kandahar* testifies to the urgency of this moral encounter, before the sun is fully behind the moon, before West and East themselves symbolize nothing but the imposition of darkness onto Afghanistan in the name of earthly or spiritual enlightenment.

### Bush's Kandahar

It is uncanny how the official US discourse on the war on terror echoes the grammatical structure that makes Makhmalbaf's *Kandahar* meaningful. Beginning in Afghanistan and stretching into the US war in Iraq, what we find are the same primary tensions (place versus placelessness, progress versus nonprogress, and light versus darkness) that map this discourse spatially, temporally, and morally. And what is equally clear is that, when considered through Makhmalbaf's *Kandahar*, each of these tensions is critical of US foreign policy ambitions in relation to the war on terror.

As in Makhmalbaf's *Kandahar*, in which one character is firmly in place (Nafas's sister) while all others wander through Afghanistan as characters out of place, this dichotomy is repeated in the US post-9/11 engagement with Afghanistan. Anchoring the US narrative on the war on terror is not a maimed girl standing for the collective category of imprisoned Afghan women but Osama bin Laden, who epitomizes the collective category of the 9/11 terrorist. In official US discourse, both collective identities—wounded women and terrorists—are located in Afghanistan. This is why US troops had to be introduced into Afghanistan, to wander the "placeless" landscape as Nafas did. For just as Nafas is in search of her sister, US troops are in search of bin Laden.

Troublingly for the US, though, after Makhmalbaf's *Kandahar*, the place and placelessness dichotomy is turned on its head in official US discourse because, as we saw in Chapter 2, even though bin Laden functions in US discourse as a stationary subject position—terrorist, US public enemy number one—he himself is anything but stationary, as the repeated reports of his whereabouts and the repeated failures by US troops to capture him evidence. Bin Laden is not only on the move; he symbolizes movement itself, as an illusive corporeal body and as a religious-political movement called al Qaeda. This could not be more worrying for US troops, whose own wanderings are at least officially reported to be restricted within the bounded space of the sovereign state of Afghanistan. If, as in Makhmalbaf's *Kandahar*, where there is movement there is hope, then hope is firmly on the side of bin Laden, al Qaeda, and terrorism, whereas US efforts to capture him, shut down his international network, and win the war on terror seem to be hopeless.

Like the spatial dichotomies of Makhmalbaf's *Kandahar*, so too is its temporal dichotomy depressingly echoed in official US discourse, for what we find in both Makhmalbaf's *Kandahar* and in official US discourse on the war on terror is the double temporal frame of necessary progress versus cyclicality. Just as Nafas urgently needs to find her sister before hope is eclipsed by darkness, so too, in official US discourse, the US urgently needs to capture bin Laden before more dark terrorist acts are committed against the West. But Nafas's journey to her sister, like all journeys in Makhmalbaf's *Kandahar*, is incomplete. The film begins and ends with her hopes eclipsed by the Taliban.

The US excursion/incursion into Afghanistan is also incomplete. US troops entered the frame of Afghanistan not knowing where bin Laden was. As major US military activities officially ended in Afghanistan with the fall of the Taliban and the establishment of an interim Afghan government, they still did not know enough about bin Laden's whereabouts to capture him. Like Nafas in Makhmalbaf's *Kandahar*, then, US military activity in relation to its anchoring objective begins and (at the time of this writing) ends at the same place, with necessary progress frustrated.

Whether because of US failures or in spite of them, bin Laden's terrorist network persists in committing terrorist acts: attacking US embassies, launching missiles at civilian Israeli aircraft, bombing a British bank and the British consulate in Turkey, to name a few. With the simultaneous bombing of four passenger trains in Madrid on the eleventh of March, 2004, America's 9/11 seemed to have been repeated as Spain's "el 11 M." El 11 M signifies not only a link to 9/11 but, of course, a link to Gulf War II. For al Qaeda terrorists claimed Spain was targeted because it supported US objectives in Iraq and because of its contribution of troops to the resulting war. Citing these very same justifications, an al Qaeda-linked group employed British suicide bombers in its July 7, 2005 bombing of the London transportation system, thereby continuing the cycle of repetition.

By widening the frame from Afghanistan to Iraq, then, the non-progressive cyclicality of the official US narrative on the war on terror is merely replayed in another location. Gulf War II, itself a redux of the war on terror in Afghanistan (not to mention Gulf War I and some would argue increasingly Vietnam), did result in the overthrow and capture of Saddam Hussein. However, the official US aim of instituting a democratic order in Iraq and making Iraq safe for the Iraqi people is nowhere near being achieved, if it is indeed achievable by the US. Far worse than US failures to bring security to post-Saddam Iraq (which echoes US failures to secure Afghanistan outside of a small zone around Kabul) is the mirroring of US security tactics by those of Saddam's, primarily the torturing of Iraqi prisoners in the Abu Ghraib prison (which itself recalls US treatment of suspected terrorist "detainees" in Camp X-Ray at Guantanamo Bay).

All this renders it pretty difficult for the US to claim to be on the side of goodness and light rather than on the side of evil and darkness in the final dichotomy explored in Makhmalbaf's *Kandahar*. For how can one sustain the dichotomy of holding that democracy promotion and humanitarianism are good versus holding that fundamentalist fanatics (e.g., the Taliban, bin Laden, Saddam, and terrorists) are evil when US good intentions (assuming they were good intentions) lead minimally to questionable acts and arguably to evil ones?

Read onto the US war on terror, Makhmalbaf's *Kandahar* is a damning critique of US post-9/11 foreign policy. And yet President Bush latched onto this film to help to justify his bombing of Afghanistan. How is this possible? How, in light of Makhmalbaf's *Kandahar*, could the US claim to be making a positive (moral) difference in Afghanistan?

One factor that begins to explain the Bush administration's use of the film is its release date. Although it was screened in art houses and at film festivals before 9/11, most Americans first heard about and saw *Kandahar* in November 2001, a mere two months after 9/11. This timing could not have been better for the Bush administration. Traumatized by the events of 9/11, many US citizens were urgently asking, "Why do they hate us?" Though this question can be read as positioning US citizens as politically innocent victims of international events, it can also be understood as an expression of moral uncertainty. Indeed, one would be hard pressed to find another moment in US history when so many Americans were so self-awarely in search of a moral compass, when so many of them asked not just why they hate us but the follow-on question: "And what should we do about that?"

What the Bush administration did about it was to declare its war on terror, which the vast majority of US citizens supported at the time. When the Taliban refused to turn over Osama bin Laden, the administration declared war on Afghanistan and began its bombing campaign of terrorist training camps and Taliban positions. The US response to 9/11, then, was aggressive and vengeful but not (necessarily) moral, except in the stark terms of seeing terrorists as "evil doers" and Americans as "do-gooders." But, of course, setting the United States up as a nation of do-gooders was itself a problem, for how could this extensive bombing campaign, which disrupted and destroyed the lives of so many Afghans, be seen as doing good?

This is where the Bush administration turned to *Kandahar*. Never mind that *Kandahar* offers a damning critique of foreign adventures in Afghanistan. More importantly for the Bush administration, *Kandahar* represents a non-Western vision of Afghanistan as a country in need of humanitarian assistance. As such, what *Kandahar* offered the Bush administration was the key to transform its bombing mission in Afghanistan from vengeful to helpful, as long as it justified its war in Afghanistan on humanitarian grounds.

That is precisely what it did. Laying claim to those figures who both in the film and in international humanitarian discourse most needed international assistance—the wounded women of Afghanistan—the Bush administration embellished its justification of the war in Afghanistan from capturing Osama bin Laden and disrupting terrorist training in that country to rescuing Afghan women. In November 2001, not only did George W. Bush and UK Prime Minister Tony Blair offer this justification; their wives, Laura Bush and Cheri Blair, were paraded before the press to argue the case for Afghan women. In the first full-length radio address ever given by a US First Lady, Laura Bush told Americans in November 2001, "Afghan women know, through hard experience, what the rest of the world is discovering: The brutal oppression of women is a central goal of the terrorists...The plight of women and children in Afghanistan is a matter of deliberate human cruelty, carried out by those who seek to intimidate and control. Civilized people throughout the world are speaking out in horror— not only because our hearts break for the women and children in Afghanistan, but also because in Afghanistan we see the world the terrorists would like to impose on the rest of us...Fighting brutality against women and children is not the expression of a specific culture; it is the acceptance of our common humanity, a commitment shared by people of good will on every continent" (L. Bush, 2001).

Conveniently for those rehearsing the official US story on the war, what symbolizes the oppression of Afghan women to Westerners—the burqa—is the very symbol Makhmalbaf uses in *Kandahar* to symbolize what imprisons Afghan women. In official US discourse, this point is made both in the US Department of State's *Report on the Taliban's War Against Women* (2001), released immediately after Laura Bush's radio address, and in the comments of the First Lady at the Republican National Convention three years later. Laura Bush told delegates, "After years of being treated as virtual prisoners in their homes by the Taliban, the women of Afghanistan are going back to work...And wasn't it wonderful to watch the Olympics and see that beautiful Afghan sprinter race in long pants and a tee shirt, exercising her new freedom while respecting the traditions of her country" (L. Bush, 2004).

From its non-Western perspective, then, *Kandahar* functioned in this particular Western discourse as a cinematic lifting of the veil on Afghan women and, more broadly, on Afghanistan itself while it made an urgent plea for international humanitarian assistance for Afghanis to the

English-speaking world.[4] The Bush administration embraced this plea as if it had become as enlightened as the spiritually transformed US doctor in the film who treats Nafas.[5] "We may not have gone to Afghanistan for all the right reasons," the Bush administration could say to itself and to the American people, "but now we've seen the light and are fighting for humanitarian causes."

Makhmalbaf's film is clear that fighting is not the way to achieve any moral causes in Afghanistan. The US bombing campaign, then, is not the sort of moral re-envisioning of Afghanistan that the filmmaker (much less many feminists in and beyond Afghanistan; see Molloy, 2002 and Rosenburg, 2002) was calling for. Yet, from the perspective of the official US story, this criticism is easily dealt with. For the Bush administration could respond, as it did in practice, that Makhmalbaf's vision of a humane Afghanistan cannot be realized as long as the Taliban are in control of Afghanistan and of Afghan women. Makhmalbaf's film, like all the stories he depicts within it, can be viewed as incomplete. In the official US story, the United States was capable of bring Makhmalbaf's story to a happy ending; however, it could do this only by going a step beyond Makhmalbaf, by reminding him and the world that it is sometimes necessary to use military force to realize humanitarian goals, to complete humanitarian visions. And, of course, in making this argument, the Bush administration suggested that by bombing Afghanistan, the United States was making a (moral) difference in Afghanistan.

## Who we really are

What *Behind Enemy Lines, Black Hawk Down*, and *Kandahar* tell us when read together is that "becoming a moral American" requires more than US moral leadership or self-referential US heroism. It requires broadening the scope of the US moral engagement from one with some self-referential US *we* to one with a US *we* with a real humanitarian mission in the real world of the war on terror. To become this moral American, these films tell us, we must be more than morally confused soldierly sons who rescue our own sense of morality. We must rescue the feminized others who are the real victims in the war on terror, be these Afghan women or the feminized states of Afghanistan and later Iraq.

Being aware of this trajectory toward becoming a moral American, we can finally embrace another US *we*: the morally enlightened humanitarian. This US *we* expresses who we really are in the official story of the war on terror. And this US *we* is the foundation of another

US moral grammar of war, in which enlightened US do-gooders fight morally unenlightened evil doers not for our own self-interest but for the good of all humanity.

As the necessary object of rescue by US soldierly sons, the feminine in this latest US moral grammar of war functions as the final necessary supplement to a meaningful answer to the question "What does it take to make a (moral) difference in the war on terror?" What it takes, these films suggest, is for the United States to assist separated sisters or wounded women to complete their unfinished journeys by removing evil forces who stand in their way. This, it seems, is the humanitarian spirit of the US intervention into Afghanistan. But, of course, in helping the sisters of Afghanistan complete their journeys toward living humane lives, the United States is also helping itself to complete its journey toward becoming a (heroic) humanitarian. In this gesture of humanitarian assistance to the women of Afghanistan, the United States seems to escape the circle of self-referential humanitarianism it seemed to exercise in the 1990s.

However, has the United States really escaped its self-referential claims to heroism and humanitarianism in this particular inflection of its moral grammar of war? Is it really humane to use an objectified feminized (and often Orientalized) other to make our own claim to a subjectified masculine self? And can finding our subjectivity in an objectified other ever amount to anything other than (reflected) self-referentiality?

From the perspective of the official US story, the answers to these questions are yes, yes, and who cares. America's mission is too important to get sidetracked into "politically correct" conversations about gender or imperialism. And, indeed, as the films *Behind Enemy Lines* and *Black Hawk Down* remind us, the US humanitarian mission is so important that the United States cannot let anyone stand in its way, foe or friend (e.g., NATO or the UN).

Established as a response to 9/11, this humanitarian US moral grammar of war was also applied to Gulf War II. It was used to deflect criticisms that the Bush administration's war on Iraq was about Bush Jr. and his (father's) cohorts attending to the unfinished business of Gulf War I waged by Bush Sr., primarily the removal of Saddam Hussein from power (see Chapter 6) or securing access to Middle Eastern oil reserves. Sometimes justified as cleansing Iraq of dangerous "weapons of mass destruction" (which at the time of this writing have failed to materialize and many doubt ever existed) and at other times justified as a response to al Qaeda terrorist activities in Iraq (a claim that lacked and still lacks any evidence), the Bush (and Blair) administrations could always fall back on the justification that this was a humanitarian war.

No one in the West argued that Saddam Hussein was not a brutal dictator, and few argued that removing him from power would not improve the lives of the vast majority of everyday Iraqis. However, many in the United States and in other Western states hesitated at what they viewed as the conquest of another feminized state rather than a humanitarian rescue mission of Iraqi citizens. All they saw in Iraq was the United States again securing itself in relation to an objectified, feminized other. On this unofficial reading, this hardly amounted to the United States making a (moral) difference; rather, it merely repeated the official nonprogressive, myopic American morality against which so many in and outside the United States cautioned the United States after 9/11 and in the build-up to Gulf War II. Rather than securing an enlightened, humanitarian US *we*, US actions as narrated in unofficial stories about the war on terror increasingly marked the Bush administration's evocation of this US *we* as both hypocritical and dangerous, as the failures of Afghanistan, whether to secure the state or to rebuild the country for its people, replayed themselves with a vengeance in Iraq.

When, in the spring of 2004, images of US soldiers abusing Iraqi prisoners circulated in the global media, any credible claim the United States made to an enlightened, humanitarian *we* for its post-Vietnam era band of brothers (and, in this case, sisters) was lost. Never mind that these atrocities did not represent the actions of every US soldier, much less every US citizen, or that the soldiers responsible were condemned by the US public and subjected to courts martial by the US military. As far as the wider world was concerned, the United States, which always claims the moral high ground, had exposed its "true" moral character to the world. This US *we* was not, as *Behind Enemy Lines* claimed, one that necessarily exercised US moral leadership on behalf of its reluctant European allies (such states as Germany and France, who opposed Gulf War II). Instead of those European allies appearing as they do in *Behind Enemy Lines* as dangerously inactive, the US *we* of Gulf War II appeared to be dangerously overactive.

Even if (and this is a huge *if* ) one gives the Bush administration the benefit of the doubt, arguing that it had the best of intentions in its humanitarian projects toward Afghanistan and Iraq, these three films together raise a troubling question about how one becomes a moral America(n). That question is this: Is it ever possible in practice to live up to the ideals of enlightened humanitarianism, especially when we define our "moral mission" for ourselves? If the answer is no (and I think it is), this does not mean that humanitarianism as an ideal must be abandoned; it means that when *we* attempt to act as humanitarians, we must make sure we begin by respecting those we claim to be helping. Otherwise, we are only really helping ourselves and, as Makhmalbaf's *Kandahar* suggests, probably doing harm to (feminized) others.

Not only is this not the sort of (moral) difference we want to make; it is morally disquieting, for one way or another, the feminized other eventually finds a way to get our attention. Like the pictures from the Abu Ghraib prison that circulated in the global media, our moral mistakes come back to haunt us. Unlike Fowler in *The Quiet American*, there really is no way for us to make peace with these ghosts, nor should there be.

If this is who we really are, then who we might become must be a US *we* that does not mistake the feminine as a passive, willing object of our moral rescue but sees it as an active moral agent in its own right. Put differently, we would be well advised not to let our morality eclipse the morality of those we wish to help. For if we make this moral mistake, we risk plunging ourselves into moral darkness.

# 5  Who we really are (vigilantes)

The trio of films—*Behind Enemy Lines, Black Hawk Down*, and *Kandahar*—underscores just how risky it is in the morally uncertain post-Vietnam era to base US morality on a claim to be helping a feminized other, especially when that other does not want the kind of help the United States has to offer. Furthermore, these films emphasize the difficulty of grounding US morality in America's post-Vietnam war sons. For however much these soldierly sons intend to carry on the moral traditions of their WWII fathers, their humanitarian missions, arguably like this generation of myopic Americans, risk helping only themselves and often hurting others. In the face of America's failure to sustain humanitarianism in the war on terror, these films lead us to consider whether it might be less risky to base US morality on ourselves and ourselves alone. In other words, instead of claiming to be helping others, *we* could avoid this moral quagmire by owning up to the fact that we are only helping ourselves.

Another pair of films—Collateral *Damage* and *In the Bedroom*—does just this. In the spirit of 9/11, both films ponder how a traumatized US citizenry ought to respond to unbearable grief. In very different ways, *Collateral Damage* and *In the Bedroom* consider the morality of a vengeful US *we* as the basis of a post-9/11 moral grammar of war. In so doing, what they give us is another inflection of who we really are: a solitary US *we* out for a justifiable "eye-for-an-eye" type of revenge that is not rooted in a claim to be protecting the humanity of others. Far from it, when some forms of humanity get in our way, it is our moral duty to "take them out."

What is striking about *Collateral Damage* and *In the Bedroom* is that both films play out their stories of vengeance in the father–son relationship. In both cases, a contemporary US(-based) father deals with the death of his US son by murdering his son's killer. Not only do fathers return center stage in these films; these fathers do not make the same mistake that post-Vietnam era US sons did: they do not treat the feminine as a passive object that willingly bends to their desire to rescue her (or, when they do, they soon learn their mistake and correct it). In *Collateral Damage* and *In the Bedroom*, the feminine (represented by morally questionable meddling mothers) bears ultimate responsibility for these fathers' unbearable grief and is the source of their moral insecurity. It is only by silencing meddling mothers, these films suggest, that *we* can rescue US domesticity after 9/11. This silencing of the feminine could not occur more differently in each film. In *Collateral Damage*, the meddling mother is murdered; in *In the Bedroom* (which features two rival meddling mothers), one meddling mother is marginalized from happy US home life while her rival's vengeance is indulged to murderous effect.

What we have here, then, are two claims to a US *we* based on a vigilantism that is not (ultimately) about rescuing the feminine but about marginalizing or murdering it. As such, it could not be more different than the US *we* that formed the basis of an official US humanitarian moral grammar of war.

## Collateral Damage

A foreboding soundtrack introduces *Collateral Damage*. As increasingly thick clouds of smoke overlay the black background of the title sequence, urgent short-wave radio chatter about a fire joins the music. Fade in and out the names of the film's director (Andrew Davis) and its star (Arnold Schwarzenegger). Fade in the film's title in white lettering that gives way to a fiery red. The music explodes just as a yellow fireball fills the screen. Among the flames are firefighters battling a blaze in an occupied tenement building. Gordy Brewer (Arnold Schwarzenegger), one of the firefighters, attempts the heroic rescue of a helpless old woman, against the better judgment of his colleagues. As stairwells collapse and the screen again fills with fireballs, the film cuts to a close-up of a white US woman safely at home in bed, her eyes jumping open as the soundtrack explodes. Cut to a long shot of the woman in bed awaking from her nightmare, the film's opening fire. She is alone. It is early morning, and someone from her bed is clearly missing. Fade up Gordy's voice from another room as the woman, his wife, searches the house for him. Anne Brewer (Lindsay Frost) finds her husband helping their young son Matthew (Ethan Danpf) put together a futurist spaceship.

Cut to scenes of the happy family: the relieved wife with her husband and son, father and son showering together, and mother and father arranging for their son to see the doctor that day as he awoke with a sore throat. The arrangement is this: Anne will take Matthew to the doctor and Gordy will meet them in the nearby café to collect his son.

Cut to extreme long shot of the Los Angeles skyline, which locates the action.

Cut to mother and son (complete with the toy he made with his father that morning) entering the café after their appointment. As mother and son settle into the café awaiting Gordy (who is late), we see an L.A. police officer (Cliff Curtis) drive up on his motorcycle. He is a traffic cop distributing tickets, but this cop seems to be more interested in an approaching caravan of official cars than in policing traffic. When Gordy drives up, he tells the officer he will just be a minute, as he is there to pick up his child. The distracted officer is fine about it and walks away. Father and son spot one another just as the officials in the caravan exit their vehicles and enter the Colombian Consulate next door.

A bomb originating from the cop's motorcycle explodes, destroying much of the Consulate and killing several people in the adjacent café, including Anne and Matthew Brewer. As Arnold tries to make his way to his family, he is hit by a passing taxi. This time, there is no heroic rescue. Gordy not only fails to help his family; he experiences the reality of his wife's dream, the loss of his family.

This opening sequence of *Collateral Damage* establishes the successes and failures of the contemporary American family in relation to the US state. By giving us the middle-class, happy, heterosexual white characters of mother, father, and son, we see in this family not only the stability of a happy home life but the promise of future US families who will repeat this domestic bliss (symbolized by son Matthew). What we have here is the same traditional US family who served as the foundation of a post-WWII moral grammar of war, much like the family of Rafe, Evelyn, and their son Danny from *Pearl Harbor*. Yet on closer inspection, the Brewer family is nothing like the traditional post-WWII family. For the fulcrum of this US family is not (originally) American; he is Austrian. Though *Collateral Damage* never marks Gordy Brewer's (Arnold Schwarzenegger's) nationality, Arnold's accent and status as an icon of Hollywood cinema do this for us. Unlike the US-born but Australia-raised Mel Gibson of *We Were Soldiers,* there is no way cinema goers can mistake Gordy Brewer as (someone raised in the) United States. Conversely, Arnold Schwarzenegger is one of America's success stories. As a former body builder, he is literally a self-made man who immigrated to the United States, pursued his ambition to become a movie star, married into American "royalty" (the Kennedy family), and ultimately became governor of the state of California. What Arnold embodies, then, is the fulfillment of the American dream. Arnold is iconic not only of a Hollywood star but of a further foundation of the US family: the self-made immigrant.

Leaving aside Arnold's sociopolitical body to consider Arnold's cinematic body, what we notice is that Arnold's body often symbolizes perfect fatherhood. In his most famous role as The Terminator, Sarah Connor (Linda Hamilton) proclaims the reprogrammed protective Terminator of *Terminator II* to be "the perfect father" for her son John, a figure echoed in *Collateral Damage* in the futurist toy Gordy makes for his son Matthew. However, Arnold is even more than the perfect father; he is the perfect—and only necessary—parent. This is established in the comedy *Junior*, in which Arnold (with the help of Danny DeVito) usurps the power of reproduction by giving birth to his own child. Even though Arnold eventually pairs up with the owner of baby Junior's egg (Emma Thompson) and Danny DeVito reconnects with his pregnant divorced wife, the feminine as the reproductive basis of these US families is marginalized in, if not superfluous to, this film. Yes, women can still have babies, but in every case with the help of men. More important, as Arnold's pregnancy proves, men can have babies with virtually no help from women (so long as they are willing and able to steal a human egg).

When one ties Arnold's symbolic function as the fulfillment of the American dream to the reproductive dream of marginalizing women from their traditional roles as reproductive of the family, the result is the foreshadowing of another (American) dream: the establishment of future US families on the masculine alone. As it is portrayed in *Collateral Damage,* women may have the babies, but ultimately it is the heroic US father who ought to raise them. Moving from the usurpation of reproduction to the usurpation of parenting, *Collateral Damage* not only returns the US father to his traditional patriarchic role; it also insulates fathers (and sons) from the disruptive potential of the feminine (like the one that troubled the US *we* in its humanitarian missions in Afghanistan and Iraq). For in this American dream, the feminine is erased soon after reproduction is achieved and therefore does not function as a foundational figure for this future American family.

It is with the realization of this additional American dream that

*Collateral Damage* ends, with Arnold establishing a new US family free of all (disruptive) feminine foundations. Apart from being seen through Arnold's symbolic body, none of this is established in the film's opening sequence. Indeed, quite to the contrary, the Brewer family seems to represent the ideal US family, and Anne Brewer seems to be the perfect mother/wife. She hardly represents the feminine as the meddling mother who I have suggested is the target of this revenge film. Yes, it is her idea to take Matthew to the doctor that fateful morning, locating mother and son in harm's way; however, as the film renders clear and as Gordy (Arnold) confesses, neither mother nor son should have been there at the time of the bombing, for Gordy was late meeting them. The responsibility for their deaths, then, is claimed by the mournful Gordy.

However, as Gordy laments that the responsibility for the death of his wife and son are his and his alone because his family should not have been in the café, CIA agent Peter Brandt (Elias Koteas) interjects, telling Gordy, "No, the bombers shouldn't have been there." The responsibility for the death of this perfect post-WWII US family, the film explains, is not this successful immigrant father but destructive international forces that, unlike Gordy (and Arnold), have not been properly integrated into the traditional American dream and which occasionally succeed in violently penetrating the boundaries of the US state. This is what destabilizes the US family and what destabilizes its (future) foundational claim to fatherhood.

Indeed, the terrorist responsible for the bombing (who is, of course, the traffic cop with the exploding motorcycle that Gordy encountered as he rushed off to meet his family) proudly articulates his mission of bringing insecurity within US borders. Known as *El Lobo* (Spanish for "the wolf"), this Colombian terrorist sends a message to US officials that is broadcast on US television and watched by Gordy.

> EL LOBO: The bombing was an act of self-defense against America's war we know. As long as America continues its aggression in Colombia, we will bring the war home to you, and you will not feel safe in your own beds. Colombia is not your country. Get out now. (Making a gesture of slapping one hand violently into another, he continues.) Sangre o libertad (blood or liberty).

El Lobo's statement not only establishes the terrorist mission of disrupting US home life; it also lays the blame for this disruption on a prior disruption: US interventions in Colombia (through the US global war on drugs). Foreign terrorist acts in the US homeland, El Lobo contends, are the fault of the US government itself, and they will not stop until the United States stops meddling in Colombia's internal affairs.

Needless to say, this reading of terrorism was not likely to be one that would go down well with the majority of post-9/11 US citizens. Regardless of whether US citizens supported their government's policies in Colombia, what they surely did not condone was a terrorist response to these policies, of bringing the war in Colombia to the United States. And, of course, quite uncomfortably, El Lobo's justification for terrorism in the US homeland echoes al Qaeda's justification for its attacks in New York, Washington, D.C., and Pennsylvania. Furthermore, *Collateral Damage* emphasizes that the United States was fighting the wrong war in September 2001: the passé war on drugs rather than the pressing war on terror. In light of this, it is not surprising that *Collateral Damage*, a film that was originally scheduled to be released in early October 2001, had its release date postponed until February 2002.

However, of course, as a mainstream Hollywood film, *Collateral Damage* offers the terrorist's justification for his actions only so it can immediately discredit this justification, or really its consequences. For the bomb El Lobo planted failed to kill any of its intended targets, claiming the lives of such innocent victims as Anne and Matthew Brewer instead. Immediately after El Lobo's statement, the news broadcast Gordy is watching cuts to an interview with the political spokesman of El Lobo's terrorist group. Not only does this spokesman describe El Lobo as a freedom fighter rather than a terrorist; when pressed to comment on the deaths of Anne and Matthew Brewer, he admits that their deaths are regrettable but makes no apology for them. For in war, these things happen. As he puts it, "It is called collateral damage."

The spokesperson's statement effectively dehumanizes Gordy's wife and son, a move that, needless to say, infuriates Gordy. Indeed, this insensitive statement is the film's first justification for Gordy's vengeance. He wastes little time in exercising it. That night, Gordy breaks into the headquarters of the political wing of El Lobo's terrorist organization, trashes the place, and demands to know where The Wolf is, only to be interrupted by US government officials who have the headquarters under surveillance.

This first justification for Gordy's vengeance has nothing to do with meddling mothers and everything to do with feuding fathers. On the one hand, we have Gordy, an immigrant American father who, in the face of personal loss, acts out his vengeance against the Colombian terrorist organization that murdered his family. On the other hand, we have a Colombian terrorist, claiming a kind of national paternity, vengefully attacking the US home(land) on behalf of the Colombian people. When we later learn that El Lobo is himself a father of an adopted son and we see Gordy's actions increasingly position him as symbolic of a pure US patriarchy, this feuding fathers motif is further strengthened.

Given all this, why am I claiming that *Collateral Damage* is a film that justifies its vengeance by targeting meddling mothers who symbolize the disruptive feminine that undermines the contemporary foundational US family? The answer lies not with Gordy Brewer's wife Anne but with El Lobo's wife Serena (Francesca Neri).

Gordy meets Serena when, after Brandt admits to Gordy that "justice for your wife and son isn't a priority right now" and that El Lobo is believed to have returned to Colombia, Gordy does precisely what an FBI agent warned him not to do: take justice into his own hands. Gordy travels to Colombia with one aim in mind: to murder El Lobo. Gordy's mission is a just one because, from his perspective, the US government is treating his family as a kind of second-order collateral damage. From Gordy's perspective, their deaths are not the regrettable effects of US military operations, but *a lack of justice for their deaths* is the regrettable effect of US policy decisions. For first it is CIA protocol and then it is US government prohibitions that allow El Lobo to go unpunished.

These failures and insensitivities of the US government to bring Anne and Matthew's killer to justice, then, are the second justification for Gordy's vengeance. This justification not only reminds a US viewing public of the interagency disputes between FBI and CIA that many US citizens see as the real cause of the government's failure to anticipate 9/11 (claims that continued to circulate in the hearings of the US 9/11 Commission); they also set up Gordy's third justification for vengeance: protecting the United States, himself, and his future US family from the meddling Colombian mother Serena, because it is Gordy's vigilantism that takes him to Colombia.

Gordy's presence in Colombia delights both Colombian terrorist El Lobo and CIA agent Brandt. El Lobo learns of Brewer's presence as he is complaining to his officers about how "Americans hide behind family values, false ideas. They have forgotten the reality of war." Interrupted with the news about Brewer, he continues: "Excellent. Take a fireman from Los Angeles. When America hears the story, they cry...Capture him. We hold him for ransom, and they will pay...If they don't pay, we kill him."

It is Brandt who made sure the terrorists knew that Brewer was in Colombia because Brewer's capture could be the means whereby Brandt convinces the US government to resume its counterterrorist activities in Colombia, activities that were suspended after the bombing. Indeed, we learn that the reason the bombing occurred in the first place is because Brandt and other US officials were at the Consulate to pitch to the Colombian government an unauthorized plan to attack the guerrillas. For bringing the Colombian war to the United States, as one US senator claims, Brandt is relieved of his post in the field and assigned to a desk job. Ignoring his restrictions, Brandt returns to the field and sets Brewer up to be kidnapped by the terrorists, gambling that the US public will recognize in this event the need for continued US counterterrorist activities in Colombia.

Brewer is not only the pawn of a terrorist kidnapping plot and of CIA agent Brandt. He is, most important, the pawn of Serena. Gordy meets Serena and her young deaf-mute son Mauro (Tyler Garcia Posey) in the guerrilla zone when, as Serena engages in a heated conversation with motorcyclists who nearly hit Mauro, Gordy comes to their rescue. Of course, the whole thing is a setup, for the motorcyclists are members of El Lobo's terrorist organization. Gordy is unaware of this or of Serena's connection to El Lobo as Serena introduces herself and her son, telling Mauro that Gordy is a friend. As their conversation ensues, Gordy is encircled by the terrorists who are intent on capturing him. However, Colombian officials interrupt them, arrest Gordy, and throw him into prison.

Eventually, El Lobo's forces do kidnap Gordy, after he dramatically breaks out of —predictably—a fiery prison, infiltrates the guerrilla zone, and explodes a cocaine production plant. He even nearly manages to assassinate El Lobo. However, when Serena and Mauro approach the grenade Gordy has planted, he flashes back to the deaths of his own wife and son, warns them off, and protects them from the explosion with his body. This warning to them also serves as a warning to El Lobo, who escapes unharmed and finally succeeds in capturing Gordy.

It is only when the captive Gordy awakes to Serena tending his wounds that he learns she is El Lobo's wife. Her care and sympathy for Gordy are immediately contrasted to her terrorist husband's feelings for the prisoner. When El Lobo enters Gordy's cell, he not only banishes his wife from the prison with a look of disgust but again expresses his distain for Americans in general.

EL LOBO: You Americans are so naïve. You see a peasant with a gun, you change your channel. But you never ask, "Why does a peasant need a gun?" Why? Because you think you are the only ones who have a right to fight for independence.

GORDY: Independence to do what? To kill my wife and my son?

EL LOBO: I remember your face, from Los Angeles. That was the face of a man who saved lives. Now your face has changed. Do you think your wife and son would recognize you now?

GORDY: I remember your face, too. The smile, just before you killed them. You're gonna pay for that.

EL LOBO: Well, it seems we are both willing to kill for a cause. What's the difference between you and I?

GORDY: The difference is I'm just gonna kill you.

Put differently, in Gordy's murder of El Lobo, there will be no collateral damage, a point he has already proved in his rescue of Serena and Mauro from his first assassination attempt on El Lobo. For Gordy's disrespect, El Lobo beats Gordy, in stark contrast to his wife, who tended to Gordy's wounds. Later, El Lobo and Serena argue about the prisoner.

EL LOBO (angrily): Why do you want to keep him alive?

SERENA (emphatically): Because he saved my life.

The fight continues with screams and shouts. When El Lobo says he will kill the American tomorrow, Serena has had enough and leaves her husband to his ranting. Gordy, peering through a crack in his cell, sees and hears the entire scene, some of which is spoken in English.

Even given their contrasting treatment of and attitudes toward Gordy, Gordy is suspicious of Serena and demands to know why she is helping him. "Because you saved my son," she tells him. For the mourning Gordy, there could be no better reason to extend care to someone. In contrast, Gordy's reply—"And your husband killed mine"—reiterates the basis of Gordy's unbearable grief and motivation for his actions.

Up to this point, the film has worked hard not only to distinguish El Lobo from Serena (they may be married, but they seem very much to have been cut from different moral clothes); it works hard to distinguish El Lobo from Gordy. Both are men willing to kill for a cause, but whereas El Lobo will tolerate collateral damage, Gordy will not. However, then the caring, understanding, and presumably trapped Serena offers a wrinkle into this neat dichotomy between vengeance for a good moral cause (represented by Gordy) and vengeance for a bad moral cause (represented by her husband). As she explains to Gordy, her husband was not always like this. He was a teacher in Guatemala when she met him, but when troops led by US military advisors attacked their village and killed their infant daughter, he changed into "a man consumed by hate and triggered by rage. He is like you," she tells Gordy. By contextualizing El Lobo's rage, Serena in a single stroke erases the difference between Gordy and her husband.

Even though Gordy resists Serena's characterization of him, her words not only resonate like a warning to him (Gordy: I'm not like him; Serena: Not yet); they also bond Gordy and Serena together as two people who do not want to be like El Lobo.

> Gordy asks Serena: What about you? If you are working with him, you are no better than he is.
>
> SERENA: What would you have me do?
> GORDY: Help me stop him.
> SERENA (sadly, regretfully): It's too late.

But maybe it is not too late. For we next see Serena packing, distractedly, and the next morning when she helps Gordy escape, the bond between this repentant wife and mother and the man who, unlike her husband, respects the line between justified murder and unjustified murder, is cemented.

> SERENA (to Gordy): I'm trusting you with my life, and my son. Claudio [El Lobo] has gone to Washington to plant another bomb. I can't be a part of it anymore. They'll [the US government] protect us, won't they?
> GORDY: If they won't, I will.

At this moment, Serena and Mauro become Gordy's substitute wife and son whom Gordy heroically protects from bombs, bullets, and minefields. He even protects them from CIA agent Brandt who, on the pretext of rescuing Gordy, catches up with the three fugitives after destroying the terrorist camp. When Gordy explains that El Lobo is about to plant a bomb in Washington, that Serena is El Lobo's wife, and that only she can identify the target, the three are flown to D.C. in an attempt to foil the bombing.

As El Lobo plants a bomb in D.C. and prepares to escape through a series of underground tunnels by motorcycle, Serena, accompanied by Gordy, Mauro, and Brandt, attempts to identify El Lobo's target from a situation room in the US State Department. Eventually, she identifies Union Square, where we see El Lobo dropping off a suitcase. Gordy reassures her that she has done the right thing, but Serena looks anxious and unconvinced. When the US Secretary of State and the Under Secretary of State for Latin American Affairs announce they will depart shortly for Union Square, Serena asks to go to the restroom. Mauro refuses to go with her, which angers Serena. In response to his refusal, Serena violently slaps one of her hands into the other. A stunned Gordy tells her Mauro will be fine with him and encourages her to go alone. Very quietly Serena answers, "Okay." After a long, anxious look at her son, a look that further confuses Gordy, she exits.

And then the penny drops. Gordy realizes he has seen this gesture before. This is the very gesture that El Lobo made when he claimed responsibility for the Los Angeles bombing. Gordy grasps what this means for who Serena really is. She is not a trapped mother and wife but a full-fledged terrorist and, as a full-fledged terrorist, she is part of this terrorist plot. Just as Gordy figures this out, we learn that the Union Station bomb was a hoax, and we suspect, as Gordy does, that the real bomb is in the State Department, targeted as top US officials gathered there.

Gordy rushes out of the situation room in pursuit of Serena, only to find that she has killed her restroom attendant and is about to make a cell phone call that will explode the State Department bomb. As he watches her pressing numbers on her keypad, Gordy flashes back to Los Angeles, where he remembers a disguised Serena making the cell phone call that triggered the bomb in her husband's stolen motorcycle. She, as much as El Lobo, killed Gordy's wife and son.

For Gordy, Serena does not just equal her husband's crimes; she surpasses them. For this time, the terrorist bomb is not planted in a vehicle outside the building; it is concealed in her son's toy, the toy Mauro (like Matthew Brewer before him) insists on taking with him everywhere. Serena has not only left this toy behind to explode; she has left her son there to explode with it, after she warned him with her gesture: sangre o libertad—blood or liberty. By choosing to stay with Gordy rather than accompany his mother to the restroom, Mauro has chosen blood, death. This explains Serena's reluctance to leave him, her long anxious look, but leave him she does, nevertheless. And even though her son is holding the toy/bomb as she is making the call that will detonate it (something she does not see but she could have suspected), she makes the call anyway. As such, Serena is hardly a fitting substitute for Anne Brewer, for she sacrifices her own (adopted) son in the name of her terrorist cause.

However, as this is, after all, an Arnold Schwarzenegger film, our hero snatches the toy/bomb from Mauro's hands, sends the bomb sailing toward the sky through a smashed window just as it explodes, and shelters Mauro from the explosion. In the meantime, Serena escapes to the tunnel below, where her husband rescues her on his motorcycle. Gordy chases them, but they get away, so he uses a control panel to lock the exit gates, forcing their return. In the meantime, taking a fireman's axe, he hacks open gas pipes that create an explosion when Serena returns and fires her gun at Gordy, but this, of course, is not enough to kill the bad guys. A fight scene ensues, in which Gordy first kills Serena by electrocuting her with the control panel and then kills El Lobo by throwing the fireman's axe into his heart.

Gordy's vengeance is now fulfilled, both by making El Lobo experience the loss of his wife (and maybe his son, although El Lobo never reacts to this) and finally by killing him.

The film ends with Gordy asking "Where's the boy?" Just then, Mauro spots the man who murdered his parents, runs toward him with open arms, and is scooped up in Gordy's embrace. This marks not only the mutual adoption of father and son by one another but also the establishment of a new US family consisting of two male refugees, one successful and one now destined to become successful. As this new American family leaves the scene of the bombing, a voice-over news broadcast tell us that Gordy has been awarded the Presidential Medal of Freedom, the highest decoration a US civilian can receive. The final credits roll.

The ultimate US family of *Collateral Damage* could not be more different from the white, heterosexual nuclear family we began with in WWII's *Pearl Harbor*. Though heterosexuality (as far as we know at this point) remains intact, every other foundation of this US family is transformed, for this US family is multiethnic, multiracial, and multinational. As such, it might speak to the multicultural moment in the United States and its promise of difference living in harmony within one state.

Yet, there are some extremely troubling aspects to this new US family. On the one hand, this family of refugee father and son is not just multi-everything; it is also fully assimilated (or about to be fully assimilated) into the traditional script of what it means to be a US citizen. Gordy (as Arnold) has already been assimilated into US-ness, and now, extending his fatherly protection, Gordy will see to the assimilation of his vulnerable, voiceless adopted son Mauro. At its best, what we have here is a kind of happy multiculturalism transformed into a happy US-ness; at worst, we have a gung-ho neocolonialism that resecures US borders from foreign influences by incorporating them into the US *we*. However, because this US *we* respects the line between justifiable vengeance and collateral damage, it is not only moral, it is heroic. For ultimately, this US *we* saves lives while dealing violently with those who would take lives.

According to the film's director, Andrew Davies, "…A hero is basically someone who cares about human beings, who ultimately tries to be part of the innocent, the unspoken for, who represents the downtrodden, who represents the voiceless, the people who don't have a say in their lives and their world and tries to give them a dignity and a humanity that they otherwise wouldn't have…I still think heroes are ones that save lives not take lives" (*Collateral Damage* DVD, 2002).

By inscribing heroism in this way, the US *we* of *Collateral Damage* is not only heroic; it is humane. And its humaneness—its humanitarianism —is strikingly like that which we saw when we read *Behind Enemy Lines, Black Hawk Down,* and Bush's *Kandahar* together. However, there is a crucial difference to the heroic humanitarianism of *Collateral Damage*. For at the end of this film, there is no feminine to trouble the moral claims made by this stereotypical masculine *we*. Feminine forces, such as Serena, cannot be trusted, whether they remain attached to foreign foes (as the willing wife of El Lobo) or reattach themselves to US heroes (as the symbolic substitute wife of Gordy). The feminine always ends up saying and doing too much. Unlike Mauro, the voiceless son whose silence can be interpreted by viewers as strengthening this heroic humanitarian US *we*, Serena as the feminine herself cannot be captured, cannot be captivated, and thus must be killed.

So *Collateral Damage* ends with a purified patriarchal US family that reinscribes not only what it means to be humane (heroic) and securing (assimilate or kill the foreign other) but what it means to be American (a successful or bound-to-be-successful immigrant). This invented US family reinvents not only the US *we*; it reinvents a US moral grammar of war that justifies an eye-for-an-eye-style vengeance, which some claim was what propelled official US actions in Afghanistan and Iraq. Indeed, the film cinematically rearticulates the official justification for America's war on terror uttered by President George W. Bush in the immediate aftermath of 9/11: "Either you are with us, or you are with the terrorists" (Bush, 2001b), which is more or less exactly what Gordy tells Serena.

## In the Bedroom

If *Collateral Damage* is an ultimately uplifting, heroic action-adventure film released to make post-9/11 US citizens feel good about themselves (Schwarzenegger, 2002), *In the Bedroom* (based on Andre Dubus's short story, "Killings;" Dubus, 1996) is a dark, contemplative American tragedy that instead multiplies America's moral tragedies with layer on layer of moral uncertainty. Like *Collateral Damage*, it does this by focusing on the figure of the meddling mother.

In the style of an art house film, *In the Bedroom* tells its story at a slow but steady pace.

> The film begins aurally. Over a black screen, we hear a summer breeze, then sea gulls, then an excited woman who could be laughing or crying. Cut from black to an extreme long shot of a field of tall, brown grasses. A woman's legs are visible in the upper left hand corner of the screen. She is running into the field, across the screen. As she runs, we see only her legs. As the camera pans up to show the woman from behind, we see a man chasing after her, diving to catch her but missing. At this, she lets out one of several small screams. Cut to another extreme long shot of the pair racing across the field, past a New England-style house. As the woman approaches the camera, we finally see her face. She is smiling broadly, as is her pursuer.
>
> Cut to several close-ups of the couple kissing, looking adoringly at one another, touching one another lightly. In these shots, we realize that the woman is significantly older than her lover. She is well into (and possibly out of) her thirties; he is barely into his twenties. She is Natalie Strout (Marisa Tomei); he is Frank Fowler (Nick Stahl).
>
> NATALIE: I love it here.
> FRANK: I know you do.
> NATALIE: I can feel my life, you know?'
>
> Their fingers entwine as a grin breaks out across Frank's face, the camera then cutting to the leafy green tree above them, seemingly sheltering this idyllic couple while suggesting a dreaminess about them.

Fade in the film's title against a black background. Fade up the sound of a baseball game on a car radio.

Cut to black. Cut to the source of the radio, a large Ford pickup truck wandering the streets of this small Maine town. Dawn is breaking. The truck stops at Natalie's house, where she awaits Frank and his father Matt (Tom Wilkinson) with her two young sons, Duncan (Christopher Adams, about 5 years old) and Jason (Camdon Muson, about 7). Frank and Matt collect Jason for a day of lobster fishing. This is Frank's summer job. He is a university graduate biding his time before graduate school in architecture in the fall. Jason, seated between Matt and Frank, exchanges a warm smile with Frank. The truck drives past the harbor. Cut to scenes inside the dockside Strout fish-canning plant, owned by Natalie's father-in-law.

Cut to Frank skippering his lobster boat. As Frank empties his traps, his father Matt disables the pincers of each crustacean. When Matt comes across a one-clawed lobster, he shows it to Jason.

MATT: Oh boy. See what happened to this poor fella?

JASON: What?

MATT: Well, look, it lost an arm. The trap has nylon nets, called heads, two side heads to let the lobster crawl in, and inside what they call a bedroom head to hold the bait. Keeps them from escaping. You know the old saying, "Two's company; three's a crowd?"

Jason nods yes.

MATT: It's like that. You get more than two of these in a bedroom and chances are something like that's gonna happen.

Frank produces another lobster and tells his father, "Dad, show him this one."

MATT: Well, older females—like this old gal—they're the most dangerous, especially when they're growing berries.

JASON: Berries?

MATT: Yeah, eggs, you see (pointing to the eggs on the pregnant lobster). She could take out two males, no problem...But this fine lady, she has it easy 'cause the state says we have to let her go.

In this introduction, not only is the film's title explained, but the danger of "older females," especially those who (like the lobster) are about to give birth or who (like Natalie Strout) already have young to protect, is emphasized. As Matt Fowler puts it, "She could take out two males no problem." And that, in a way, is what Natalie Strout, the first meddling mother of *In the Bedroom,* does. Natalie is in the process of divorcing her violent husband Richard (William Mapother), who is a popular athlete and heir to the Strout fish-canning industry and whose life has gone downhill since high school. In the meantime, Natalie has embarked on a summer fling with young Frank. Not only are Natalie and Frank from different generations (as the opening sequence close-ups establish); they are from different economic classes and have different family responsibilities. Natalie is an uneducated working-class wife and mother responsible for two young sons; Frank is an overeducated middle-class son of a physician father and school teacher mother; his only responsibility seems to be to himself and to his potential (both intellectual and as a progenerator of the next generation of Fowlers).

From Richard Strout's point of view, Frank is making his bedroom very crowded and, as a result, increasingly crowds what should be Natalie's and Natalie and Frank's private space. He does everything from crashing his son's birthday celebration held in the Fowler's backyard to breaking repeatedly into the marital home, threatening Natalie and suggesting he move back in to punching Frank in the face when he discovers him at Natalie's.

As Richard's violence increases, Frank's parents, and particularly his mother Ruth (Sissy Spacek), become increasingly alarmed. Ruth has solicited assurances from Frank that the relationship with Natalie is not serious, assurances she does not believe. After Richard assaults Frank, Ruth demands Frank end the relationship sooner rather than later, but Frank has other ideas. He misses an interview (whether for school or career is unclear), staying home instead to fool around with Natalie. He suggests to Natalie that he delay going to architecture school for a year, and he shares with Natalie his fantasy of raising her children with her. Surprised and overwhelmed, Natalie first protests and then is at a loss for words. As Frank is caught between his growing love for Natalie and her boys and his mother's demands that he end his affair, it is unclear what he ultimately decides. He confides in his father that he is thinking of becoming a lobsterman full time rather than going to graduate school, meaning he will be around for Natalie. However, soon after, when his mother asks if he has spoken with Natalie (meaning dumped her), he lets on that he has. And this does seem to be the truth of the matter, for we next see Frank on the phone back in the Fowler home seeming to accept a position working or studying with a famous architect. However, in the middle of this call, another call comes through. It is young Jason, panicked. We do not hear the call, but Frank is distressed and tells Jason he will be right over.

Frank arrives at Natalie's. Richard, in his violent rage, has trashed the place and then fled. Moments later, Richard returns. Frank sends Natalie and the boys upstairs for their own safety, promising he will not let Richard reenter the house but, of course, because Richard has broken into his own home so many times before, we are not surprised when he does it again. As the camera follows Natalie, first with her two sons in an upstairs bedroom, then making her way down the stairs, we hear a gunshot. Natalie runs down the stairs. Richard has shot Frank in the face, killing him.

Frank's murder fulfills the promise of the film's title. When there are three in a bedroom, one of them is going to be physically harmed, if not killed, especially when there is an older female involved. Never mind that Natalie is not directly responsible for Frank's murder or that it is Jason, not Natalie, who begs Frank to protect them from Richard. It is Natalie's involvement in Frank's life, and that alone, that makes him a target for her wild husband's frustrated desire to reconcile with his estranged wife.

Frank's murder also shatters the film's idyllic images of domestic bliss, whether they are of Frank's dreams of domesticity with Natalie or of the happy home life he shares with his loving parents. From his parent's point of view, Frank's murder (like the murder of Matthew Brewer in *Collateral Damage*) echoes the tragedy of having one's future brutally and suddenly destabilized thanks to the murder of a beautiful, lively son. In so doing, the film plunges Frank's parents into unbearable grief, grieving not only Frank's death but the end of their dreams and their brutal return to reality. As one commentator put it, *In the Bedroom* (like *Collateral Damage*) thereby "tapped into deep collective emotions stirred by the terrorist attacks on New York and Washington: shock, grief, anger, and the desire for revenge, in that order" (Lodge, 2002; also see Holden, 2001). And because it is a realistic story about "real" people in small-town America rather than an action-adventure picture in which Arnold blows up the bad terrorists, the portrayal of shock, grief, anger and the desire for revenge in *In the Bedroom* was arguably more chilling and stirring to everyday US citizens watching it in cinemas in November 2001 because they could more easily identify with these characters and these contexts.

Just as many post-9/11 US citizens did, the Fowlers immediately experience shock and anger at their sudden loss of their son and of their domestic security. Their anger and desire for revenge become tangible only when it emerges that there is no eyewitness to Frank's murder, that Richard (claiming manslaughter) will be released into the community on bail, and that his murder trial (which is likely to result in a far shorter sentence than they had originally expected) will be significantly delayed. Just like Osama bin Laden, Richard Strout seems to be getting away with murder.

All this is beyond what Ruth Fowler can bear, especially when she and Richard start crossing paths in town. This not only leads to Ruth's further emotional deterioration. Her understandable emotional difficulties begin to express themselves in her relationship with Matt, culminating in each of them blaming the other for their son's death. Ruth claims Matt did not stop Frank's relationship with Natalie because he lived out his fantasy to have Natalie himself through their son, whereas Matt claims Ruth was always too judgmental of their son (i.e., she was always an overbearing, disapproving, controlling meddling mother). The only way back to the domestic peace (if not domestic happiness) the Fowler's enjoyed before their son's death, it seems, is to take justice into their own hands and get rid of Richard Strout, the constant reminder of their loss and unhappiness.

This is precisely what they do. Matt kidnaps Richard at gunpoint and makes Richard drive them back to his apartment. The frightened Richard keeps trying to justify his murder of Frank, thinking Matt is going to kill him.

RICHARD: Dr. Fowler, it was an accident. I'm going to jail to pay for it. If I ever get out, I'll be an old man. Isn't that enough?
MATT: You're not going to jail...See, it's the trial. We can't go through that, my wife and I. That's why you're leaving. I got you a ticket. My wife keeps seeing you. I can't have that anymore.

The relieved Richard packs while Matt plants in the apartment evidence that Richard has jumped bail. Still held at gunpoint, Richard drives them to Matt's best friend Willis's country retreat, consisting of more than 300 acres of private land. Richard, who to this point had taken Matt at his word that he is helping Richard get away, worries when they turn onto Willis's secluded property.

But when he sees Willis (who he knows), he is reassured. Matt then makes Richard face him, claiming he wants him to carry a suitcase—and then Matt shoots the defenseless Richard in cold blood. There is no struggle; there is no pretext, apart from revenge. As the wounded Richard tries to crawl away on the ground, Matt shoots him a further two times, finally killing him. It transpires that this was the plan all along, to make the authorities think Richard jumped bail so they would not look for his body or for his murderer.

The men bury Richard's body on Willis's property, park Richard's car near the railway station, and part company as dawn is breaking. Matt returns home through the back door, strips and cleans himself, and then makes his way through the semidark house to the bedroom. There Ruth awaits him, sitting up in bed smoking a cigarette.

RUTH: Did you do it?

Matt gets into bed, turning on his side away from Ruth. He is clearly shaken, staring into space and holding himself.

RUTH: Are you all right, Matt?

After a long pause, Matt speaks.

MATT: There was a picture of him and Natalie on the wall.
RUTH (concerned and confused): What does that mean?
MATT: The way she was smiling...
RUTH (almost pleading): What?
MATT (each word spoken deliberately, with short pauses between each word): I don't know.
RUTH: Matt?

When Matt will not, cannot, answer, Ruth makes her way down stairs, telling Matt he must be hungry. "Matt, do you want coffee?," she calls up to him.

Matt says nothing. Instead, he shifts in his bed, notices the Band-Aid on his finger from when a lobster pinched him earlier, and removes it. The wound has healed. Matt lets out a deep sigh.

Cut to a long shot of the exterior of the house, then an extreme long shot of the neighborhood of pristine white houses, then to several more extreme long shots of the town and the harbor. Cut to black. Roll credits.

*In the Bedroom's* ending has been interpreted as bringing moral closure to the Fowlers. With Richard finally out of their lives and vigilante justice done, Matt breathes a sigh of relief, his physical (cut finger) and emotional (loss of son) wounds finally healed or healing. Maybe, as David Lodge argues, Matt's healed finger is "a heavy symbolic hint that he has achieved a kind of closure, and an implicit endorsement of his action," whereas the final long shots express a return to normality more generally, in the home, in the community, and in post-9/11 America (2002). Maybe, but I wonder whether things are not more complicated than this, for everything else in Matt's final scene suggests he is far from certain about what he has done, that he remains so deeply troubled by the whole affair that he cannot even face his wife.

I would agree with Lodge that the film does give us moral closure, but not for Matt: only for Ruth. It is Ruth who, even though she is concerned about her husband, is buoyant about Richard's death. It is Ruth who returns to the routines of domesticity, making her husband breakfast, asking him if he wants coffee. Matt, on the other hand, tosses and turns in bed, his final sigh possibly marking the contrast between physical healing and emotional healing, between his wife's return to normality and his own inability even to get out of bed.

On reflection, it is not at all surprising that Ruth and Matt would feel differently about Richard's murder. Ruth wanted Richard dead. When Matt returns to their bedroom, she does not ask, "Are you okay?" but "Did you do it?" And once she knows Matt did do it, her story of her son's death has finally come to a just end. Matt, on the other hand, remains deeply troubled, not only because in seeking justice for his murdered son he, too, has become a murderer, but because it is unclear that Matt ever wanted this kind of justice. Matt's response to his son's death was much more about emotional withdrawal than it was about seeking vengeance. Yes, Matt was angry when it appeared that Richard would get off with a light sentence, but he did not go around saying, "I want Richard Strout dead." Instead, he sought evidence that officials in the legal system might be able to use in their case against Richard. It seems, then, it was only Ruth who got what she wanted, not Matt.

That Ruth's response to her son's death would be more dangerous than Matt's makes perfect sense when we recall how gender functions in this film and when we reconsider the film's opening sequence. As we already know, *In the Bedroom* tells us that "older females" who are protecting their babies are the most dangerous. As Matt explains to young Jason, "She could take out two males easy." The *she* here is, of course, the pregnant lobster Matt is holding, whereas the scene as a whole—about dangerous older females and crowded bedrooms—marks

Natalie as the dangerous female who will symbolically "take out" both Frank and Richard. Had this mother not meddled in Frank's life, the film tells us, Frank would not have died (nor would Richard).

When we think back to the opening of the film, we realize that from its very first image, *In the Bedroom* sets up the danger of the meddling mother. This is the scene of an unidentified woman running through a grassy New England field. As several critics have pointed out, what this opening invokes is the realist painting of Maine resident Andrew Wyeth (Lodge, 2002). However, it does more than that. It is a cinematic simulation of a particular Wyeth painting, "Christina's World." As Philip French explains, "Initially, that painting of a young woman lying in the grass looking up a hill towards a house, looks like a rural idyll, but a closer study of the picture and its accompanying paintings tells us that the woman is a cripple, painfully dragging herself along and that she isn't, in fact, a young beauty but has a gnarled peasant face" (2002).

"Christina's World" invokes the dangers of what cannot be properly identified by playing on the deception of appearances. As the film opens, we cannot identify Natalie, for we see only her legs. We cannot identify Frank except as a male figure who dives for her in a field. We cannot even identify the emotion of the scene. Is it playful or threatening? Is Natalie laughing or crying? Do her screams signify danger or joyous excitement? Only later do we realize Natalie symbolizes all these things simultaneously but, at this moment, in this opening, what we see and hear are either unclear or deceptive. When Natalie's beautiful, smiling face finally comes into view and when she exchanges loving looks with Frank, we know that these lovers occupy the realm of fantasy, not reality. Read as a series of paintings about Christina, we know that at some point the film, like Wyeth, will turn its viewers and characters around to look at the darker reality foreshadowed here.

There is something else foreshadowed in this opening. For just as Wyeth's paintings suggest that the physical body of Christina represents multiple women (or impressions of woman), so too does Natalie's physical body in *In the Bedroom* stand not only for herself but for the category of "meddling mother." In so doing, Natalie's unrecognizable body is also misrecognizable. This laughing/crying/screaming woman racing across a grassy New England field could as easily be Ruth Fowler as she could be Natalie Strout. This link between Ruth and "Christina's World" is further symbolized by the book Ruth reads at bedtime, a biography of the Wyeth family. What this means is that Ruth is not only another meddling mother; she, like Natalie, is a potential threat to her family, for she is another older female out to protect her young. However, because of her smothering, overprotective ways, she ends up taking out two males, easy: her beloved son Frank and her son's killer. What this means is that *In the Bedroom* is about Ruth's vengeance, a vengeance that—for Ruth's peace of mind and Ruth's alone—transforms her husband into a murderer.

That it is Ruth who is the vigilante and Matt who is her mere proxy emerges from their different responses to their son's death before Richard's murder. As we know, Matt pursues official justice (seeking evidence to help the courts to convict Richard) while Ruth finds Richard's presence more and more unbearable. Interestingly, these two different responses to their son's death map onto different US and world responses to the 9/11 terrorist attacks. Read through post-9/11 US foreign policy, Matt represents the unofficial desire of many in and beyond the United States to have al Qaeda brought to justice by bringing its members before the International Criminal Courts of Justice. Ruth, on the other hand, represents the official US government view, one that (as Matt explains to Richard) cannot put itself through long trials and repeated court appearances but instead wants justice done now. And if the only way to speed justice along and ensure its outcome is to take it into one's own hands, then so be it. Just as Ruth won out over Matt, so too did official US foreign policy, first in Afghanistan and later in Iraq, win out over national and international opposition.

In the immediate aftermath of 9/11, the majority of US citizens found that they could stomach revenge attacks in Afghanistan against al Qaeda and the Taliban. There is a logic, after all, in taking out terrorist training camps of those terrorists who admit that all US citizens (and Jews) are their targets. However, it was harder for US citizens to support what many saw as revenge attacks by President George W. Bush against Saddam Hussein, attacks that seemed to have more to do with Bush family honor than with honorable US conduct. So, it is not surprising that, just like the Fowler family, the US "family" increasingly split over US foreign policy in Iraq to the point that (at the time of this writing) one US reservist serving in Iraq claimed conscious objector status and faced court martial and prison rather than return to what he saw as dishonorable duty in Iraq.

Taking this analogy between the Fowler family and the US family one step further, what this means is that if Ruth represents official US foreign policy *and* a meddling mother, US foreign policy is akin to a meddling mother. It may act out of a desire to protect its young but, like Ruth Fowler, this desire for justice may end up taking out its own son(s).

On this reading, then, *In the Bedroom* hardly provides the United States with moral closure, nor does it ultimately endorse vengeance as a necessary, morally certain undertaking. Instead, this film speaks to the dangers not only of meddling mothers but of moral certainty, demonstrating how moral closure for one member of the US family (Ruth, the Bush administration) may well morally destabilize another member (Matt, US citizens/soldiers). As such, the film underscores how vengeance, far from resecuring the traditional US family, instead rips it apart.

## Who we really are

Vigilantism is an undeniable motif in post-9/11 US foreign policy, in Afghanistan or Iraq. As such, it is an undeniable part of the US *we*. Whether in official US foreign policy or in films such as *Collateral Damage* and *In the Bedroom*, this US *we* is justified in taking the law into its own hands when official channels of justice fail. Never mind that such films as *Collateral Damage* and *In the Bedroom* attribute these failures to the US justice system. The broader, official argument is that it is *international* justice that is time consuming and ultimately unreliable. Their inconvenient locating of the failures of justice aside, these two films seem to offer the US *we* a way out of the moral quandaries into which the humanitarian US put us. For unlike the humanitarian US *we*, the vigilante US *we* unapologetically claims to be working on its own behalf. Though (as in *Collateral Damage*) it may still allow for integrating voiceless children into the US family, this US *we* does not make the mistake of taking the feminine as its passive object of rescue. Indeed, it does not bother to rescue the foreign feminine at all, preferring instead either to marginalize it or to murder it, but always to hold it ultimately responsible as the source of moral mistakes.

All this begs the question, "Is this a safer strategy for the US *we* to follow or does it in the end backfire?"

It certainly seemed to backfire in the film *Collateral Damage*, to the point that at least initially it appeared to be one of the biggest cinematic casualties of 9/11. As noted earlier, the release of *Collateral Damage* was postponed from November 2001 until February 2002 but, even then, it opened to all manner of protests. There were objections that the film stereotyped Colombians as one-dimensional, drug-dealing terrorists and, more important, that the portrayal of US firefighters as vigilantes dishonored their heroism on 9/11 (reported in Ebert, 2002). And, of course, there is the obvious point that the film seemed to be hopelessly behind the times, fighting as it did the passé war on drugs rather than the new war on terror.

In light of this, the film's distributor embarked on a huge publicity campaign to reinvent the film. The film's star, Arnold Schwarzenegger, went on the talk show circuit to claim that "seeing *Collateral Damage* would buoy Americans' spirit" (Lawson, 2002). The film's producer, Steven Reuther, claimed in the press notes that "Since Sept. 11, *Collateral Damage* has become a term that we've all had to digest. The journey that Gordon Brewer takes in this film has become more understandable for everyone" (quoted in Caro, 2002). And the DVD of the film included a special feature called *The Hero in the New Era* in which director Andrew Davis and star Arnold waxed lyrical about how they hated terrorism and how US firefighters were heroes (*Collateral Damage* DVD, 2002).

*Collateral Damage* ended up doing very well at the box office. If anything, 9/11 did the film a favor, saving it from being another overlooked mediocre Arnold film to just a mediocre Arnold film but one that Americans (who in the wake of 9/11 caused *Die Hard* and *Rambo* films to top the list of video rentals and put *Black Hawk Down* number one at the box office; Lawson, 2002) wanted to see. Even the Super Bowl seemed to be on Arnold's side, featuring as it did a series of public service commercials that linked cocaine use to financing terrorism (Mitchell, 2002), thus rendering America's fight in the war on drugs relevant to its fight in the war on terror.

Not surprising is that a film that reinvents the foundational US family could also reinvent itself, but *Collateral Damage* still faced a few problems it could not quite overcome. One of these was that it halfway humanized its terrorist (Berardinelli, 2002a). Never mind that Cliff Curtis, the New Zealand actor who played the terrorist El Lobo, often plays villains and Arabs (as he did in *The Majestic, The Insider*, and *Three Kings*), thereby allowing El Lobo to be consumed by US audiences as "a Colombian version of Osama bin Laden without the fanatical religious element" (Puig, 2002). This is a man with a wife and son, a man who turned to vengeance for the very same reason Gordy Brewer did (because he lost a child), and a man who is allowed to take Americans to task throughout the film, questioning so-called American family values and claiming that "When Americans see a peasant with a gun, they turn the channel. But they never ask why a peasant needs a gun. Why? Because they believe they are the only ones allowed to fight for independence." El Lobo's statements question not only official US policy toward Colombia, but the self-perceptions of everyday Americans about themselves. In this way, it is loaded with interesting, if utterly simplistic, answers to the question many Americans asked themselves in the wake of 9/11: Why do they hate us? As such, *Collateral Damage* could have been reinvented as an antiwar film, which is why its Hollywood director, producer, star, and distributor worked so hard to repackage it as an uplifting tale of US heroism and humanitarianism that upheld rather than troubled traditional American values.

There is a second way in which *Collateral Damage* functions not as a celebration of American values and of contemporary American families but as a warning to Americans: this is in its use of gender. By placing so much blame on meddling mothers that the film ends by reconstructing the contemporary US family as composed of father and son but no mother or sister, the film succeeds in banishing the disruptiveness of the feminine. However, it leaves us asking, At what cost? The cost for the feminine is clear enough: marginalization or death, and always moral blame. But what is the cost for the masculine, for the US family, and for the US *we* that this family constructs as the basis of its moral grammar of war?

*Collateral Damage* never answers these questions, nor are they easily answered, especially when *Collateral Damage* is read against *In the Bedroom*. For if the pat answer to these questions is that what is stereotypically feminine keeps what is stereotypically (hyper)masculine in check, then how do we make sense of the fact that in *In the Bedroom* it is the meddling mother who is the source of vigilantism, not her husband (who merely carries out her wishes)? Indeed, Ruth Fowler's vigilantism is arguably purer than that of Gordy Brewer's for, unlike Gordy, Ruth never even momentarily attempts to rescue anyone other than herself. Unlike Gordy, who substitutes Serena and (then just) Mauro for his dead family, Ruth never reaches out to Natalie or her sons, thereby replacing her lost family with this new one. Quite the contrary: when Natalie comes to make peace with Ruth, Ruth slaps her across the face with the back of her hand.

As both films render clear, the United States has little to fear from either hypermasculine men, such as Gordy, or weak husbands, such as Matt, even though both end up being murderers. Rather, in a reversal of the masculine=aggressive/feminine=nurturing stereotype, the really scary figures that disrupt contemporary US families are meddling mothers. Reversals of such stereotypes are nothing new; just recall the string of Michael Douglas films from *Fatal Attraction* to *Disclosure* to *Falling Down*. Such reversals, whether about class, gender, sex, or race, are noteworthy not so much in themselves (as they often represent a backlash against gains made by the underdog) but because of how they work.

So, how do they work in these post-9/11 films? Picturing mothers as bad and fathers as nurturing (even when they are murdering murderers) in these films not only removes any guilt on the part of US citizens in eschewing troubling rescue missions of the feminized other and acting only on our own behalf. They also explicitly tell us what danger looks like: danger is feminine, even when it appears to be a nurturing mother. Furthermore, they tell us where this dangerous feminine is located in relation to the US family and the US state. In *Collateral Damage*, the disruptive meddling mother Serena is an alien terrorist who occasionally weasels her way into the US state and almost into the US family. As such, Serena is a disruptive force *to* the US state and US family. In contrast, the disruptive meddling mothers Natalie and Ruth from *In the Bedroom* are traditional, all-American girls. What this means is that, unlike Serena, they are not disruptions *to* the US state and US family but disruptions *in* them. As such, Natalie and Ruth are even more dangerous than the Colombian terrorist Serena, for they have not infiltrated the US homeland; they *are* the US home front itself (as Evelyn was in *Pearl Harbor*). As such, US males cannot just "take them out" as Gordy "took out" Serena but instead end up being dangerously manipulated by them (as they are in *In the Bedroom*).

Here we have our final reversal, for what all this means is that what US fathers and the US state traditionally try to secure (women, a feminized US home front) is actually the source of their own insecurity. Who we really are, then, are not just unselfconscious vigilantes; *we* are vigilantes whose very need for vengeance ends up destabilizing our very selves. Read through post-9/11 US foreign policy, this means that US homeland security brings the United States further insecurity in the home(land). And this is why a vigilante US *we* ultimately backfires against any attempts by the official US story to incorporate it. For this is the real collateral damage of *Collateral Damage* and *In the Bedroom* that the official US story cannot gloss over: that hypersecurity breeds hyperinsecurity, in individuals, in families, in states, and in the world.

Ultimately, who we really are (vigilantes) always threatens to become just another iteration of who we wish we'd never been. Given this, it is not surprising that antiwar protests (especially against the US-led war in Iraq) have sometimes rightly, sometimes wrongly, harped on the similarities between US actions in Gulf War II and the lost US war in Vietnam. The challenge for the US *we* is to become someone who can think about the relationship between justice and security differently. However, to do this, *we* need to think about the feminine, as family member and as US home front, differently.

# 6 Who we might become

The vigilante films *Collateral Damage* and *In the Bedroom* highlight just how difficult it is in the post-9/11 United States to tell a straightforwardly positive story about who we really are. In the Bush administration's official discourse, *we* may wish to be humanitarians, and *we* may even know ourselves to be virtuous. However, when our power is mixed with our unbearable post-9/11 grief, it is difficult to distinguish our claims to be a moral America(n) from accusations that *we* are actually vigilantes. As we saw in *Behind Enemy Lines,* this is why official American tales of who we really are so often get charted through our WWII past, a seemingly simpler time when bad guys were bad guys (Fascists, Nazis) and *we* were the undisputed good guys.

The reason why this mythologized American WWII story is so appealing to many Americans is not only because it gives us clear good guys versus clear bad guys; it seems to suggest a solution to the age-old problem of how to balance morality with security, a problem of great urgency for the post-9/11 United States. As articulated in the five films discussed in Chapters 4 and 5, this is the problem of balancing our humanitarian desires against our vigilante impulses.

Harking back to WWII, the film *Pearl Harbor* tells us that we can find this balance rather simply. All we have to do to have both justice and security is to construct a homefront that is worth defending (expressed as woman/mother/nation) as the basis of our patriarchal projection of power and justice internationally. In this way, the (usually) white, happy, heterosexual nuclear family is not just a convenient national myth; it is an international necessity for any United States-led just world order.

However, that was all in the past. Since WWII, we have had failing fathers in *We Were Soldiers,* wayward sons in *Behind Enemy Lines* and *Black Hawk Down,* and finally meddling mothers in *Collateral Damage* and *In the Bedroom* (not to mention vigilante fathers) who disrupt the homefront by functioning as America's enemies. On the basis of this complex contemporary cinematic retelling of who *we* are as US family and US nation, it seems unlikely that *we* will return to our idealized US past as anything but a happy memory that we cannot now relive. This presents America and Americans with a serious problem. For if contemporary narratives of the US nation succeed only in presenting America and Americans in a sustained, positive moral light when considered through an idealized US past, then how can *we* possibly be moral America(ns) in the post-9/11 present? Put differently, how is it possible to tell a positive story about who we really are without always telling it through the past positive story of who we think we were?

What is at stake in these questions is not just some feel-good factor in US self-perceptions. More importantly, what hangs in the balance here is the contemporary US relationships between justice and security, which has profound implications for contemporary global governance. The pressing post-9/11 question is this: How can *we* strike a balance between justice and security, between morality and military power, in our post-9/11 world without its being an ill-fitting echo of how we solved the problem of justice and security in our WWII past?

The answer is to move from the past not to the present but to the future, from who we think we were to who we might become.

It is an unlikely pair of post-9/11 films—a blockbuster directed by Steven Spielberg and a documentary directed by Michael Moore—that move US citizens out of the past and into the future. On the one hand, these films move the US *we* into the future because both concern themselves with a future time. Spielberg's fictitious *Minority Report* (based on Phillip K. Dick's story of the same name; Dick, 2002) is set in the not-too-distant future of 2054, whereas Moore's fact-based *Fahrenheit 9/11* addresses itself to a future that (at the time of the film's release in the summer of 2004) was almost on us: the 2004 US Presidential elections.

However, this is not the most important way in which these films engage the future. More important, both films have been linked to critiques of the Bush Doctrine of Preemption: the doctrine that holds that it is morally defensible for the United States to use force against a perceived foreign foe to prevent future harm against itself, even though that perceived foreign foe has not yet attacked the United States. Articulated by President Bush in a speech on June 1, 2002, preemption was the Bush administration's primary justification for embarking on Gulf War II (Bush, 2002b). Saddam Hussein, the administration argued, had weapons of mass destruction that he was likely to use against the United States at some time in the future, even though he never threatened to do so. Coincidently, *Minority Report*, a film that critically explores a US domestically applied system of preemptive justice, was released in the United States later that same month and was immediately linked by film critics to the Bush Doctrine of Preemption (Edelstein, 2002a; Lithwick, 2002; Lott, 2002).

It took another two years before Moore's film *Fahrenheit 9/11* was released into US cinemas. By then, the Bush Doctrine had played itself out in the Iraq war, a war that was becoming increasingly unpopular with many US citizens. Among other things, Moore's film traces the implementation of the Bush Doctrine in Iraq and its consequences for Americans and for the American family.

In telling their stories about preemptive justice, both *Minority Report* and *Fahrenheit 9/11* explore the relationship between crime and consciousness (and crime and the unconcious) individually and collectively and what that relationship(s) means for the post-9/11 US relationship between morality and power, justice and security. This chapter traces how, in reconsidering the relationship between justice and security, each film articulates a moral grammar of war that, quite strikingly, is based on a reactivated feminine. For in both films, it is the feminine (albeit a very different feminine in each case) that is the keystone of a sustainable, positive expression of who we might become.

Reactivating the feminine might seem to be an unlikely course to chart for post-9/11 films about the future of American justice, given the dangers that the feminine embodied in the contemporary families of *Collateral Damage* (enemy alien without) and (especially) *In the Bedroom* (dangerous homefront within). And yet, given that both *Minority Report* and *Fahrenheit 9/11* play off the vigilant genre—with the main *Minority Report* character John Anderton flirting with vigilantism and with *Fahrenheit 9/11* director Michael Moore arguably practicing vigilante journalism by taking US Presidential electoral justice into his own hands—this move is less surprising. For in these films, what both empowers and restrains the justice of these vigilantes is the unruly feminine. This renders the destabilizing feminine the perfect location from which to launch these very different critiques of the Bush administration's official policies of security.

## Minority Report

*Minority Report* combines futuristic film noire with Spielberg sentimentality to tell a tale about preemptive justice. Set in the District of Columbia in 2054, the film stars Tom Cruise as Chief Inspector John Anderton of the police department's Division of PreCrime.

PreCrime, as its name suggests, is designed to catch criminals before they commit their crimes. What causes PreCrime to function is the "precogs" (the precognitives), twin brothers Arthur and Dashiell and the girl Agatha (Samantha Morton), whose exposure in the womb to their mother's hallucinogenic drugs endowed them with the "gift" to see the future. However, their gift is actually a curse, for the future they see is that of murders that are about to happen. By downloading the precogs' visions and then artfully interpreting them, the Division of PreCrime (whose most talented man in the field is Anderton) is able to catch the criminals before they actually murder their intended victims.

The film's opening sequence not only illustrates how PreCrime works (in this case, by preventing the death of Sarah Marks and her lover Donald Dubin at the hand of her husband, Howard); it establishes the film's central motif: the relationship between the *I* and the *eye* and the relationship between the "I/eye" and the "we/nation."

The film opens to ominous sounds of cymbals, reminiscent of both the thunder of an approaching storm and the quickening of the human heart. These sounds foreshadow both the action that is about to take place and its pace, for the images we are about to see come in quick flashes, never lasting more than a few seconds and sometimes lasting for only a few frames.

Over a black screen, the credits and the film's title fade in and out. Fade in over-lit, blue-tinted lava lamp-like shapes. As the soundtrack continues, the shapes form into a close-up image of a man and a woman kissing. Faded in over this image is a pair of scissors. To a cymbal crash, the scissors violently slide off the screen, seemingly pushed. Cut to an image of the male lover struggling in a bathtub. Cut to a different man in a suit walking upstairs, with scissors in his hand, to the woman and her lover kissing, viewed through a pair of eye glasses sitting on a bedside table, to the couple in bed, with the suited man standing over them. The male lover rushes off the bed toward the bathroom when the suited man confronts the woman, slashing down at her with the scissors in his hand. Cut to the bathtub, where the suited man's arm is drowning the male lover.

Up to this point, all the action has been shown in a forward linear progression, even though it is jumpy, partial, and dreamlike. From this point on in the dreamlike sequence, the action jumps between forward and backward temporalities. Cut to backward action shot of bloody water rushing back into the bathtub, then a forward action shot of the male lover running from the bed to the bathroom as the suited man chases him with the scissors.

Cut to the face of President Abraham Lincoln with one eye poked out, scissors protruding through the opening. A small boy is holding the President's paper head in one hand and a pair of scissors in the other.

Return to the suited man standing in the upstairs bedroom. As he raises his glasses to put them on, he says to the woman (in bed with her lover), "You know how blind I am without them." In this same hand that holds his glasses, the suited man also holds the scissors. We see this action from various views, with the horrified woman in the background. "Howard, don't cry," she tells him. At this, the suited man/Howard turns around and violently slashes the woman with the scissors.

Cut to the scissors in water from the overflowed bathtub, with the water moving backward; to the wounded woman in bed struggling to breathe; to water flowing back into the bathtub, with the terrified male lover sitting in it. Water then falls onto the floor.

Cut to a close-up of the female victim. Fade to a close-up of another woman's eye, then to an extreme close-up of the vivid blue eye of the precog Agatha. In a rapid zoom-out shot, the camera retreats from Agatha's eye to show all of Agatha's pale white face. She is wearing what appear to be large headphones, and her head is surrounded by a hazy, milky, bluish background.

AGATHA (very slowly, overenunciating): Mur-der.

As she speaks, her face is submerged a few inches below the surface of the milky blue liquid. Air bubbles escape her lips. Her eyes remain wide open.

This is the end of the dreamlike sequence, which from the time we see the first image until we cut away from the submerged Agatha runs for a mere 60 seconds. The ending of this sequence is marked not only by Agatha's close-up (which seems to establish that she is author of the dream/premonition) but by replacing the hazy, partial, rapid succession of dream shots with crisper, more predictable images (albeit still blue-washed and over-lit) presented though linear progressive, real time-like editing and in the absence of the clash-filled soundtrack.

Cut to a machine laser-cutting grainy wood into two round, reddish balls. The machine releases the balls into a maze of clear tubes. The camera follows the balls as the first comes to rest at an exit labeled *VICTIM*. The ball is inscribed with two names: Sarah Marks (the woman) and Donald Dubin (her lover).

Cut to John Anderton (Tom Cruise) entering the futuristic PreCrime building. As Anderton enters the building, situating subtitles fade in and out on the screen: "Department of PreCrime," "Washington, D.C.," "The year 2054."

Cut back to Agatha receding deeper into the water, eyes and mouth open, wearing a distressed expression.

Cut to the second ball as it lands at the exit labeled *PERPETRATOR*. It reads: "Howard Marks" (the suited man).

In view of "remote witnesses" whom we see on separate screens in the background, Chief Inspector Anderton prepares to review the evidence generated from the precogs' premonitions. Donning electronic gloves that allow him to manipulate images on the clear screen before him, Anderton artfully conducts the precog-generated images to his selected music, Schubert's *Unfinished Symphony*. As Anderton tries to piece together the predicted crime, the film cuts back and forth between his assembly of predicted events and real-time events in the Marks' household. As Howard looks for his eye glasses, Sarah helps their son memorize the Gettysburg Address, and their young son makes an Abraham Lincoln mask by cutting out Lincoln's eyes, Anderton and his men draw closer and closer to the soon-to-be crime scene, finally descending from the sky like jet-packed angels just in time to rescue the would-be victims. For his premeditated (but not yet committed) crime, Howard is haloed. He is forced to wear an electronic headband that incapacitates him physically while securing his unconscious. Once haloed, he will be shipped to the Hall of Containment, a kind of purgatory between thought and thoughtlessness, where he will be held indefinitely. This is the end of the opening sequence.

What we have in this opening sequence is not just the seeds of a moral dilemma—arresting a man for a crime he thought about but did not (yet) commit means the man is not (yet) a criminal—but a particular way to think about this moral dilemma: through a complex series of I-to-eye and I/eye-to-we/nation relationships. To unpack these relationships, it is helpful to consider how *Minority Report* plays on (and with) vision.

Even though the film is obsessed with eyes, one of the first things the film establishes is that eyes do not provide us with the clearest insights. Howard Marks (our would-be murderer in the opening sequence) "sees" that his wife is having an affair even though he is not wearing his glasses and claims to be blind without them. Marks' physical lack of visual clarity is mirrored by the experience of the film's viewers, who use their eyes to scan the film's first 60-second sequence without being able to make proper sense of it. It is only once these images are understood not as visions but as previsions that they begin to make sense. Visions are made by the eye; previsions are made by the unconscious, by the mind's eye. And while the eye is always linked to an *I* (to a human subject), the mind's eye might well be subjectless.

This, the film tells us, is how we should think about the precogs. As Anderton explains the precogs to a detective, Witwer (Colin Ferrell), who has come to investigate the workings of the Department of PreCrime before the D.C.-wide program becomes a national program, "It's best not to think of them as human." The precogs, three drugged, twenty-something human bodies suspended in a milky, amniotic-like fluid with electrons downloading their mental images, are regarded by the public not as humans but as deities. They appeared to the state as a miracle six years earlier and ever since have become a holy trinity allowing the state to uphold justice. Even the PreCrime investigators play on these ideas, calling the room that houses the precogs the *temple* and referring to themselves as more like priests than police.

If the precogs are the holy trinity who seem to see one collective vision with their one collective unconscious eye (itself a symbol of deification),[1] it is the priestly police who (like any priests) are the human interpreters of this vision. It is they who connect the subjectless single eye of the precogs to the subjective *I* of the state (which, because it is a collective subjectivity, is always also a *we*). This is Anderton's job, for he is the eyes and the *I* of the state. Using his physical eyes and his conscious mind, Anderton interprets the precogs' visions of the evil unconscious of would-be murderers to enable and enforce state justice.

From the perspective of the Department of PreCrime and the many US citizens who end up voting for PreCrime to go national, this system of literally blind justice (blind because the precogs see with their minds, not with their eyes) is perfect. If there is an error in the system, it could not rest with the deified precogs but only with their human interpreters. In other words, prevision (the unconscious subjectless eye) is perfect, whereas vision (the conscious subjective *I*) is imperfect. The task of Detective Witwer, who works for the US Attorney General and represents "the eyes of the nation now upon us" (as the head of PreCrime puts it), is to check for human error in the PreCrime system before it goes national.

However, things of course are more complicated than this. *Minority Report's* opening sequence does not just establish the benefits of prevision over vision; it suggests that prevision, like vision, might suffer from limitations. The film does this in at least two ways.

First, the opening sequence contains not two violent stabbings but three. It is not only Sarah Marks and her lover who are stabbed; it is also President Abraham Lincoln whose eyes are cut out by the Marks's young son. Lincoln is a complex US president who is revered by many Americans for guiding the Northern states to a victory in the Civil War and thereby becoming the father of a new nation, one that was premised on and promised to uphold the ideals of liberty and freedom for all men regardless of race. As such, Lincoln stands as a president who could see beyond the turmoil of his present situation and recover and more broadly interpret America's founding ideals of justice for all in a materializing, reconfigured nation. Yet to achieve this ideal prevision of America—to arrive at this moral US *we* of who we might become— Lincoln was also the first US president to suspend the right of habeas corpus (the right not to be held indefinitely without charge). Lincoln, then, denied individual civil liberties to Americans as a means toward ensuring his vision of collective liberty, of justice for all, by providing security for all. This was how Lincoln domestically solved the problem of the relationship between justice and security during the Civil War.

Almost a century and a half later, President George W. Bush seems to hark back to Lincoln's domestic solution to solve America's international problem of balancing justice and security in its war on terror.[2] In the United States-led war in Afghanistan in 2001, the Bush administration distinguished between enemy soldiers and enemy combatants, the latter suspected of being terrorists somehow linked to the al Qaeda network. These enemy combatants were not treated as prisoners of war but instead were shipped to the US military base at Guantanamo Bay, Cuba, where the majority of them have been held without charge ever since. US treatment of these suspected terrorists violates not only the Geneva Convention but the US constitutional requirement of habeas corpus. However, the Bush administration maintains that the suspension of the civil liberties of these terrorist suspects is necessary to the security of the United States in its war against terror.

Over the next three years, the Bush administration extended the scope of its preemptive justice measures from deeds to (pre)thoughts. The US Justice Department did so domestically by claiming that US citizen Jose Padilla (also known as Abdulla al-Muharjir) was involved in the initial stages of a plan to explode a dirty bomb somewhere in the United States, labeling him as an enemy combatant, which enabled his transfer from the criminal justice system to the military justice system, and holding him indefinitely without charge since May 2002. Defending the Bush administration's handling of Padilla, Deputy Defense Secretary Paul Wolfowitz explained, "There was not an actual plan. We stopped this man in the initial planning stages," meaning that attaining a conviction in criminal court would have been virtually impossible (Lithwick, 2002). Padilla, then, is being held for what the Bush administration thinks he thought, not for what the Bush administration can prove he was about to do, much less did. The criminal act here has not just moved from the deed to the thought; it has moved from the conscious thought to the unconscious one. For, as Wolfowitz puts it, "There was no actual plan." To the extent that consciousness comes into play here at all, it relates not to Padilla's prethought plan but to the Bush administration's moral geography of terror (see Shapiro, 1997 and Agnew, 2003) as the consciousness through which all acts and now thoughts and prethoughts must first be securitized and then—and only then—formally judged.

President Bush extended the scope of preemptive justice internationally when, on June 1, 2002, he announced what has come to be called the Bush Doctrine of Preemption. Claiming that America's Cold War practices of deterrence are insufficient in America's new war on terror and making a veiled reference to Iraqi President Saddam Hussein, the President explained, "Containment is not possible when unbalanced dictators with weapons of mass destruction can deliver those weapons on missiles or secretly provide them to terrorist allies. We cannot defend America and our friends by hoping for the best. We cannot put our faith in the word of tyrants, who solemnly sign non-proliferation treaties, and then systematically break them. If we wait for threats to fully materialize, we will have waited too long...[O]ur security will require all Americans to be forward-looking and resolute, to be ready for *preemptive action* when necessary to defend our liberty and to defend our lives" (Bush, 2002b; my italics).

By March 2003, the Bush Doctrine of Preemption became the principle justification for the United States-led war in Iraq, known as *Operation Iraqi Freedom*. As the President explained in his March 19, 2003, address to the nation, "The people of the United States and our friends and allies will not live at the mercy of an outlaw regime that threatens the peace with weapons of mass murder. We will meet that threat now, with our Army, Air Force, Navy, Coast Guard, and Marines, so that we do not have to meet it later with armies of fire fighters and police and doctors on the streets of our cities" (Bush, 2003).

Lincoln's and Bush's beliefs are eerily echoed in the PreCrime slogan, "To ensure that that which keeps us safe also keeps us free." That the

Marks's young son is stabbing Lincoln through the eyes suggests that Lincoln's (and PreCrime's and now maybe Bush's) vision and prevision of America as a land of liberty achieved through the suspension of individual civil rights needs to be re-envisioned. That Lincoln's eyeless face becomes this now fatherless son's mask for his school recitation of the Gettysburg Address confirms that this change in perspective is imminent.[3]

The second way in which the opening sequence implies the limitations of prevision is in its naming of the precogs. Viewers learn that the precogs are named Arthur, Dashiell, and Agatha. Because the blue-washed film of *Minority Report* constantly reminds viewers of the film noire genre, it does not take much thought to realize where the precogs names came from: Sir Arthur Conan Doyle, Dashiell Hammett, and Agatha Christy. What is striking about the precogs' names is that they are not the names of famous detectives but of famous detective writers; they are the authors of stories rather than the assemblers of facts. This makes perfect sense when we consider the relationship between the precogs and the police, in which the precogs generate images that Chief Inspector Anderton scans for clues and assembles into a coherent timeline that predicts future injustices. However, by naming the precogs after authors rather than detectives, the film suggests two things. First, it suggests that like good detective novels, precog visions are (potentially) fictitious in nature. Second, it suggests that just as these three detective writers use different styles to tell distinct stories, so too might the three individual precogs tell the same story in different ways. Indeed, they might even tell different stories.

It is this possibility that the precogs might disagree, that they might generate conflicting previsions, that Anderton discovers when the precogs predict that Anderton himself will commit murder in three days' time. As Anderton learns from the cocreator of the PreCrime system, the eccentric Iris Hineman (Lois Smith), though the precogs are never collectively wrong, Agatha sometimes sees things differently, producing a *minority report* of the predicted crime. If Anderton, who is predicted to kill a man he has never even heard of, much less met, can prove that Agatha sees his future differently, he might be able to clear his name and escape eternity in the Hall of Containment.

Of course, all this presents problems for Anderton. Anderton is a true believer in the PreCrime system, a system to which he has devoted himself since the disappearance and presumed murder of his young son Sean. Had PreCrime existed when Sean was taken, Anderton convinces himself, Sean would be alive today. Sean's disappearance and presumed death led not only to Anderton's devotion to PreCrime but to the breakup of his marriage and his addiction to narcotics. Instead of enjoying his white, happy, heterosexual nuclear family as he did in the past, Anderton now revisits them as homemade holographic movies with which he interacts in his drug-induced state. Now that Anderton stands accused by the only thing he has left in the world to believe in and the only legal channel for this mourning father's vigilante impulses—the justice of PreCrime—he will either end up losing his (un)conscious life (by being haloed for his crime) or losing his faith in PreCrime (because if Anderton does not commit the predicted murder, this means the system is not perfect).

As a criminal on the run, Anderton ceases to be the *I* and eyes of the state and instead comes under the constant surveillance of other state eyes. There are those of Anderton's fellow officers and Detective Witwer, but more menacing is the constant mechanical surveillance of Anderton's eyes: routine public transportation ID scans, billboard scans leading to personally directed advertisements, and shop scans that lead to sales pitches based on his purchasing history. Most disturbing of all are the mechanical spiders used by the police to identify all warm bodies in dangerous locations, such as the tenement in which Anderton hides out.

John Anderton's only hope of evading detection by the state is to stop being John Anderton. And to do that, John Anderton must "swap" his *I* and his eyes for those of another. In a sleazy backstreet operation, this is precisely what Anderton does. While Anderton is blindfolded, shielding his new eyes from light so that he does not go blind, the spiders invade his building to check all *I*'s/eyes. When Anderton's clever attempts to evade them ultimately fail, the spiders shine a bright light into his left eye. This not only confirms that, to the state, Anderton is a new/another man; it fulfills an earlier prophecy told to Anderton by his eyeless drug dealer: "In the land of the blind, the one-eyed man is king." When Anderton (who has kept his old eyes so he can use them to break into the temple and steal Agatha to download his minority report) loses one of his old eyes down a drain, the prophecy's fulfillment is repeated. However, repeating it means that the new Anderton is a mix of his old vision and his new vision, allowing him to see what he needs to see in the past, albeit differently. Indeed, Agatha's persistent question to Anderton is, "Can you see?" With these eyes, Anderton ultimately does.

Before Anderton can see what Agatha wants him to see, he must settle his own fate. Anderton ultimately succeeds in downloading Agatha's previsions about his predicted crime but, to his bitter disappointment, Agatha did not see events in Anderton's future any differently than did Arthur and Dashiell. Agatha does not provide Anderton with a minority report, or at least not the sort of minority report Anderton expected. Instead of offering an alternative vision of Anderton's crime (for she has none), Agatha repeatedly tells Anderton, "You can choose," which amounts to a minority report on predestination itself and raises the question, "If you know your future, are you doomed to fulfill it?"

Mindful of his future, Anderton does choose. When he discovers that his intended victim is the abductor of his missing son Sean, Anderton tells Agatha, "I *am* going to kill this man." However, when he comes face to face with his intended victim, a tearful Anderton instead chooses to arrest the man, only then to discover that the whole thing was a setup. Anderton's intended victim was promised money for his family in exchange for his own death at Anderton's hand. Desperate for the money, the man grabs Anderton's gun, still in Anderton's hand, and shoots himself. This suicide looks exactly like the murder the precogs predicted. And for this "crime," Anderton is eventually arrested, haloed, and contained.

What we have at this point, then, are two failures in the PreCrime system that are both located on the side of prevision rather than that of vision. On the one hand, because the precogs produce only images but no text, they either cannot always distinguish between or cannot communicate the distinction between murder and suicide, thereby leading to the conviction of an innocent man like John Anderton. However, even more important, prevision fails because when would-be criminals know their own future, they can choose to act differently. In Anderton's case, this means deciding not to kill his son's killer; in Saddam's case, this means not stockpiling or using weapons of mass destruction. Overall, what this means is that, under particular circumstances, previsions are not the same thing as predestination.

Thus, using prevision, even the precogs cannot always answer in the affirmative to Agatha's insistent question, "Can you see?" Through his encounters with Agatha, eye swaps, and lost faith in PreCrime, Anderton finally does see what Agatha hoped he would: that his boss Lamar Burgess (Max von Sydow) murdered her mother Ann Lively, who threatened the future of PreCrime because she wanted Agatha back. Anderton solves the mystery of Ann Lively's disappearance (which is really a death) because, this time, Agatha does have a minority report, but it is a minority report that can be understood only when viewed through a different eye/I.

Agatha's question to Anderton—"Can you see?"—might be restated then as "Can you become someone who can see otherwise?" Anderton does so only when he is forced to, when this would-be criminal must swap out his original eyes to avoid detection by the state. Even so, this one-eyed man of *Minority Report* is never quite king, especially an enlightened one, because though Anderton may be our action hero (our man on the run throughout most of the film), he is not really much of a detective. He was wrong about PreCrime, he was wrong about his boss (whom he trusted) and Detective Witwer (whom he mistrusted), and he was initially wrong about Ann Lively's death.

*Minority Report* is not about this clever man saving the day; it is about his repeated failure to see things clearly and his search for clarity in all the wrong places (PreCrime, drugs, memories of his lost family). Strikingly, every time Anderton loses the trail, it is a woman who sets him straight. Agatha pleads with him to see her prevision about her mother's death properly. Iris Hineman informs Anderton that there is such a thing as a minority report and that it is always held by the most gifted of the precogs, the girl. And Anderton's ex-wife Laura (Kathryn Morris) takes no time to figure out that Lamar Burgess has betrayed Anderton, at which point she rescues him from prison and convinces Anderton's ex-colleagues to cooperate in a plot to expose Burgess.

*Minority Report*, then, locates invention (Iris), knowledge (Agatha), and meaningful action (Laura) not in our male hero but in the feminine, for without the feminine guiding Anderton at every turn, one-eyed or not, he would not see a thing. Instead, Anderton would be more like the one-eyed soldier in the final shot of the haunting Vietnam War film *The Quiet American*, a figure who symbolizes a loss of (international) perspective rather than a re-envisioning of the world though the knowledge that vision and prevision ultimately fail.

*Minority Report* tells us that the choice between these two very different ways of seeing and these two very different previsions of who we might become is ours. *We* can choose; we can be moral America(ns) not just by refusing to commit crimes but, more important, by insisting on seeing the world, including our own world, differently. To do this, we must begin by reconsidering the relationship between justice and security. First, we must admit that vision (surveillance of what people do, as in intelligence that claimed to show Saddam Hussein stockpiling weapons of mass destruction) and prevision (surveillance of what people [should not] think, as in Jose Padilla's not-yet plan to explode a dirty bomb in the United States) fundamentally fail to provide security and fundamentally fail to provide justice. Second, we must see that the PreCrime dream of securing the body by securing the unconscious always leads to dehumanization, whether through the deification of troubled "children" (the precogs) or the detention of *I*'s whose "eyes/windows to the soul" may have been misread (be these of the detainees of Camp X-Ray or of Jose Padilla).

In making its case against equating *I*'s with eyes—identity to the unconscious—the film implies yet another way in which the state might act immorally. When the state accuses someone of a future crime, might it not set in motion a chain of events that actually leads to the fulfillment of that accusation? Is this not what happened to Anderton, a man who literally ran into his victim because he was running away from the state? As one reviewer put it, "Take away the accusation, and there would be no question of his (Anderton['s]) committing a criminal act. The prediction drives the act—a self-fulfilling prophe[c]y" (Berardinelli, 2002b). Even though Anderton did not fulfill this prophecy (he arrested his intended victim, who then committed suicide), the point remains: accusations based on an equation of identity and the unconscious are dangerous. In Bush's war on terror, more than anything else it is the administration's exercise of preemptive justice that seems to cement the sympathies of at least some of the accused with the terrorists with whom they are accused of sympathizing. If we can see this, then who we might become is not only a moral America(n) but a more secure one.

Overall, the moral grammar of war in *Minority Report* is one that demands a re-envisioning not only of our positive stories about who we really are (humanitarians) but of our past stories of who we think we were. *We* need to look again at the vision and prevision of Abraham Lincoln (and now George W. Bush) through their questionable decision to attain state freedom by suspending individual freedoms, including the freedom of (pre)thought. On this the film is clear. What it is less clear on is the role that the feminine plays in rendering possible this reworking of the relationship between justice and security.

As pointed out earlier, it seems to be Agatha's insistent question— "Can you see?"—that enables the change in Anderton's and ultimately America's perspective. It is the feminine that renders possible America's moral re-envisioning of itself, the world, and itself in the world. The film implies that to become a moral Amerca(n), *we* would be well advised to take careful note of what the feminine is showing us.

Yet, even as it portrays the feminine as innovative, intelligent, and active, *Minority Report* caricatures each of its female characters though gender stereotypes, so much so that the film at best sends mixed messages about the feminine and what it wants *us* to see.

Iris, the coinventor of PreCrime, is not just cast as an innovative scientist and (as her name implies) a messenger to the gods (for it is she who tells Anderton of the minority reports). Pictured as she is living in ier secluded home protected by killer plants, Iris is not so much colorful as dangerously eccentric. Furthermore, we learn that it was never Iris's intention to use the precogs to create the perfect justice system. Her eye/iris was not meant to link the unconscious to criminality; instead, looking through her eye/iris of compassion, Iris's desire was to save these children who became precogs. Iris, then, is less scientist than she is motherly humanist, which adds to her disruptive character.

Agatha, the seer of the future and the keeper of past knowledge, is portrayed as innocence itself. She is a troubled child who through no fault of her own sees a troubling future. However, in her characterization, Agatha's innocence is taken to the extreme, for more than anything else, Agatha resembles an infant. She lives in the Temple with the other precogs, cradled in a womblike pool of what might be amniotic fluid or mother's milk, dressed in what the film's costume designer referred to as "an embryonic kind of covering" (*Minority Report* DVD, 2002). Even though it is Agatha whose minority reports have the capacity to destroy the state's system of justice, this disruptive potential is downplayed by casting her as utterly dependent, inside and outside the Temple. On the inside, she is nurtured on a mix of mother's milk (drugs) and motherly love (by her caregiver). On the outside, she is dressed and walked by her abductor Anderton and, after the demise of PreCrime, cocooned in a remote island home with the twins. Nor is it Agatha's intention to bring down PreCrime. Rather, her repeated question to Anderton—"Can you see?"—is a plea for his help in bringing her mother's murderer to justice, not a desire to dismantle the justice system itself.

Finally, Anderton's wife Laura, who is the feminine embodiment of meaningful action, is always first and foremost characterized as wife and mother. She first appears in Anderton's home movie holograms as his wife, after establishing that she is also the mother of his child. Later, the present Laura, ex-wife of John, explains that she left her husband because every time she looked at him she saw their dead son. The final shot of the film shows the future Laura reunited with her husband John and pregnant with their future child. As these cameos of Laura illustrate, regardless of how pivotal Laura is to bringing down the PreCrime system, she is always tied historically, narratively, and visually to reproduction. Reproduction and, indeed, rebirth are her most meaningful acts.

Taken together, all three main female characters of *Minority Report* are stereotypically feminine. All are introduced to viewers first in a home setting. All their desires are familial: to help troubled children, to get justice for a mother, to get justice for a husband. And their ambitions are private, not public. What this means is that no matter how much they privately assist Anderton in his public quest to dismantle PreCrime and enable America(ns) to rethink the relationship between justice and security, what is always brought to our attention about these women is that they secure what is traditionally domestic: the white, happy heterosexual domestic family.

This is no small contribution to the state, for on this foundation the literal and figurative rebirth of the nation is rendered possible (Michel, 1989; Berlandt, 1997; Coontz, 2000). However, by once again functioning as homebodies, do not the women of *Minority Report* resemble the WWII women in *Pearl Harbor*, relegated to be the role of homefront, however much this role fails to capture what they are really up to? As such, do not these women ultimately lack credit for making meaningful moral action and find themselves cast as stagehands, marginalized to the wings in the patriarchal performance of the nation's rebirth? This is, after all, John Anderton's/Tom Cruise's movie about a father's desperate search for his lost son/fatherhood.

These concerns seem to be all the more convincing when we note that *Minority Report* ends for John Anderton very much where it began: with a happy holographic image of family come to life, first technically and then biologically. It is a sentimental ending, with Anderton lovingly stroking Laura's pregnant belly. Does this not mean that, in *Minority Report*, who we might become is merely a future echo of who we think we were: the foundational family of WWII?

The answers to these questions are both yes and no, for what we find in *Minority Report* is that the feminine is cast in not just one role but two. Through the film's use of stereotypes, the feminine functions as we have long seen the feminine function: as that which secures the home. However, by rendering the feminine more innovative, intelligent, and meaningfully active than its male lead, the film makes a claim to the disruptive potential of the feminine to destabilize the state. However seemingly contradictory this dual casting of the feminine may seem to be, I would argue that is it utterly consistent, for what this future feminine does is combine what we knew about the feminine in the past (Evelyn of *Pearl Harbor*, a figure who always fought for home and family) and what we know about the contemporary feminine (Ruth of *In the Bedroom*, a figure who seems to only fight for herself, albeit under the guise of fighting for her family). By combining the stereotypical role of the past feminine with its disruptive potential in its contemporary role, *Minority Report* directs this disruptive potential away from its own seemingly selfish private aims to more collective and ultimately public/national aims.

What this means in *Minority Report* is that the feminine functions to secure the home/nation while destabilizing state policies (e.g., homeland security domestically and preemptive justice internationally) that might destabilize it. In so doing, it is not only itself safely contained in the home(land); the feminine also contains rather than fuels the vigilante impulses of the masculine.

Thanks to this dual function of the feminine—for the home and, as the moral force of the homeland, against anything that might destabilize home/nation (including state policies)—*our* US character is transformed. *We* emerge as a subject very much like the new John Anderton, who can see differently both because he relies on previsions to see the future or to secure the unconscious for the state and because, like Anderton, *we* have one eye on the past (one old eye) and one eye on the present (one new eye). This, *Minority Report* tells us, is what it takes to become a moral America(n). And this, it promises, is who we might become in the future.

## Fahrenheit 9/11

Michael Moore's 2004 film *Fahrenheit 9/11* takes "seeing differently" as its goal and, like *Minority Report*, it ultimately employs this same domesticated but disruptive feminine figure to render possible its re-envisioning of who we might become.

Moore's film begins with a black screen, against which fireworks appear. The camera pans down to a campaign platform on election night, where Al Gore and Joseph Lieberman celebrate their victory in the 2000 Presidential election. As this scene rolls, we hear Michael Moore in voice-over ask, "Was it all just a dream? Did the last four years not happen? Was it a dream, or was it real?"

This is Moore's introduction to his history of US politics during the nearly four years of the administration of President George W. Bush. It begins with the events that led first to "something called Fox News" and finally the US Supreme Court's putting George W. Bush in the White House. It traces the Bush presidency prior to 9/11, during which time the new president spent 42 per cent of his time on vacation and declared in front of cameras in August of 2001 that he did not spend much time thinking about Osama bin Laden. It recaps the horrors of 9/11 itself by virtually repeating how they are displayed in Alejandro Gonzales Inarritu's short film, one of those that comprises the compilation *11"09"01*. We hear the collapse of the Twin Towers but see only a blank screen. After this long moment, Moore cuts to the shock and horror of ordinary people in the streets caught up in this tragedy.

The film then recounts the Bush administration's reaction to 9/11: its war in Afghanistan, its policies for homeland security, its passage of the Patriot Act, and finally its war in Iraq against Saddam Hussein. Along the way, Moore suggests that the Bush family's ties to the Saudi royal family—particularly their shared oil interests—largely account for the Bush administration's actions and inactions in its war on terror. The United States did not invade Iraq, Moore suggests, for the reasons the administration says it did (primarily, that it was a security threat to the United States because of its weapons of mass destruction and Saddam's links to al Qaeda, neither of which has been proven). It invaded Iraq for its own personal, elitist reasons (to secure the interests of US companies linked to the Presidential Bush and Vice-Presidential Cheney families, such as the Carlyle Group, Unocal, and Halliburton, and to avenge Saddam's attempt "to kill my Dad," as George Jr. puts it in the film).

On this summary, most people would agree. Judging from commentators' reviews, however, what they would vehemently disagree on is how they would describe Moore's telling of this story. How should the film be characterized? Is *Fahrenheit 9/11* a documentary, or "by mixing sober outrage with mischievous humor" does it "blithely [trample] the boundary between documentary and demagoguery" (Scott, 2004)? If "Michael Moore doesn't so much make documentaries as make movies with documents" (O'Brian, 2004), might his film be better described by comparing it to something else altogether: "muckraking social satire" (Hoberman, 2004); "an op-ed piece" (Ebert, 2004); "an editorial cartoon" (Scott, 2004); or "a beer commercial" (Gitlin, 2004)? Does Moore's "high-spirited and unruly exercise in democratic self-expression" (Scott, 2004) reduce the broader political value of his work, or does the genre he seems to have created of "first-person polemic or expressionist bulletin board, or theatrical Op-Ed piece" become more politically effective?

Differing answers to these questions have led to differing opinions about the film as a whole. Some reviewers hated the film; of these, Christopher Hitchens is the most scathing. He writes, "To describe this film as dishonest and demagogic would almost be to promote those terms to the level of respectability. To describe this film as a piece of crap would be to run the risk of a discourse that would never again rise above the excremental. To describe it as an exercise in facile crowd-pleasing would be too obvious. *Fahrenheit 9/11* is a sinister exercise in moral frivolity, crudely disguised as an exercise in seriousness. It is also a spectacle of abject political cowardice masking itself as a demonstration of 'dissenting' bravery" (Hitchens, 2004).

Far more reviewers offered (sometimes qualified) praise for the film, describing it as a "brilliant battering ram" (Travers, 2004) or as "incendiary, excitable, often mawkishly emotional but simply gripping: a cheerfully partisan assault on the Bush administration" and an "inflammatory polemic" (Bradshaw, 2004). Still others were of two minds about the film. Describing *Fahrenheit 9/11* as "the liberals' *The Passion of the Christ*" (the 2004 Mel Gibson film that was the darling of some of the religious right), David Edelstein confessed of the film, "It delighted me; it disgusted me. I celebrated it; I lamented it. I'm sure of only one thing: that I don't trust anyone —pro or con—who doesn't feel a twinge of doubt about his or her response" (Edelstein, 2004).

How I would describe *Fahrenheit 9/11* is as a minority report, and in some respects a *Minority Report*, on the Bush administration. First, *Fahrenheit 9/11* offers a minority view of US politics through the genre of vigilante journalism: a watchful reporting style that claims to exercise a superior brand of (real) justice thanks to the personal involvement of its witness(es). Second, it does so, as does *Minority Report*, by focusing on the same key themes (state censorship, the reliability of vision, and the relationship between crime and consciousness) to tell its futuristic tale of post-9/11 American morality. Finally, in a fashion similar to that in *Minority Report*, it ultimately establishes who we are as moral America(ns): by reactivating the role of the feminine.

That the film is about censorship is immediately evident from its title. Combining the word *Fahrenheit* with a number is a reference to Ray Bradbury's famous novel, *Fahrenheit 451*, published in 1953 (the height of the McCarthy era). Setting his story sometime in the future, Bradbury tells of a time when reading the written word is banned. What people read instead are images: static as well as moving pictures. Newspapers, for example, look like compilations of comic strips, broadsheets of wordless picture panel followed by wordless picture panel. And television has so intruded into everyday life that each home has several wall-sized screens. Firemen in Bradbury's future society do not put out fires; they start them, for it is these state workers who are responsible for seizing and burning any surviving books. The story's title, *Fahrenheit 451*, refers to the temperature at which paper burns.

As depressing as all this sounds, it is important to note that Bradbury's tale of state censorship and the suppression of individual rights is also a tale of political resistance. To circumvent state authoritarianism based on a dangerous anti-intellectualism, a growing number of common citizens have taken it on themselves to memorize great books and then to pass their knowledge on to future generations. *Fahrenheit 451*, then, is a story about how, when everyday individuals band together to remember the past, they constitute both a political threat to the present authoritarian state and our best hope for a future in which we will all enjoy individual freedoms.

With its tag line, "The temperature where freedom burns!," *Fahrenheit 9/11* boldly proclaims that the future is now. What Moore's title inplies is that Bradbury's nightmare of state censorship arrived in the United States on 9/11, and America's best hope for a better future is to remember its past, not the McCarthy era but the more immediate past of the Bush presidency, so that Americans will not repeat it. By releasing his film in the run up to the 2004 US Presidential elections, Moore has made no secret of the fact that *Fahrenheit 9/11* is part of his personal campaign to make sure George W. Bush is removed from the White House (Younge, 2004).

In the run up to the summer 2004 US release of *Fahrenheit 9/11*, Moore's points about censorship, made implicitly through his film's title and explicitly through his film's discussion of such things as the Bush administration's implementation of the Patriot Act, became issues surrounding the screening of his film as well. When the Disney corporation, whose subsidiary Miramax had purchased the film, refused to distribute *Fahrenheit 9/11*, the film was bought back by Miramax cofounders Harvey and Bob Weinstein and marketed under an additional tagline, "The Film They Did Not Want You To See." Then such groups as Move America Forward tried to pressure individual US theatres into not showing the film (O'Brian, 2004; Younge, 2004).

Some have claimed that this censorship storm was of Moore's own making, helping him to win the coveted Palme d'Or for Best Picture at the Cannes Film Festival (Anthony, 2004; Kermode, 2004) and thereby hyping *Fahrenheit 9/11*. It is difficult to assess the truth of such a claim. What is not difficult to assess, though, is that *Fahrenheit 9/11* became a must-see film in the United States and beyond. The film grossed $21.8 million in the United States in its first three days: that's compared to *Harry Potter*, which took in just over $11.4 million during the same period (Brockes, 2004). As of early August 2004, the film had earned $100 million in the United States alone, rendering it the highest-grossing "documentary" of all time, and it was still playing in cinemas (Yahoo Movies Box Office Charts, 2004).

Not surprisingly for an overtly political (and politically divisive) film such as *Fahrenheit 9/11*, the film's success led to more cries against it, taking the form of a documentary called *Michael Moore Hates America*, a book called *Michael Moore is a Big Fat Stupid White Man* (a play on Moore's book *Stupid White Men*), and even accusations by the conservative group Citizens United that Moore violated federal election laws because he has admitted that his goal was to impact the November 2004 Presidential elections (Younge, 2004).

All this is to say that censorship is something that Bradbury's novel and Moore's film have in common. Having said this, though, there are clear differences in Bradbury's original story and Moore's riff off it.

In Bradbury's story, the past to be remembered is not of state censorship but of the great intellectual traditions represented by great literary works that preceded it. *Fahrenheit 451,* then, is as much a critique of the dystopia of the McCarthy era as it is a celebration of the intellectual utopia that preceded it. In contrast, Moore never makes the claim that the more distant past (say, the Clinton presidency) was better than the present; he merely emphasizes just how bad the near past under Bush has been and how tragic it would be to repeat this near past in the near future. As such, there does not appear to be a utopian vision in Moore's film, just a warning about our current and possibly future dystopia (a point to which I return later).

Undoubtedly, the biggest difference between Bradbury's novel and Moore's suggested equivalence to it concerns the very different ways in which each regards the written word in comparison to the visual image. By highlighting the trivializing of information through the image while celebrating the retention of information through the memorization of the written word, Bradbury's hierarchy of words over images could not be clearer. Rightly or wrongly, Bradbury argues that the simplicity of images and their easy manipulation puts pictures on the side of anti-intellectualism, whereas the complexity of words and their ability to cut through and complicate what we see is the epitome of intellectualism.[4]

Writing in the early 1950s, a time in which images were rapidly invading American homes through television, novelist Bradbury's celebration of the revolutionary potential of the written word is not difficult to understand. Half a century later, it is equally understandable why filmmaker Moore would reverse this hierarchy. For now, do *we* not live in a "visual age" in which "life takes place on screen" (Mirzoeff, 1999)? And if that is the case, does it not make sense that political arguments are most effective when rendered visual?

This is the implicit case made by Moore's film. *Fahrenheit 9/11* is much more than the splicing together of Moore's best-selling books *Stupid White Men* (2002) and *Dude, Where's My Country?* (2003), even though much of the information in each book is found in Moore's film. Rather, it is a visual (and aural) tour de force that powerfully appeals to the mediatic American mindset. As such, *Fahrenheit 9/11* is arguably less interesting for what it says than for how it says it.

How the film tells its story is through the presentation of "pictures that seem to speak for themselves" (O'Brian, 2004). These images come in the form of censored media clips of "what they didn't want us to see"; popular images that *we* have all seen before and therefore instantly understand; and underreported first-person accounts of what *we* actually saw for ourselves. The censored clips come in three varieties: pre-rolls, post-rolls, and non-rolls. Pre-rolls are bits of footage taken while the camera is rolling but before the footage is fed live on television; post-rolls are bits of footage taken after the live feed while the camera is still rolling; and non-rolls are footage that was not broadcast.

In the style of Kevin Rafferty and James Ridgway's 1992 documentary *Feed* (about the New Hampshire primaries), *Fahrenheit 9/11* runs embarrassing pre-rolls of a collection of Bush administration officials, from Condoleeza Rice to Paul Wolfowitz to the President himself, as they preen themselves for the camera (Bradshaw, 2004). In these takes, we see Wolfowitz soak his comb in his own saliva and then run it through his pompadour; that's disgusting and funny. What is more disturbing is President Bush's practicing facial expressions immediately before he goes live to tell the US public that the United States is at war with Iraq. Though humorous, these pre-rolls are not necessarily politically effective, for do not all of us fix ourselves up and rehearse before we go on camera? And, if that's the case, does that not mean that the critical story told by these pre-rolls can be told about anyone? Indeed, those familiar with Rafferty and Ridgway's film know that these very same types of shots were used to question the character of then-Governor Bill Clinton, a knowledge that neutralizes the political effectiveness of using these types of images against Bush administration officials.

It is Moore's use of post-rolls that is more effective. Two post-rolls in particular stand out. There's the footage of President Bush on a golf course, golf club in hand, talking tough about terrorism to a group of journalists. Then, without missing a beat, the President turns to the real business of the day and tells the journalists, "Now, watch this golf swing." However, the most damning post-roll in the film was also probably the most important post-9/11 non-roll. Taken on 9/11, it shows the President sitting in that infamous Florida elementary school classroom. *Fahrenheit 9/11* shows us what we have all seen before: an official whispering into the President's ear, "The nation is under attack," after a second plane hit the Twin Towers; then it shows us what the President did in response. He sat there for a full seven minutes. Because no one told him what to do, Moore suggests, the President continued to read *My Pet Goat* with the children. What is shocking about this post-roll is not only the images it presents but the fact that these images had never before been shown to a mass US audience. What is also shocking about these images is that they seem to speak for themselves. But they do not.

Never mind that Moore makes these seven minutes real for viewers by taking nearly seven minutes to present them, thereby allowing viewers to feel this time as well as to see it. These seven minutes are intercut with Moore's account of how, prior to 9/11, the Bush administration ignored warnings of an imminent terrorist attack and cut funding to fight terrorism. Jumping back and forth between the seemingly bewildered Bush and this back story, Moore speculates in voice-over what Bush must have thought during those seven minutes: Who screwed me? Was it Saddam, the Taliban, the Saudis? Undoubtedly, this seven-minute post-roll/non-roll speaks volumes, but, like any image, precisely what these seven minutes say—what they mean—is not self-evident. Those on the right might interpret these images as showing the President setting an example of calm for the American people. Had the President acted differently, "leaped from his stool, adopted a Russell Crowe stance, and gone to work," he might well have been criticized by some on the left for either "being a man who went to war on a hectic, crazed impulse" or as someone who expected the attack, used it to solidify his power, and who "couldn't wait to get on with his coup" (Hitchens, 2004).

I am not trying to make a case for reading these seven minutes one way or another. Rather, I am trying to make the same point that Bradbury made in *Fahrenheit 451*: that we cannot trust the image alone, a point Moore makes himself, albeit very differently, in *Fahrenheit 9/11*. For if Moore trusted images alone, he would not have needed to set his pictures to provocative soundtracks. REM's "Shiny Happy People" accompanies scenes of the Bushes and the Saudis socializing. The theme song from the TV show "The Greatest American Hero" ("Suddenly I'm up on the top of the world/Shoulda been somebody else") plays as Bush addresses Naval personnel and prematurely announces "Mission accomplished" in Iraq. And the music from a Marlboro cigarette ad plays as Moore wonders aloud why, in spite of a terrorist's attempt to light a shoe bomb on an airplane, up to four books of matches and two lighters can be carried by each passenger on US flights.

If Moore trusted images alone, he would not have had to mix his images and sounds calculatingly. He would not have needed to use clips from old US television shows, such as *Bananza*, to mock the collection of characters in Bush's posse or turn to *Dragnet* to underscore the administration's presumed failure to question the bin Laden family before they left the United States (a "fact" that Moore reportedly got wrong; see Kermode, 2004). Nor would Moore need to sample old Western and witch-hunt films and splice them with the sound bites of George Jr.

Overall, if Moore trusted images alone, he would not have needed to manipulate never-before-seen footage by intercutting it with popular cultural sounds and images that solicit immediate, anticipated thoughts and feelings from his American viewing public. He would not have needed to exclude images and arguments that undercut his case against Bush.[5] Further, he would not have needed to set the whole thing to his own voice-over. However, Moore does all these things, and then some. He does them because he, like Bradbury, knows that images do not speak for themselves; that is why he has to speak for them, all the while presenting himself as if he is speaking through them.[6]

Yet, all this having been said, there are some images that Moore seems to suggest are beyond manipulation. These images are what *we* saw for ourselves, first-person accounts of actual events. In 2000, *we* saw for ourselves that Gore and Lieberman won the US Presidential election. Moore tells us it was only thanks to Bush's cousin John Ellis (a Fox News executive who called Florida for Bush) and a conservative Supreme Court (some of whose members were appointed by the Reagan-Bush administrations) that George W. Bush ended up in the White House.

By 2004, Moore tells us, *we* can see for ourselves the devastation caused by nearly four years of the Bush presidency. It takes the form of failed homeland security testified to by average, ordinary, under-resourced Oregon state troopers and by average, ordinary oversurveyed US citizens subjected to the restrictions of the Patriot Act. It is shown as failed US foreign policy testified to by amputee US veterans of Gulf War II and Moore's own gruesome footage of the death and devastation US foreign policy brought to Iraq. However, probably most forcefully, it is expressed as the failed hopes and dreams of everyday Americans to believe in the integrity of their leaders.

It is this final story—of not only lost hope but betrayed expectations—that is the emotional and moral core of Moore's story. Unlike in Moore's previous documentaries *Roger and Me* and *Bowling for Columbine*, the figure who tells this story is not Michael Moore; it is Lila Lipscomb, a white working-class mother from Moore's hometown of Flint, Michigan.

Lipscomb first appears in a segment establishing how poor, and particularly black, youths are targeted by US military recruiters to enlist and fight in US wars (such as Iraq). Lila Lipscomb, a former welfare mother who now works at an employment agency designed to get people off welfare, tells Moore that the military is an excellent option for people from economically depressed Flint. She boasts that two of her children served in the military: a daughter in Gulf War I and a son in Gulf War II. To establish Lipscomb's credentials further as a true US patriot, Moore shows her hanging the American flag outside her home, something she does every day, and viewers noticing that she is wearing not only a cross around her neck but an American flag pinned to her lapel.

Moore often cuts away from Lipscomb to interview US soldiers caught up in the Iraq conflict. He shows some soldiers behaving badly by disrespecting an Iraqi corpse or by getting themselves charged up for war in a very *Apocalypse Now* way by playing music with the lyrics "Burn, Motherfucker, Burn." Mostly, however, he shows US soldiers who feel betrayed. One serving soldier tells Moore that if he saw Secretary of Defense Donald Rumsfeld, he would tell him to resign. Another soldier who did a tour of duty in Iraq tells Moore that he will refuse to return, no matter the consequences. And a number of veteran amputees discuss their disillusionment with the war and with their aftercare that each of them so tragically embodies.

However, Moore always returns to Lipscomb and her story. What we learn from Lipscomb is that her son Michael had reservations about going to Iraq but did so because it was his duty to go. Once over there, he wrote to his mother that the war was not justified and that she should do everything in her power to make sure that George W. Bush was not reelected. A tearful Lipscomb sits on a sofa surrounded by her mixed-race family as she reads this letter, which she received a week after she got the news that her son's Black Hawk helicopter was shot down and he was killed. In a move echoing Moore's attempt in *Roger and Me* to confront General Motors Chairman Roger Smith about the 1980s closing of the Flint GM plant, Lipscomb goes to Washington to confront President George W. Bush about his betrayal of her and her son but, again echoing Moore's experience, she is refused entry into the White House, only to be confronted in the adjacent Lafayette Square by an angry prowar woman who shouts at her, "This is all a set-up," to which Lipscomb replies, "My son is dead. That is not a set-up."

What Lipscomb represents is not just a mourning mother but the moral center of a betrayed America. *We* have been betrayed by the Bush administration, Moore's film proclaims. As if in reply to Agatha's question from *Minority Report* ("Can you see?"), Moore's answer is a resounding yes. *We* can see that we have been lied to by the Bush administration, which apparently is the only reason why Americans supported the suspension of some civil liberties (by passing the Patriot

Act) and supported the Bush administration's war in Iraq. And because *we* can see, we, like the characters of *Minority Report* who had their futures foretold, can choose. *We* do not have to relive this nightmarish prevision: four more years of the Bush administration. Instead, *we* can vote George W. Bush out of the White House.

This is Michael Moore's moral grammar of war in *Fahrenheit 9/11*. Becoming a moral America(n) for Moore involves recognizing that *we* were not dreaming, that the past four years did happen and that even though America and Americans did horrible things during those years, these things were not *our* fault. *We* are basically good but, because we were lied to, *we* did not see what was really going on. Thanks to Moore's turning the "eyes of the nation" back on the big *I* of George W. Bush and his administration, *we* know more than before because *we* have seen what *we* were not allowed to see before. And so the moment has arrived for *us* to act morally. Acting morally begins by acting at home: by voting George W. Bush out of the White House. This is Michael Moore's prevision of a moral America.

Like all moral grammars of war, Moore's makes sense only when expressed through a particular US *we* that is located in relation to specific gendered, familial relations. The first thing to notice about Moore's US *we* is that it is both hyper-individualized and utterly collectivized at the same time. Its individualism lies in the populist spirit of Moore's work, expressed through his insistent first-person perspective. As Gary O'Brian argues of Moore's film, "Its fiction is that one man—not a lecturer or a representative of a political party, but somebody you might meet at a party or in a bar—is telling you according to his own lights what's been going on in the world lately …[A]t every step, he reminds you in devastating detail how ineptly or deceptively others have told their versions of this same story. The proof of their ineptitude or deception is that he's telling things you haven't heard before, and showing you pictures that seem to speak for themselves. It's not a story about a well-hidden conspiracy: all you have to do, he implies, is look around. You could set outside the room where you're sitting and pick up the trail anywhere, right on the street" (O'Brian, 2004). Moore's populist US *we*, then, is about every one of *us*; it is about *me*.

Yet this *we/me* is utterly collective. For Moore's US *me* is firmly embedded in a particular collective category: the relatively downtrodden economic and social class that does not form part of George W. Bush's base. And that transforms Moore's US *me* into a US *we*. We are the many middle-class (but mostly working-class) Americans who have suffered at the hands of these elite few and their neoliberal economic politics that benefit "them" but not "us." Moore emphasizes this point is his closing voice-over to *Fahrenheit 9/11*. Speaking of America's poor and their historical relationship to US wars, Moore ponders aloud, "It is hard to understand how the worst off are the first to step up so we can be free. All they ask in return is that we don't send them into harms way unless it is absolutely necessary. Will they ever trust us again?"

In this closing voice-over, Moore positions himself as if he is not a part of this US *we*, as if he is part of some *they* that has done the US *we* harm. This is both ironic and strategic. It is ironic because the less-off *we/me* that is the moral center of *Fahrenheit 9/11* is the moral center of every Michael Moore documentary. The only difference between past films *Roger and Me* and *Bowling for Columbine* and this film is that, in the earlier films, it is Moore himself who embodies this US *we/me*. That in *Fahrenheit 9/11* this task falls to Lila Lipscomb makes strategic sense, for it allows Moore to claim to be speaking as a mournful *them* when he is really speaking for an *us* that reflects *him*.

Lipscomb's embodiment of the moral American *we* is strategic in another sense: it enables Moore to consider the relationship between crime and consciousness from a seemingly objective perspective. Like *Minority Report*, *Fahrenheit 9/11* objects to the state's extended criminalization of consciousness and the unconscious, whether domestically (by increased surveillance of peace activists and other everyday Americans) or internationally (through the Bush Doctrine of Pre-emption). In making these objections, both films reverse the relationship between crime and consciousness. *Minority Report* does so by raising public consciousness of the crimes of Lamar Burgess, which are crimes of the state. *Fahrenheit 9/11* does this by raising everyday Americans' consciousness about the crimes committed against it and in its name by the Bush administration.

And like *Minority Report*, it is the feminine—in this case, an everyday, poor American mother in a mixed-race family—who renders possible this plot twist against the state. She is the link between her martyred soldier son and the all-too-unaware American public. There is no better figure to bring about *our* consciousness raising than Lila Lipscomb. This is because Lila Lipscomb knows (as the film *We Were Soldiers* knows) that American soldiers are mainly moral and we should respect and celebrate them, even if the wars they fight are unpopular. She also knows, however (as Makhmalbaf's *Kandahar* and *Minority Report* know), that America's (presumably) moral vision can be eclipsed by unjust state practices. It is for this reason (and not the simplistic patriotic reasons of *We Were Soldiers*) that testifying to what one has seen is a moral necessity.

Lila Lipscomb, then, is someone who can offer her testimony to the failures of state policy while keeping her patriotism intact. Unlike Michael Moore, who is accused of being against everything and nothing at the same time,[7] Lila Lipscomb is not against "America." She is not even against war, but she is firmly against this war and against this president's reelection because he got *us* into this war. Lila Lipscomb moves many American movie-goers to tears when she speaks of her loss and her determination to change US policy by changing the US president. Unlike Moore, when Lipscomb is accused of a set-up or of scoffing at power, viewers generally feel pained by this accusation, for this is not a woman who indiscriminately scoffs at power; she is a woman who represents America's loss, *our* loss. In ways that Michael Moore never could, Lila Lipscomb represents the sacrifices of the American homefront, *our* sacrifices. She is not some traditional, stereotypically inactive homefront (Elshtain, 1995; Michel, 1989). Rather, Lila Lipscomb is that unruly feminine (Irigaray, 1985) who, in her determination to (re)secure the US home (front), is willing to destabilize not only US state practices but the US President himself. In *Fahrenheit 9/11*, then, Lila Lipscomb—not Michael Moore—is *our* champion, for Lila Lipscomb is who (American) movie-goers and Americans more generally trust.

*Fahrenheit 9/11* would be just another Michael Moore film if it were not for Lila Lipscomb, and this is something that Moore himself seems to appreciate. Lipscomb explained in an interview, "Michael Moore said he'd already been around America interviewing all different types of people [for the film]. It was the most incredible experience; he was sitting in our living room and all of a sudden, during the talking and sharing, a tear fell from his eye. His producer said afterwards, 'Michael found it, he found it, he found what the movie was going to be about!'" (Brockes, 2004).

What a Michael Moore movie is always about is Moore's use of sounds and images to speak "truth" to "power." Truth is located in working-class or otherwise oppressed (usually racialized) Americans; power is located in oppressive (usually white) American elites. As such, Moore's films are always domestic tales that redress the balance between justice and security. *Roger and Me* is about the unjust closure of a GM plant that led to the economic insecurity of its workers. *Bowling for Columbine* is about the unjust promotion of America's gun culture by elites and industries that led to the destabilizing of all Americans, especially children. And *Fahrenheit 9/11* is about the unjust lies of George W. Bush and his administration that led to destabilizing not only America's poor, who fight Bush's wars, but to destabilizing the very idea of a moral America as the champion of democratic freedoms for all.

Moore's picture of America, which seems to speak for itself, is based on two ideals: the first utopian, the second dystopian. Moore's utopian ideal is the populist belief in the goodness of everyday Americans. Moore's dystopian ideal is that in bringing forth the goodness of everyday Americans, the means seem to justify the ends. Moore's means do not involve burning books; instead, they involve burning images that seem to speak for themselves but are spoken for by Moore into the eyes/souls of movie-goers.

Caught between Moore's utopian ideal and his dystopian tactics is Lila Lipscomb. Lipscomb might be read not only as a good, everyday American with a story Moore must bring to the US public—a story that, incidentally, Moore discovered after it was made public in the US news magazine *Newsweek* (Brockes, 2004)—but as Moore's means toward achieving his own ends. For this most domestic of domestic US figures, the grieving mother of a soldierly son, speaking her mind to a President of the United States who refuses to listen, symbolizes the unruly homefront who, in attempting to secure home/nation, is in perfect opposition to the Bush administration's war in Iraq. As such, Lipscomb (like the women of *Minority Report*) challenges the past WWII function of the feminine as a docile US homefront/woman who needs protecting and as the stage from which the projection of US patriarchal power into the world is made possible.

Lipscomb is well aware that she is voicing homefront opposition to Bush's war in Iraq. What she may be less aware of is that, by doing so in a Michael Moore film, her very personal *I/me* is translated into Michael Moore's specific US *we*. Yes, Lipscomb is working class; yes, she is a mother in a mixed-race family; but that does not mean that she supports the many things that Moore's US *we* embodies. The only content to her opposition to Bush's war in Iraq is her son's objections to that war and his untimely death. She makes no argument about oil pipelines or Bush–Saudi ties or stolen elections or the overzealous Patriot Act coupled with the failures of homeland security. However, by functioning as the moral center of Moore's film—as "what the film is about"—Lipscomb is fused with all of this and more/Moore. Indeed, there are two things that theater goers regularly recall after seeing *Fahrenheit 9/11*: those seven minutes when Bush read *My Pet Goat* and Lila Lipscomb. There is no connection between these two images except the connection Moore makes between them.

In speaking against one patriarchal projection of power, Lipscomb seems condemned to speak for/as another, for within the frames of

Moore's film, speaking against Bush's project means speaking for Moore's project. And though the masculinities that inform them could not be more different (Bush's Wild West cowboy versus Michael Moore's working-class, racially sensitive new-age guy), how they authoritatively speak for the domestic (be it state or mother) suggests that they are both patriarchal, even while they embody strikingly different political projects.

When articulated outside the frames of Moore's film, Lipscombs' project sounds altogether different from Moore's. In an interview with *Guardian* newspaper reporter Emma Brockes, what Lipscomb conveys is her loss of certainty in the idea that "the government knew best" about Iraq, and that has made her question all authority. As Brockes reports, "Now, instead of telling them to trust authority, Lipscomb is raising her seven grandchildren to question it. 'I tell them: If you don't understand something, ask. And if you still don't understand it, go to the next level. And the next. And the next'" (Brockes, 2004). Lipscomb, then, is asking Americans to think. Moore, in contrast, seems only to be asking Americans to see and, because of the way in which images function in a Michael Moore film, "seeing" may not mean "thinking" at all, unless it is about letting a morally certain Moore think for "us."

By seeming to swap his *I* for Lipscomb's eyes, Moore does succeed in powerfully reconsidering the post-9/11 US relationship between justice and security, and that, it has to be said, cannot be dismissed lightly. This might be among the reasons why at the end of his ambivalent review of *Fahrenheit 9/11*, David Edelstein concludes that the film is "an act of counterpropaganda that has a boorish bullying force. It is, all in all, a legitimate abuse of power" (Edelstein, 2004). However, I wonder whether this supposed swap ever takes place, for how Moore uses Lipscomb in *Fahrenheit 9/11* is not to mouth the extremely complex and varied moral objections many Americans have to Bush administration's security policies but as a mask for his own morally certain opposition to the moral certainty of the Bush administration. In *Fahrenheit 9/11*, then, Moore seems to perform the very same gesture on Lila Lipscomb that the Marks's young son performed on Abraham Lincoln in the opening sequence to *Minority Report*: he pokes her eyes out and replaces them with his own. There is an eye swap here, but it is not Moore's for Lipscomb's (as it appears to be) but Lipscomb's for Moore's.

Ultimately, what this means is that Lila Lipscomb's dual feminine roles in *Fahrenheit 9/11* may have contributed to containing the policies of the US state and undermining the credibility (if not the re-election) of the administration of the US President. However, they failed to contain Moore, to bring him back from the brink of his vigilante journalism. Instead, it is Lila Lipscomb who was contained and, in containing her, what was also contained was the possibility to re-envision the post-9/11 relationship between justice and security in anything other than the morally certain terms shared by both Bush and Moore: "us"/good versus "them"/bad.

All this leads me to conclude that Moore's abuse of power is not legitimate. Moore's cooption of the face of Lila Lipscomb as his own *I* is surely not the moral act it purports to be. It could not be more different from what Moore's film suggests it is: a swapping of Moore's eyes for those of Lipscomb. Nor does Moore do what Anderton does in *Minority Report*: retain one old eye of his own and combine it with one new eye (that of Lipscomb). All "eyes/*I*'s" in *Fahrenheit 9/11* belong to Michael Moore, and that's a shame for, in spite of all the potential to explore different oppositional perspectives in this film, Moore never sees things differently, whether these things are US policies or US administrations or moral dichotomies. All he insistently asks, indeed demands, is that *we* see things differently by seeing through his eyes/*I* and his pictures.

While Lipscomb's "eyes/*I*" is always co-opted and framed by Michael Moore, there is another *I* that the *Fahrenheit 9/11* cannot contain: the *I* suggested by its title. Turning the eyes/*I* of Ray Bradbury back onto the *I* of Michael Moore, Bradbury would surely see in *Fahrenheit 9/11* many of the things he warned America(ns) about in his novel *Fahrenheit 451*.

## Who we might become

Considered together, what do *Minority Report* and *Fahrenheit 9/11* tell America(ns) about who we might become?

By drawing a rather devastating picture of who *we have* become in the Bush administration's war on terror, both films warn us that justice and security both in the United States and as it is projected by the United States abroad are dangerously out of balance. Who we might become and, indeed, who we must become, is a nation willing to get this balance right.

How *we* can do that is first by reconsidering the relationship between crime and consciousness. It is not possible, *Minority Report* tells us, to police the unconscious by drawing an equivalence between thinking about doing something bad and actually doing something bad. No matter how many times *we* might be right in our suspicions, preemptive justice is unjust if *we* are wrong even once. What this means is that while both Lincoln and Bush for a time had the extralegal authority to suspend the individual civil rights of suspected, would-be criminals, neither of them had the moral authority to do so, however well intentioned they may have been.

*Fahrenheit 9/11* is more scathing about President Bush's lack of moral authority, criticizing the President not only for the Bush Doctrine of Preemption but for everything from his dubious "election" as president through his handling of 9/11 and his wars in Afghanistan and Iraq. There is no question that the President is acting immorally, according to Moore for, in Moore's moral economy, America's elite have no moral purchase on goodness. So Moore spreads the word by raising *our* consciousness about the criminality of our elite leaders.

Whether articulated as a failure of the system or a failure of a political/ economic class, both films ultimately make a similar point: that *we* chose badly when *we* chose either a system (PreCrime) or a leader (Bush) who believed more in security than in justice. However, as *Minority Report* tells us, *we* can choose, and as *Fahrenheit 9/11* suggests, if the first four years of the Bush administration were a prevision of what is to come, then because *we* already know/knew our future, *we* are/were not condemned to repeat it. The choice is/was *ours*. The trajectory for becoming a moral America(n) lies in choosing to live with increased physical insecurity if that means living with increased justice. By making this choice, future stories about who we might become can sustain a positive image of *us* as moral America(ns) in ways we failed to sustain in *our* present stories about who we really are.

But at what cost?

As articulated in *Minority Report* and *Fahrenheit 9/11*, there are serious constraints on "our" moral choices because there are serious constraints on who this *we* is. Not only does Moore's US *we* preclude the consideration of elite Americans as moral Americans (which is a huge generalization); both *Minority Report* and *Fahrenheit 9/11* in one way or another also constrain the feminine. While the feminine is depicted as intelligent, innovative, and active, it is also always somehow domesticated. This occurs in *Minority Report* by resorting to feminine stereotypes that construct Iris, Agatha, and Laura as an unruly US homefront, and it occurs in *Fahrenheit 9/11* by Moore's framing, editing, and narrating of Lila Lipscomb's particular story to that point that her morally uncertain *us* morphs into Moore's morally certain dichotomy of the morally good *us* confronting the morally bad *them*.

It is surely a step forward that these films reactivate the feminine rather than erase it (as in *Behind Enemy Lines* and *Black Hawk Down*) or discredit it (as in *Collateral Damage* and *In the Bedroom*), but how these two futuristic films reactivate the feminine is utterly problematic.

Their reactivation is never an end in itself; it is always a means toward re-enabling masculine authority in the name of re-establishing justice: to allow John Anderton to finally figure things out so he can save *us* from the system of PreCrime or Michael Moore to sound sincere so he can save *us* from the Bush administration.

By mixing the domesticated feminine who secures the US home-(front) with the public feminine who destabilizes the US state, *Minority Report* does succeed in curbing the vigilante impulses of its male hero. However, this same mixture of home(front) security and state insecurity does not have the same effect in *Fahrenheit 9/11*. Unlike in *Minority Report*, where this mixed feminine symbolically stands for Anderton's "eye of the past" mixed with his "eye of the future" (*our* passive feminine WWII past with *our* active feminine future), the only mixing we have in *Fahrenheit 9/11* is a "mixing up" of Moore with Lipscomb but never a change in vision. Having said this, however, I would still argue that because both films contain the feminine within a domestic space, they constrain how the feminine functions in terms of political resistance, for the political resistance of the feminine must always be activated by and seen through (at least one eye) of the masculine, the figure who ultimately rules the home(land).

Agatha's treatment by Anderton in *Minority Report* and Lila Lipscomb's treatment by Michael Moore in *Fahrenheit 9/11* serve as cinematic examples of contained political resistance; Colin Powell's treatment by the Bush administration serves as our example of contained political resistance in US foreign policy. This is most evidence when we position Powell as a sort of "precog." Reading the script of *Minority Report* onto the Bush administration's war on terror, we find three precogs in Bush's first term: the always-in-agreement twins, Secretary of Defense Donald Rumsfeld and Deputy Secretary of Defense Paul Wolfowitz, and the often-dissenting Secretary of State Colin Powell. It is Powell who holds the minority report on the Bush administration, not (only) because of his overcoded minority status as both an American racial minority and as an intelligent and innovative thinker but because he has consistently been located in the outsider, feminized position in that administration. First overruled when trying to build more genuine international support and a worldwide coalition against al Qaeda in the run up to the bombing of Afghanistan and then, in the run up to Gulf War II, forced to recant his assessment that Saddam Hussein had no weapons of mass destruction that could pose a threat to the United States, Powell's minority report has always been firmly contained/constrained/domesticated by the hegemonic narrative of the Bush administration...and we can all see where that has gotten us.

The case of Colin Powell is but one example, but the general point here is clear: what this means is that as long as the feminine is domesticated, it is not a reliable foundation for political resistance. This does not mean that the maternal cannot be a ground for moral political action; it means that, in claiming this feminine as such, *we* had better carefully examine how this claim is made and what this claim does. It also means that, as it is stereotypically portrayed in post-9/11 cinema, the maternal is not the only moral basis for becoming a moral America(n). Yes, these films tell us, *we* ought to see what the feminine is showing us, but maybe *we* can achieve a more moral vision of the post-9/11 world not only by looking at/as mothers. Maybe *we* can break out of the domestic altogether.

# 7 Conclusion

Having traced the transformations of the US *we* at the intersections of post-9/11 cinema and US foreign policy from past to present to future, is it now any easier to answer the question, "What does it mean to be a moral America(n), and how might we act morally in the post-9/11 era?" Because so many US *we*'s and the moral grammars of war they ground have been uncovered, the answer to this question is surely yes but, for this very same reason, because the US *we* has been so radically pluralized, the answer is also surely no. How do we know which one of these US *we*'s we ought to be, and how do we know which of them ought to ground what we ought to do?

To begin to figure all this out, it makes sense to take stock of each of the US *we*'s and the various US moral grammars of war that they render possible. So, who were *we*, who are *we*, and who will *we* be?

Who we think we were is a usually white, happy, heterosexual nuclear family. This is the US *we* that emerged from WWII; this is who we fought for. Thanks to this US *we* as the foundation of what it means to be a moral America(n), we knew exactly what it took to secure our postwar future. All we had to do was repeat what we had done during WWII: emasculate our hypermasculine/hypersexual foreign enemy and afterward oversee his moral maturation. Further, if he were incapable of maturing morally, it was not just our right but our duty to kill him. In so doing, we not only stamped US patriarchal authority onto the wider world; we secured our feminized homefront.

This foundational modern morality tale of who we think we were not only informs us about the past; it is also a gold mine for us in the morally bewildering present. So, it is no surprise that, in the wake of September 11, 2001, official US discourse drew a parallel between the events of 9/11 and Pearl Harbor. However, as noted in the discussion of "Attack on America," this WWII moral grammar of war created more problems than solutions. Yes, it made us feel good about ourselves but, aside from that, it did not enable us successfully to counter the enemy: in the 9/11 discourse of Attack on America, there are no clear enemies, no clear homefronts, no clear families, much less genders and sexualities, and no clear boundaries between any two terms. This led not only to strategic insecurity but to moral confusion, with bad guys/bad practices located where we would expect to find good guys/good practices, and vice versa.

Without ever fully giving up on the WWII moral grammar of war to understand the events of 9/11 and what America's moral response to it ought to be, officially and unofficially we recovered other US *we*'s to help to sort out the moral dilemmas we faced in the aftermath of 9/11.

Just as it was worth reminding ourselves of who we think we were/ are, it was important to remind ourselves of who we wish we'd never been. Officially, who we wish we'd never been is a nation who shunned its Vietnam War soldiers, even though they acted with so much professionalism and moral certainty that they might well express "what family ought to be" (as Hal Moore puts it in *We Were Soldiers*). But, of course, this brotherhood of Christian soldiers that Hal Moore hoped to see in his soldiers is not at all how the US family really appeared during the Vietnam War era, nor did the US family appear this way during WWII. Instead, the Vietnam War era US family was epitomized by its failing fathers: fathers who, however much they tried to, could not guarantee that their soldierly sons would inherit their moral certainties of WWII. Unofficially, as in the film *The Quiet American*, the Vietnam War reminds us that there is more we should wish we'd never been: government professionals so blinded by our own moral certainty that we crossed the line between do-gooders (fighting for freedom and democracy) and evil-doers (terrorists).

Remembering our shameful past (this haunting moral grammar of war) reminds us of what it takes to become a moral America(n). Officially, it is about making peace with our Vietnam-era ghosts by supporting our troops as they fight the war on terror; this is the morally right thing to do. Unofficially, it is about recognizing that we should never make peace with these very same ghosts for, if we do, they go quiet. And as we learned through both CIA practices in Vietnam and failed intelligence practices and their uses in the run up to Gulf War II, the quieter the ghost/spy, the more morally dangerous it is for us.

Even as our Vietnam era-past morally disquiets us, that does not mean that it expresses who we really are, for all that took place during the Cold War, when arguably both superpowers made a lot of moral mistakes. In a one-superpower world in which the United States is the only superpower, we have both the opportunity and responsibility to act not only for ourselves but for everyone. This means embracing the 1990s Western agenda of support for humanitarianism, even when it requires military intervention. This is precisely what our US soldierly sons did.

What we learned during our 1990s interventions as depicted in *Behind Enemy Lines* and *Black Hawk Down* is that it is always right to rescue the other, especially the feminized (and often Orientalized) other of Bush's *Kandahar* who is not capable of completely rescuing herself, as long as we exercise moral leadership for a just cause. And there is no higher moral cause than the prevention of genocide. Combining these lessons, we learned that the prevention of genocide is too important a task to be left to such multinational institutions as NATO and the UN. Never mind that the United States failed to intervene in some humanitarian crises (Rwanda being the most striking 1990s example); we'd rather look to our (imagined) remembered successes in the former Yugoslavia and our military failure but moral success in Somalia, where we performed as "reluctant heroes." As long as we can apply these principles in the new war on terror, we can rescue both the Afghan and the Iraqi people and see them safely to democracy and freedom. This is what it takes to make a moral difference in the post-9/11 era. This is our humanitarian moral grammar of war.

Of course, that is not the only aspect to who we really are, for what we learned from Makhmalbaf's *Kandahar* is that the feminine is not always as willing an object of rescue as we make her out to be. We surely should have remembered this from the Vietnam War and, if we need reminding, we can look to post-9/11 United States-occupied Iraq. What all this suggests is that if the feminine did not want our help—if we were not actually rescuing the feminine—maybe we were only rescuing ourselves. If that is the case, our evocation of a humanitarian moral grammar of war may be both self-referential (we only ever rescue the US humanitarian *we*) and hypocritical (our rescue missions occasionally lead to grossly immoral acts, such as the torture of Iraqi prisoners at Abu Ghraib prison).

So we turned to another US inflection of who we really are: vigilantes who take justice into our own hands. In this vigilante moral grammar of war, we are fathers (and sometimes mothers) who are suffering unbearable grief in the face of the traumatic loss of how we thought the future would appear, whether that is expressed through the loss of a son or the loss of a pre-9/11 vision of new millennial America. Thus, we forthrightly state that we are not interested in rescuing anyone other than ourselves; all we care about is getting payback. That is how we define moral justice in the films *Collateral Damage* and *In the Bedroom*.

In so doing, we have no need to rescue the feminine, not because it may well not need us or want us to rescue it but because, in this vigilante moral grammar of war, it is the (this time maternal) feminine who is the source of moral mistakes. Why would we want to rescue her? This, of course, does not mean that the feminine plays no role in this US vigilante moral grammar of war. Whether located within the United States (as the domestic homefront) or beyond it (as a foreign alien), the feminine is always cast as a morally malicious mother, whose meddling with US fathers produces murderous effects.

Though it might be tempting to embrace this vigilante moral grammar of war (fathers good/mothers bad) because it is both so simplistic and, it has to be said, so familiar, that does not mean that it is just. Causing either the masculine or the feminine to take all the blame for moral mistakes is not only silly; it is dangerous. For it binds us into an us-versus-them kind of moral logic that does not describe the world in which we live nor help us to think about how to act as a moral America(n) in the post-9/11 era. Further, it leaves completely out of balance the relationship between justice and security. Yes, it recognizes that the feminine, whether as foreigner or as US homefront, can create security and insecurity in the United States simultaneously, but might these abilities of the US homefront be put to better use? Might in their attempts to secure the home these mothers also destabilize illegitimate state policies and practices being used once again to reestablish us-versus-them dichotomies?

This is precisely how the feminine functions in America's future stories about who we might become as portrayed in the films *Minority Report* and *Fahrenheit 9/11*. By first locating the eccentric/infantilized/reproductive feminine of *Minority Report* and the economically or racially oppressed feminine of *Fahrenheit 9/11* firmly within the US home, and then mobilizing its disruptive potential to secure the home(land) by destabilizing unjust US state policies (e.g., the Bush Doctrine of Preemption), the feminine emerges in this final inflection of who we might become as itself heroic, even though its heroism is always in the service of supporting the masculine hero. In this futuristic US moral grammar of war, who we might become, then, is a nation that rebalances the relationship between justice and security, that chooses to live with increased physical insecurity if that results in increased moral security, by utilizing the disruptive potential of the stereotypical feminine to question bad state policies and practices while utilizing its stabilizing potential to secure the US home(land). That goes a long way toward deconstructing the Bush administration's us-versus-them logic of the war on terror, both between good/supportive Americans and bad/unsupportive Americans and between good America(ns) and bad (suspected) terrorists.

This genealogy of the US *we* and the US moral grammars of war tells us many things. First, it demonstrates not only that there are multiple official and unofficial US *we*'s and multiple official and unofficial US moral grammars of war both between historical periods and within them. Read together, they do not represent some mutually agreed-on, composite US *we* or US moral grammar of war but an array of complex, contradictory moral characters in competition for star billing as moral America(n). Reducing the US *we* to any one of its momentary, highly contested inflections, then, is to impose a unity—and a moral clarity—on the morally fragmented US *we*. Yet, this reduction occurs all the time: this is who we are in Bush administration rhetoric on the war on terror; this is who we are in Michael Moore's equally morally certain tale that opposes this official story; and this is very often who we are to the rest of the world (a world we all too often reduce to an equally uncomplicated *them*; see Sardar and Davies, 2002). This is all very easy and provides us with moral certainty, but it is not necessarily moral itself.

The second thing that this genealogy demonstrates is how the possibilities and limitations of each of these US *we*'s and their moral grammars of war come into relief when considered through gender and sexuality and through film and family. What my insistence on reading these US *we*'s and moral grammars of war through the intersecting texts of post-9/11 cinema and official US foreign policy discourse does is to draw out the various ways in which the US family romance plays itself out popularly and politically by articulating what it means to be a post-9/11 moral America(n). In so doing, it shows how the moral history of the US character is constructed in the moral movements not only within and among the imagined character(s) of the gendered and sexualized family and nation but in their complex relationships between the "real" and the "reel."

Having considered all these US *we*'s and their resulting moral grammars of war and along the way dispelling the myth of some unified moral America(n), I am left wondering whether any of them individually articulates a US *we* that we would like to be(come). Every official US *we* fails to represent either US history or the US family in anything close to the forms they actually took. Let us consider the historical US *we*. That US *we* may have acted heroically during WWII, but this was a belated and partial heroism, for the United States entered WWII well after its long-suffering European allies asked it to. And in the meantime, the United States (like the majority of its allies) turned a blind eye to the Nazi treatment of Jews to the point that the United States repeatedly delayed increasing its quota on European Jewish immigrants. Instead, the United States finally entered WWII only after it was attacked by the Japanese, and how the United States won the war was by becoming the only nation in history to ever drop a nuclear bomb on its enemy.[1]

Not only is the US official memory of WWII history conveniently sketchy; so, too, is the US official history in Vietnam, Bosnia, Somalia, Afghanistan, Colombia, and Iraq, all the foreign locations that star in post-9/11 US cinema. In some respects, this is to be expected, for most of these post-9/11 films are fictions that play on/with facts but do not claim to represent them accurately. However, in other ways, this is terribly troubling when we consider how popular cinema is conflated with US foreign policy, not only to remember the present as past (by re-releasing *Pearl Harbor* after 9/11 as parallels were officially drawn between 9/11 and WWII) but to justify going to war in the present (as in Bush's use of *Kandahar*). What is more, the history of some US wars is forgotten altogether. No one of whom I know made a post-9/11 film about the ongoing Korean Conflict, which would have reminded us of the unfinished post-9/11 disputes between North Korea and the West regarding North Korea's very real development of nuclear capabilities. And the only popular US film about Gulf War I is the 1999 film *Three Kings*, a film that implies that it was largely the US betrayal of the repressed Iraqi people that rendered necessary not only years of sanctions against Saddam Hussein's government but Gulf War II.

Aligned against these partial, official memories of US history, of course, are other histories. *The Quiet American* disturbs US official stories about the Vietnam War; Makhmalbaf's *Kandahar* questions all foreign interventions into Afghanistan (including US involvements decades earlier); and *Fahrenheit 9/11* claims to set the record straight on the Bush administration and on Bush's wars. In the spirit of further complicating the official US story, even *Three Kings* (preceded by its director David O. Russell's new documentary about Gulf War II) was given a theatrical re-release in US cinemas in the Fall of 2004 (Waxman, 2004).

Though this is surely encouraging, there are several problems with how these films complicate official US history. For example, none of these films was distributed to anything like the number of screens as films that supported the official US story. We know of the distribution disputes about *The Quiet American* and *Fahrenheit 9/11*, but also a film such as *Kandahar* found a more substantial audience in the United States (and the United Kingdom) only once it was co-opted by the Bush (and Blair) administrations to support its war on terror by liberating

Afghan women. So, this leads to a second problem: that unofficial US histories are all too easily co-opted by the official US story. Though this sort of co-option is not always possible (as Michael Moore's *Fahrenheit 9/11* demonstrates), that does not mean that a film will not run into other problems. In the case of *Fahrenheit 9/11*, Moore's disregard for anything approaching a balanced account of US politics over the first four years of the Bush presidency and his complete lack of analysis of al Qaeda's rhetoric of evil and hate (which parallels while opposing that of the Bush administration; see Agathangelou and Ling, 2004) led to heavy criticism of the film by both the right and the left. And even the re-release of *Three Kings* and Russell's accompanying documentary about Gulf War II function only as qualifiedly critical retrospectives that do not ultimately oppose the official US story. For *Three Kings* does not question US intervention in Gulf War I, only the fact that we did not finish our humanitarian mission, something that comes through in Russell's Gulf War II documentary.

All these are predictable problems for films that in any way contest official US history. What for me is even more lamentable is how these very films that question official US history so often support another official US story, the one grounded in a family romance based on stereotypical relations of gender and sexuality. This is particularly evident when we consider how all these films— whether official or officially opposed—represent the feminine.

The moral character of the feminine in all these films is extremely varied. It appears as the morally neutral stage on which masculine struggles for power work themselves out and from which masculine power is projected: internationally (WWII's *Pearl Harbor*); the morally supportive wife and mother (Vietnam's *We Were Soldiers*); the morally ambiguous concubine (Vietnam's *The Quiet American*); the morally good but struggling separated sister (the contemporary *Kandahar*); the malicious meddling mother (the contemporary *Collateral Damage* and *In the Bedroom*); the moral source of just opposition to state policies and practices (the futuristic *Minority Report* and *Fahrenheit 9/11*); or as an absence altogether (in 1990s *Behind Enemy Lines* and *Black Hawk Down*).

Yet, in spite of these different moral inflections of the feminine, all these films (save one) position the feminine in exactly the same place: the heterosexual home(land). In every case but that one, the feminine functions as the girl back home or the supportive or meddling mother or the sister attempting to reassemble her home by saving her sister. What this means is that the feminine is always domestic and domesticated in official and unofficial stories about who we think we were/

are, who we wish we'd never been, who we really are, and who we might become. This holds true even in those films in which the feminine is cast as an absence, as in *Behind Enemy Lines* and *Black Hawk Down*, for in these films about soldierly sons, we all know that the feminine is off-screen because she is back home.

There is only one post-9/11 film discussed here—*The Quiet American* —that does not (successfully) domesticate the feminine. Indeed, *The Quiet American* does not offer any functional families/domestics/nations with which we can positively identify. However, when we remember that it was not the controversy-courting *Fahrenheit 9/11* but the far more subtle *The Quiet American* that struggled to be screened in the United States after 9/11 and that this film was among the least viewed of the post-9/11 films discussed here, *The Quiet American* very much seems to be the exception (and the exception we almost did not see) that proves the rule. Yet, it is only the exception with respect to home-(fronts) but not with respect to heterosexuality; even though the feminine in *The Quiet American* spills over and around the boundaries of home(land), like the rest of these films it is always firmly heterosexual. As such, the film still announces that there are clear boundaries around moral practice, suggesting that this line is always drawn at same(-sex) relationships.

It is for this reason, because the US *we* is almost always premised on a feminine that is domesticated in a heterosexual nuclear family, that I wonder whether any of these US *we*'s and the moral grammars of war they enable are worth embracing. I raise this concern not only because all these stories about the feminine and the past, present, and future families it enables express the way we never were, to borrow Stephanie Coontz's phrase (2000). I do so because grounding our national stories about who we think we were/are, who we wish we'd never been, who we really are, and who we might become on this domesticated heterosexual feminine expresses a fundamental limit on how we might rethink morality, both domestically and internationally. And this has already had consequences for how we have acted as moral America(ns) in the post-9/11 era.

For example, even though (as discussed at length in Chapter 2) the 9/11 Attack on America was launched by an international terrorist network of mostly free-floating cells with no traditional homefront, President Bush almost immediately equated fighting the war on terror with fighting particular states in the new axis of evil. This enabled the United States to bomb Afghanistan and disrupt terrorist training camps there, but this did not enable the United States to achieve either of its other stated aims: to defend the US homefront by capturing Osama bin

Laden and to instill democratic freedoms in Afghanistan to be enjoyed by the Afghan people, especially its women.

By claiming that the war on terror was a fight between domestic sovereign nation-states, the Bush administration also drew a moral boundary around its war on terror, a boundary that prevented categorizing the 9/11 attacks as international criminal acts carried out by specific individuals in the name of a specific organization or cause (or both). As such, the United States would deal on its own terms with this situation and with those who rendered it possible. As we know, this eventually led the United States to declare some of those whom it captured in the Afghan War "enemy combatants" and to ship them to the US Naval Base at Guantanamo Bay's Camp X-Ray, to be held indefinitely without charge, without trial, and without the usual protections of the Geneva Convention. Those who *are* eventually charged and tried will face the justice of a US military tribunal, not a US criminal court (unless the US Supreme Court intervenes), because that is how the Bush administration has decided to deal with them.

Had the Bush administration not domesticated the war on terror, not drawn a boundary around terrorist acts and those who perpetrated them (thereby making the claim that the United States and the United States alone has the moral authority to "bring them to justice"), it still could have made its case for bombing al Qaeda training camps in Afghanistan in accordance with international law by claiming that these actions were taken in self-defense. It still could have made the case that the Taliban and al Qaeda were so mutually supportive of one another that both needed to be held responsible for the events of 9/11 and targeted militarily. And it still could have "brought to justice" prisoners in the resulting disputes.

Yet, paradoxically, if the Bush administration had *not* used the language of domestication to fight its so-called war on terror, the fight against terrorism might actually have been more certain, both politically and morally. US military actions in Afghanistan could have targeted not a state and its citizens but specific individuals and activities, a move that could have spared the lives and livelihoods of many Afghan civilians and rendered postconflict reconstruction more effective. Those brought to justice could have appeared before the International Criminal Court and benefited from international treaties regarding the humane treatment of prisoners in custody. Further, however much linking the Taliban and al Qaeda may have been justified in the case of Afghanistan, had the sweeping policy of linking terrorists to states not existed, this policy could not have served as a precedent to help to justify Gulf War

II, a war that had no proven link to al Qaeda before it was fought but, since its execution, has turned Iraq into another al Qaeda cause.

None of this would have necessarily resulted in the capture of Osama bin Laden but, in the case of bin Laden, a figure who defies traditional US rhetoric of the enemy, especially one contained in a foreign domestic space or containable within a traditional reading of gender and (hetero)sexuality, it is hard to see how the Bush administration strategy of domestication in its war on terror was ever appropriate for this goal anyway. With bin Laden cast as the metaphorically queerest figure in contemporary foreign affairs, it at first seems to be utterly ironic that the Bush administration (which supports a constitutional amendment banning same-sex marriages and regards all queers and queer practices as immoral) would have attempted to place bin Laden within any home(land). However, of course, when considered again, this strategy is completely consistent with the Bush administration's official morality, for it is only by placing bin Laden firmly in someone else's home(land), Taliban-run Afghanistan, that it could once again draw the moral boundary of heterosexuality (the basis of the traditional US family) around the US home(land). Then again, as al Qaeda's infiltration of the US home(land), materially on 9/11 and psychologically ever since, illustrates, all that was merely wishful thinking on the part of the Bush administration. And none of it helped the United States to achieve its stated goals of protecting the US homefront, much less doing anything like what it promised to do for the Afghan and (later) Iraqi people.

Instead, what the Bush administration's strategy of declaring war on an emotion/terror (as much as on the individuals and states who caused Americans to feel this emotion) did was two things. First, it rendered many Americans more afraid. They feared not only the world beyond their borders but, through hype by everchanging color-coded homeland security alerts, they feared their everyday worlds (Weber and Lacy, 2004; Masumi, 2004). As David Fincher's *Panic Room* (2002) so aptly illustrated, like the US treasury bonds sought by the intruders into Jody Foster's home-based panic room, what destabilizes the United States always seems to be located in the very heart of the home(land) and in its unsecurable (heterosexual) familial relationships (see Chazan, 2003). Second, the Bush administration's war on terror scared many outside of the United States, not necessarily terrorists and not only civilians in Afghanistan and Iraq or in the Arab world more generally but America's traditional European allies. For example, by November 2002, a poll suggested that one-third of Britons believed that President George W. Bush—not Osama bin Laden or Saddam Hussein—was the greater threat to world peace (Wisdom Fund, 2002).

In view of all this, why did the Bush administration declare war on terror? Further, why did it insist on drawing a political and moral domestic, heterosexual boundary around its war on terror? Let me suggest three answers to this question.

One answer is that this was the easiest thing to do. By declaring war on terror and in the same breath geopolitically situating terror within specific sovereign nation-states, the Bush administration constructed a very simple and very clear us-versus-them moral and spatial dichotomy. Osama bin Ladin, the Taliban, and Saddam Hussein were all bad to the point of being morally irredeemable, and all were out to get America and Americans. So, the war on terror was really a war of self-defense, and wars of self-defense are morally just wars (Falk, 2001a and 2001b).[2] This is how the Bush administration's argument works morally, and its moral simplicity is attributable to its spatial simplicity: the moral US *we* is located within the US homeland and the bad (would be) terrorists and their supporters are located outside the US homeland.[3] This means that the US targeting of Afghanistan and later Iraq is both morally justified and geopolitically neat, requiring none of the worries about located terrorists and terrorist targets discussed in Chapter 2. And, of course, by targeting Afghanistan and Iraq, the Bush administration appeared to be acting decisively, even when many have consistently argued that the roots of anti-Americanism that fueled attacks on US targets before, on, and after 9/11 are to be found in the unresolved Israeli–Palestinian conflict, a conflict that the Bush administration's war on terror has further fueled.

A second answer is that the Bush administration's boundary around its war on terror allowed it to claim that what it was fighting, terror/ fear, was located primarily outside the United States and what it was fighting for, security/freedom from fear, was located within the US homeland. That is why the Bush administration needed to create the Department of Homeland Security: to keep Americans safe. However, in keeping them safe, Homeland Security also kept them afraid. Indeed, the Bush administration consistently repeats two claims to the American people: the world is a very scary place (be afraid), and President Bush is making the world a safer place (we are winning the war on terror/ securing the US homefront). In addition to scaring many Americans, this contradictory message offered the American people the problem (the war on terror; the Bush presidency) as the only solution to that very problem. This was a powerful message, one that of course played badly abroad but one that the Republican Party at least believed was playing well enough domestically to make it the cornerstone of their successful re-election platform for candidate Bush in 2004.

A third answer to the question of why the Bush administration drew this specific political and moral boundary around its war on terror is that had it *not* done so, it would have had to acknowledge the authority of international law in matters pertaining to terrorism specifically and to warfare more generally. This would have meant that the Bush administration would have had to acknowledge the authority of the International Criminal Court of Justice, the jurisdiction of which over US states people, soldiers, and citizens the United States has consistently denied. Had the United States not domesticated its war on terror morally and politically, likely those US soldiers tried before US military tribunals for torturing Iraqi prisons during Gulf War II would have found themselves answering to the International Criminal Court as well. Further, there would have been nothing to stop some states from calling for the prosecution of President Bush along with UK Prime Minister Blair for their uses of faulty intelligence as one of their primary justifications for Gulf War II. What is unknowable is whether anyone, from suspected al Qaeda terrorists to presidents to prime ministers, would have been charged or convicted by international courts, but it would have made a lot of moral difference to how the war on terror is being fought if US accountability were not so insistently self-referential (e.g., we believe we are doing the morally right thing, so we are moral).

What all this means is that, in the way in which the Bush administration has chosen to fight its war on terror, a strategy of domestication based on traditional understandings of gender and sexuality makes good *political* sense because it is politically safe. It just does not necessarily make good *moral* sense (not to mention, good military or strategic sense), and that may go some way to answering the question many Americans have been asking themselves since 9/11: Why do they hate us? One answer is surely that even though President George W. Bush has been described as America's "most prominent moralist" (Singer, 2004), being a moralist and acting morally are not necessarily the same thing (also see Sardar and Davies, 2002). Additionally, the more the US public supports its now re-elected president, the more confused (or merely cynical) the rest of the world seems to be about the moral claims the United States continues to make in the name of its moral America(ns).

Of course, it is worth remembering that many Americans do not support their president; indeed, many argue that George W. Bush was never elected president but was merely appointed to the post by the US Supreme Court the first time and "stole" the vote in Ohio the second time. Even before he became president, then, George W. Bush faced enormous opposition by a substantial number of US citizens. That opposition is not only about Bush's "election" as president but about how he has conducted the US war on terror. Though there was significant but only small-scale US opposition to Bush's war in Afghanistan, there was substantial US opposition to his war in Iraq. By the time Bush campaigned for his second term, the protests in New York City, the cite of the Republican National Convention, were so considerable that they were being compared to the infamous anti-Vietnam protests at the Democratic National Convention in Chicago in 1968.

Even so, the answer to America's moral dilemma about how to become a moral America(n) never could be (and ultimately was not) as simple as Michael Moore made it out to be: vote George W. Bush out of the White House. Bush comes by his morality honestly, for it is embedded in US history and certainly in US foreign policy, dating back to at least President Woodrow Wilson, our president before and during WWI. Further, as I have tried to point out, this American morality is found not only in our official foreign policy; it saturates our everyday lives through popular culture and our popular representations of gender and sexuality. Though it might have been inflected more multilaterally had John Kerry been elected president, there is no reason to believe a change in American's president would have been the only thing necessary to change American morality. Indeed, if exit polls are to be believed, President Bush was re-elected to the US presidency not in spite of his moral views but *because of them*, because they were the same views held by so many (mostly rural) Americans.

So what should we do? How might we become (differently) moral America(ns)?

Should we try to be a better nation? The easy answer is "of course," but many of the problems noted here about traditional strategies of domestication and claims to moral certainty stem from discourses of nationalism, which are always primarily discourses of home. They are embedded in the very stories we tell ourselves to distinguish ourselves and our goodness from "them" and to mark out our private space from theirs. As such, these stories and the moral dilemmas they create are by no means unique to the US *we*. Nevertheless, recourse to nationally based, traditionally home-based discourses are hardly going to solve America's moral problems.

Should we seek moral clarity elsewhere, say, beyond the bounds of the home and the nation-state? Again, the easy answer is yes, but where would we look? Looking beyond the bounds of the nation-state does not mean we will not reinvent "home" or our identity in something just as dangerous, as in Samuel Huntington's description of civilizations (Huntington, 1998). Also, we have to wonder whether moral clarity actually exists. If it does exist, how could we tell the difference between moral clarity and willful moral self-deception? Have we not ended up in the biggest moral messes when we were the most morally certain (think of Hal Moore's men being massacred in the Vietnam War film *We Were Soldiers* or Alden Pyle in *The Quiet American* or John Anderton when he worked for PreCrime). So, maybe moral clarity is not the answer either.

What if we admit our moral mistakes and embrace our moral inadequacies? Again, yes, but how would we ensure that this does not become just a sort of wallowing in our own self-pity and a very American (and masculine) strategy of controlling the conversation by turning it back on us, even if only to say, "We are bad."? That seems to be part of what occurs in Michael Moore's *Fahrenheit 9/11*, a film that heroizes its critic for being a critic, even when what he says and the means he uses to say it are not necessarily correct, fair, or morally justified. This suggests two more problems.

One problem is that the idea of celebrating our moral failures is as unbalanced as is our celebration of our moral successes. America and Americans are not all bad. The fractured, fragmented US *we* and the fractured, fragmented US citizens who compete to speak in its name may not even be mostly bad. Rather, particularly since the post-WWII US dominance of international politics, our successes, but mostly our failures, have been spectacular, playing like spectacles (and now acting as they should like specters that haunt us) in the global media.

The other problem is that in celebrating our moral failures, we again get the balance wrong by sometimes forgetting that both America's friends and America's foes make moral mistakes as well. US allies (like US citizens) have a moral responsibility to stand up to and oppose the United States when they believe its foreign policy actions are unjustified, even in the face of overwhelming US hegemonic power. Indeed, it is in these very resistances to US hegemony that that hegemony begins to erode.

Regardless of one's political views, all ought to recognize that however simplistically and one-sidedly official US discourse constructs al Qaeda members as "evil-doers" and however much one despises the Bush administration, this does not mean that al Qaeda and Osama bin Ladin have acted morally in world politics. Hating the United States and its president, then, is not a good reason to glorify US enemies, especially enemies whose recent acts and justifications for those acts are every bit as immoral as those of the Bush administration, if not far more so.

Those who need reminding of this point should not only consider international events before, on, and since 9/11 perpetrated by both bin Ladin and Bush; they should compare the terms in which each justifies their actions. If they do, what they will find is that Osama bin Ladin's discourse about Muslims struggling against infidels (Americans and Jews) is strikingly similar to that of President George W. Bush in its construction of "us"-(morally good)-versus-"them" (morally irredeemable) dichotomies (Agathangelou and Ling, 2004). Of course, the immorality of al Qaeda and Osama bin Ladin in no way excuses the Bush administration's immoral activities in its war on terror. What it does mean, though, is that (put in George W. Bush's terms) whether one is "with us or with the terrorists," neither by word nor by deed have either of these officially constructed sides succeeded in sustaining claims to the moral high ground. Because of that, merely reversing these good-versus-bad dichotomies in no way renders the world a more moral place or renders America(ns) any more moral.

So where does all this leave us? Maybe there is another option; maybe the best way to become a moral America(n) is to begin by recognizing that there is no such thing as a moral America(n). The term *moral America(n)* merely marks a place to which we may aspire but at which we will never arrive. This has as much to do with the impossibility of "being an identity" (of being a unified US *we* rather than a fragmented and always further fracturing US *we*) as it has to do with the impossibility of "being absolutely good." And this is as true for US citizens as it is for citizens of any state.

That does not mean that there is no such thing as morality, and it does not mean that the United States as the world's only superpower does not have a responsibility to take great care to try to get things right. Rather, it means that we will never get things altogether right, for the good and the bad change all the time and forever catch us out. The best we can do is two things: pay attention to what is going on (which, sadly, is one of our greatest weaknesses) and, in so doing, avoid being so blinded by our own moral aspirations and our own morality tales about these aspirations that we endlessly repeat our traditional moral mistakes.

It seems quite clear that the Bush administration did repeat America's traditional moral mistakes in its war on terror, and it did so by claiming to speak for a unified US *we* and then mobilizing this imagined character as the basis of its multifaceted moral grammar of war. As Mary Marshall Clark explains, "This dominant account portrayed a nation unified in grief; it allowed government officials to claim that there is a public consensus that September 11 was a turning point in the nation's history that has clear implications for national and foreign policy" (2002: 569). Then, of course, it allowed the Bush administration to spell out for the American people precisely what the US *we* ought to do at this particular turning point in history.

That is the official story but, quite as important, those who most directly experienced the events of September 11 reported very different reactions to that day. In her initial report of the September 11, 2001, Oral History Narrative and Memory Project, Clark noted:

> ...those interviewees who experienced the most direct and traumatic aspects of the disaster, through either proximity or loss, often feared that the violence they lived through would spark greater violence. Many whom we interviewed before October 7, 2001, the date of the first air strikes in Afghanistan, wanted publicly to record their reluctance to pinpoint the enemy in a way that would rationalize an invasion. They were particularly afraid not only of retaliation but of a technological war in which civilian populations might accidentally be attacked and falsely targeted. These statements rejected revenge as the only official response and revealed how the vulnerability of eyewitnesses and survivors translated into sympathy for other potential victims (Clark, 2002: 571).[4]

These statements remind us that the immediate aftermath of 9/11 was not marked by clarity and consensus as much as it was marked by "confusion about the origin and meaning of the attacks, which promoted a deep disquiet over the definition of the enemy in cultural as well as ideological terms" (Clark, 2002: 571) as well as a contesting of what patriotism now meant (Clark, 2002: 577). Clark reports, "We found that for most people prior assumptions about national identity and a collective sense of belonging were often not enhanced, but shaken, by September 11" (2002:577).

Clark reports that in this atmosphere of confusion, fear, and a shaken sense of national belonging, the "absence of comparisons and analogous historical experiences" to 9/11 meant that Americans had no tradition of oral culture to help them to understand and respond to the events of that day (2002: 575). This, I would argue, rendered all the more pernicious and, sadly, compelling not only traditional stories about the US *we* but the post-9/11 films through which this traditional US *we* is so often positively expressed. Indeed, Clark reports that interviewees considered a variety of filmic analogies to understand the events of that day, from *Titanic*, "drawing people's attention to the myth of invincibility" (2002: 576) to "apocalyptic imagery from films and movies, demonstrating the ways that many wrestled with questions of good and evil, life and death outside the frame of history as they had previously understood it" (2002: 577). Not understanding the times in which they were living and being increasingly bombarded with a fusion of popular and political discourses about 9/11 that equated it first with Pearl Harbor/*Pearl Harbor* and then other stories about US moral triumphs while shelving critically-self reflective films like *The Quiet American* just as it closed down critical self-reflection more generally, is it any wonder that many Americans took comfort in America's traditional morality tales after 9/11 and that the United States failed to achieve a "moral remaking" (Roseneil, 2001) of a kind expressed by the interviewees cited above?

As US citizens protested in the streets against the war in Iraq, they reopened debate, for far more of them now seemed to realize that America's traditional morality tales do not accord well with their post-9/11 realities. These stories do not describe "the enemy" or what it means to be a moral America(n) or what it means to act morally in the contemporary, post-9/11 world. This is the very reason why we ought to remember these stories about the US *we* and about US moral grammars of war. We should remember them not as "true" stories that describe who we think we were/are, who we wish we'd never been, who we really are, and who we might become. Rather, we ought to recall them as cautionary tales, tales that remind us of the dangers of collapsing "truth" with the *desire* that these stories were true, especially in an atmosphere of fear.

There is rarely security, or justice, or a just balance between them in any stories that confuse truth with desire. This might be the most moral thing worth remembering about our tales of moral America(ns).

# Notes

## 1 Introduction

1 Amy Sodaro to Cynthia Weber, New York City, February 5, 2003.
2 For more on how film functions ideologically, see Kuhn (1990) and Ryan and Kellner (1990).
3 Though it is becoming increasingly common to talk about the grammars that underlie and make meaningful everything from rhetoric to public policy, I know of no one else who uses the term *moral grammars of war*. I came up with this term while thinking about 9/11—especially through the analogy of Pearl Harbor—while reading Noam Chomski's work on grammar and syntax (1965) and Tom Bentley and Ian Hargreaves' post-9/11 considerations on the relationships between morality and ideology (2001).

## 2 Who we think we were/are

1 Chomsky's example is discussed in Elizabeth Wright's book *Speaking Desires Can be Dangerous*, which itself tropes off of Chomsky's illustration in its discussions and applications of psychoanalytic theory. See Wright (1999).
2 There is no unified notion of America or singular American imaginary. What interests me is how cultural self-representations of America—in popular film and in foreign policy rhetoric—produce and reproduce a hegemonic American national mythology of itself as if America were unified and singular. It is to this hegemonic mythology that the term *America* refers in this book.
3 *Pearl Harbor* was originally released in the United States on Memorial Day, 2001. It was generally re-released after September 11, when Americans flocked to cinemas in record numbers for that time of year. Though I do not have the figures on how many additional viewers saw the film at that time, it matters that the film was available for them to view and that the film was present in cinemas regardless of whether they saw it.
4 Throughout this chapter, I maintain a strict distinction between America's historical imaginary of Pearl Harbor and America's filmic imaginary of

that historical imaginary in the film *Pearl Harbor*, with the normal-font Pearl Harbor referring to the former and the italicized *Pearl Harbor* referring to the latter.

5   A good example comes from the case of Pearl Harbor and *Pearl Harbor* itself. History now popularly records Admiral Yamamoto's response to his attack on Pearl Harbor with the quotation, "I fear all we have done is to awaken a sleeping giant," a quotation repeated in the film *Pearl Harbor*. This, however, is not something the Admiral actually said after the attack; it is what his character was scripted to say in the film *Tora! Tora! Tora!* That Americans so readily confuse what the Admiral said with what his character says tells us something about the investment of a popular American imaginary about itself in relation to the events of Pearl Harbor, which is important to our understandings of both America and of how America politically and historically situates itself. For a general discussion of films and IR theory, see Weber (2005).

6   As will become clear, I focus on "the feminine" because of how it functions in post-9/11 cinema as the site at which morality stages its fights for certainty and uncertainty. That the location of the feminine is consistent in my reading of post-9/11 film does not mean that the identity of the feminine is consistent or stable in this reading. Rather, what the feminine is—how it is designated—varies widely not only in general cultural and political terms but practically within the pages of this text. For example, the feminine might refer to a cultural category, to a psychoanalytic categorization in which it is seen as marginal to the symbolic, or to a specific character or characterization in a film or other narrative. All these ways of understanding the feminine figure in this text. However, for the sake of simplicity, when an alignment can be made between the feminine and a character in a film or in a general script about moral America, it is this designation on which I rely most. For more on the feminine and feminine sexuality, see Lacan *et al.* (1982).

7   The script is dotted with romantic and military subplots, the most developed of which is the story of Doris "Dorie" Miller, an African-American sailor who shot down Japanese planes during the Pearl Harbor attack and who was posthumously awarded the Navy Cross for his heroism. Miller's story makes little impact on the film's overall narrative because his character never meets or is involved with any of the central characters.

8   Pearl Harbor functions in the American imaginary as a feminized figure, first as a former American colony turned state and functioning as a playground of pleasures for tourists, everyday Americans, and service people stationed at Pearl Harbor during WWII prior to its attack; and second, as the unlikely location of America's feminine homefront, which is how it is scripted in America's hegemonic imaginary. For a more nuanced reading of Pearl Harbor, see Ferguson and Turnbull (1999).

9   Ibid.

10  Evelyn's misidentification of Danny is only partial, however, for she always sees Danny as a symbolic son, even when he is her lover, which explains why she never burdens Danny with the knowledge of his pending fatherhood.

11  Hypermasculinity of an American enemy is always a complicated business, one that replies on racial and ethnic stereotypes and that simultaneously feminizes the enemy while it hypermasculinizes it. See Ling (2001).

12  Even if one queers the *Pearl Harbor* narrative, reading Rafe's and Danny's desire for one another mediated through Evelyn, the result is the same. For, ultimately, both Rafe and Danny conform to heterosexual codes of gender and sexuality, one as father and husband, the other as son.

13  The popular representations of these discourses has little to do with what they see themselves as standing for. Leftist discourses would claim to be not immoral but offering alternative moralities. Postmodern discourses claim to make room for moral choices by critiquing moral universals, thereby placing moral responsibility squarely back in the hands of everyday people. And the valuation of humor often has less to do with whether it is funny than with timing, as American comedian Bill Maher, the host of the US comedy show "Politically Incorrect," learned when he quipped about September 11, "We have been the cowards, lobbing cruise missiles from 2,000 miles away. That's cowardly. Staying in the airplane when it hits the building—say what you want about it, it's not cowardly" (comments made on the ABC television program "Politically Incorrect," September 16, 2001; see http://dailynews.yahoo.com/htx/nm/20011108/re/leisure_maher_dc_1.html).

14  For a general overview of September 11 in a critical context, see *Theory and Event* 5:4, and for a historical overview of the situation, see Halliday (2002).

15  At the time of this writing, there was no evidence that al Qaeda had any responsibility for the circulation of anthrax through the US postal service. Even so, my point is that the anthrax incidences, like al Qaeda's terrorist attacks, used America's own circulatory systems—the federal mail and US domestic air travel—against the US, rendering the question of where to find, much less strike, an enemy; a question that caused concern and confusion.

16  Comment made by Mark Duffield at the October 21, 2001, meeting of the Critical Practice Unit, POLIS, University of Leeds. Also see Der Derian (2001).

17  These reports circulated in the British press in late October 2001. By late November 2001, they were retracted when the missing fighters were spotted in Afghanistan.

18  It is possible to argue that Americans hold a positive view of the market, with the market functioning in an American imaginary not as morally neutral but as morally good. Though this may be how an American imaginary views the market itself, it is important to keep in mind that the moral goodness of the market as a whole is an effect of the moral neutrality of the market mechanism. Put differently, it is because the market mechanism is morally neutral that the market itself is good.

19  What this means is that even if the United States defeats the Taliban in Afghanistan (as it appeared to be doing at the time of this writing in November 2001) or captures and/or kills Osama bin Laden, it will not necessarily have achieved their goal of defeating and containing international terror.

# 3 Who we wish we'd never been

1 The potentially disruptive power of the feminine is suggested in a scene in which one of Lt. Col. Moore's children declares that she doesn't want to be a Catholic like her father but a Methodist like her mother. Moore puts this down to the troublesomeness of his wife, whereas his wife chides her husband that it is amazing he could think his child's stubbornness comes from anyone but himself.

2 This last point is problematic. Though the film claims to be a tribute to the North Vietnamese soldiers who died in the battle for the Ia Drang Valley as much as it is to the US soldiers who fought there, the film sends contradictory messages about how to view the North Vietnamese. In battle, they seem to swarm their US enemy so much so that they might be reduced to insects (see Palladino, 2004). Their humanity is reclaimed by letting them speak for themselves and by situating one North Vietnamese soldier in a personal context. And their intelligence is demonstrated by their thoughtful military manoeuvring that breaks through US lines and is beaten only when overwhelming US artillery support is called in. Even so, the Vietnamese are more consistently portrayed as lesser than their US counterparts. For example, Colonel Moore is always able to anticipate their next move on the battlefield, even if he doesn't always have the manpower to defeat it. And in the scene when Colonel Moore prays with Jack in the chapel, after asking for Jack's protection, he adds, "Oh, Lord, one more thing. About our enemies, ignore their heathen prayers and help us blow those little bastards straight to hell."

3 In this way, these films differ from another important post-9/11 film, *The Bourne Identity*, a film that is also very much about who we wish we'd never been. But its strategy for dealing with the trauma of who we were is first amnesia and then flight, not (as in these films) memorialization or haunting.

# 4 Who we really are (humanitarians)

1 *We Were Soldiers* is hardly the first piece to make this point about failing fathers or about failing US masculinity in general. See, for example, Jeffords (1989).

2 In *Rambo III*, John Rambo eventually gets himself caught up in a rescue mission in Afghanistan, fighting against the Soviets to rescue his old commander, Colonel Trautman.

3 For an alternative reading of Makhmalbaf's *Kandahar* as "a projection of the director's own desire to narrate a forgotten nation (back) into existence by refusing its unrepresentability", see Molloy (2002).

4 On the veil's function in Afghanistan in particular, see Khan (2001) and Rosenburg (2002). For a more general discussion of how the veil works to construct so-called Third World women, see Mohanty, 1991 and Spivak (1999). And on orientalism generally, see Said (1979).

5 And if US viewers find the nonheroic morality of the US doctor not to their liking, they can always dismiss him as an assassin, for Hassam Tantai, the African-American who plays the doctor, has been accused of being "a

Black Panther under indictment in the US for activities pursued thirty-one years ago" (Karten, 2001).

## 6 Who we might become

1  Thanks to Alana Chazon for this point.
2  First Lady Laura Bush explicitly drew a parallel between her husband and President Lincoln and their efforts to achieve both security and freedom when she addressed the 2004 Republican National Convention in New York City. Making a link to both the Civil War and to WWII, Mrs. Bush told delegates, "No American President ever wants to go to war. Abraham Lincoln didn't want to go to war, but he knew saving the Union required it. Franklin Roosevelt didn't want to go to war—but he knew defeating tyranny demanded it. And my husband didn't want to go to war, but he knew the safety and security of America and the world depended on it...And I was there when my husband had to decide. Once again, as in our parents' generation, America had to make the tough choices, the hard decisions, and lead the world toward greater security and freedom" (L. Bush, 2004).
3  The timing and implications of Spielberg's film seem to go against what the director intended, for as Jeremy Lott reported on June 17, 2002, "According to a recent Matt Drudge leak of a *New York Times* story, Spielberg has declared himself 'on the president's side' in Bush's efforts to 'root out those individuals who are a danger to our way of living'" (Lott, 2002).
4  Though Bradbury's *Fahrenheit 451* offers an insightful critique of the dangers of assuming that images speak for themselves, it of course neglects to fold this critique back onto Bradbury's privileging of words as pure sources of potential resistance. With this in mind, I raise Bradbury's critique of images *not* because I buy into his "words-over-images" hierarchy but for two different reasons. The first is that Bradbury's critique of how images might work to anti-intellectual effect is a powerful one. The second is that in raising Bradbury as his inspirational source about censorship, Moore forgets (censors?) this fundamental point raised by Bradbury, a point I will critically turn back onto Moore's *Fahrenheit 9/11*.
5  Many critics have pointed to Moore's own censorship of images and arguments. Consider, for example, Geoffrey O'Brian's comments, "This is a film about the September 11 attacks and the war on terror that omits any discussion of al-Qaeda and Islamist radicalism, while dramatically fudging its account of the Afghanistan war, and a film on the Iraq war that avoids any discussion of the nature of Saddam Hussein's regime...Iraqi life under Saddam Hussein is represented, in a sequence that seems almost a parody of the generic propaganda film, by a montage of happy wedding parties, bustling restaurants, a little boy flying a kite, a little girl going down a slide: all of it brutally interrupted by the American bombs. Moore seems reluctant to allow opposition to express any coherent argument, even if only to knock it down, just as in *Bowling for Columbine* the arguments for gun ownership rights were entrusted to an unprepared and visibly frail Charlton Heston and to the wild-eyed brother of Oklahoma

City bomber Terry Nicols" (2004). Or James Berardinelli's comments about Moore's use of Lila Lipscomb: "Maybe Moore had the good fortune to interview this particular woman while her son was still alive, so he could capture her radical shift of allegiance afterwards. But his past argues that he might not be playing things straight. Moore has a longstanding history of manipulating the truth, and we have no way of assessing whether any doctoring has been done with the Lipscomb interviews. With another filmmaker, such as Errol Morris [*The Fog of War*], we wouldn't question what's on screen. But Moore's reputation demands that we regard everything in his films with a healthy portion of skepticism" (2004). Also see Hitchens (2004) and Kermode (2004).

6 One might argue that all Moore's techniques are standard practice in filmmaking, even in the genre of documentary filmmaking. This is because film is always presented from a particular point of view, and as such is a commentary constructed through processes of selection and explication reliant on the editing of images, ideas, and sounds. In light of this, one might conclude that Moore's particular practices of editing images, ideas, and sounds to construct his strong authorial voice and his engaging film are worthy not of critique but of praise. Though there is much to praise in Moore's work (especially the political results of that work), I would not go so far as to excuse some of his filmmaking techniques on the basis that "all filmmakers—even documentary filmmakers—engage in these same practices." To do so would be to overlook a rich debate among documentary filmmakers themselves about what constitute acceptable ethical practices in filmmaking, a debate that has been raging about Moore's *Fahrenheit 9/11* since its release (see, for example, the documentary discussion list on the *Shooting People* website, www.shootingpeople.com from July 2004), not to mention Moore's earlier films, especially *Bowling for Columbine*. Furthermore, as I have already suggested, Moore's genre of filmmaking is less pure documentary than it is what I call *vigilante journalism*, a watchful reporting style that claims to exercise a superior brand of (real) justice thanks to the personal involvement of its witness(es). In this filmic genre, I would argue, ethical standards of filmmaking ought to be of the highest priority as this genre prides itself on its higher moral status *vis-à-vis* alternative forms of filmmaking. As such, it should not concern itself only with outcomes (the political ends of its storytelling) but also very much with the ethics of its storytelling itself (the means). This, I will go on to argue, is precisely where Moore's filmmaking falls short, especially when one analyzes how the feminine (Lila Lipscombe) is used as a means toward Moore's political ends.

7 These criticisms of Moore come from the character of his critiques, in which Moore seems to want things all ways. In *Fahrenheit 9/11*, for example, Moore objects to both the under-resourcing of US Homeland Security and the overly vigilant implementation of the US Patriot Act. Because of such inconsistencies in Moore's argument, audiences always get the impression that Moore is *against* something; they just don't necessarily know what the content of this opposition is. I would argue that Moore's dilemma of seeming to be against everything and nothing actually stems from his unabashed alliance with the character he constructs

in each of his films as the moral core of his arguments: the relatively downtrodden, usually working-class, often racialized moral American. By elevating the underdog to the position of the purveyor of absolute good, Moore anchors his narrative about moral America(ns) in this underappreciated character. However, because there are "good" and "bad" people in whatever class, race, gender, sexuality, you name it, doing both good and bad things all the time, Moore's moral anchor pulls him into the morally ambiguous deep waters of practical problems time and time again.

## 7 Conclusion

1 For a discussion of the US construction of a "victory culture" and its fracturing with the US dropping the bomb in Japan during World War II, see Englehardt (1995). And for a discussion of Englehardt's ideas in relation to September 11, see Weber (2003).

2 After initially claiming that the US war in Afghanistan was "the first truly just war since World War II" (Falk, 2001b), Richard Falk quickly revised this view, arguing that "With each passing day, my assessment shifts to reach the conclusion that the United States is waging an unjust war in Afghanistan..." (Falk, 2001c).

3 For a more general discussion of how inside-outside dichotomies function in international politics, see Walker (1993). Also see Shapiro (1997).

4 Clark elaborates about the stories they collected and their interviewees' searches for meaning. She writes, "These stories included expressions of wishes for world peace, a desire for increased humanitarianism and tolerance at home, and the search for personal fulfilment and meaning that included changes in relationships and patterns of living. As mentioned earlier, in sheer number these narratives dramatically exceeded the narratives of revenge that are so commonly reported on and that are used to suggest a national consensus" (2002: 576–7).

# Bibliography

Agathangelou, Anna M. and L.H.M. Ling (2004) "Power, borders, security, wealth: lessons of violence and desire from 11 September," *International Studies Quarterly* 43(3): 517–38.

Agnew, John (2003) *Geopolitics: Re-visioning World Politics*, 2nd edition. New York: Routledge.

Anthony, Andrew (2004) "Why Iraqi rebels are not freedom fighters," *The Guardian*, G4: 7, August 12.

Barthes, Roland (1974) *S/Z: An Essay*, translated by Richard Miller. New York: Hill and Wang.

Barthes, Roland (1976) *Sade, Fourier, Loyola*, translated by Richard Miller. New York: Hill and Wang.

Bentley, Tom and Ian Hargreaves (2001) "Introduction: The new ideology" in Tom Bentley and Daniel Stedman Jones (eds) *The Moral Universe*. London: Demos, pp. 5–16.

Berardinelli, James (2002a) *"Collateral Damage,"* February 8, http://movie-reviews.colossus.net/movies/c/collateral_damage.html

Berardinelli, James (2002b) *"Minority Report,"* June 21. http://movie-reviews.colossus.net/movies/m/minority_report.html

Berlant, Lauren (1991) *The Anatomy of National Fantasy: Hawthorne, Utopia And Everyday Life*. Chicago, IL: University of Chicago Press.

Berlant, Lauren (1997) *The Queen of America Goes to Washington City: Essays on Sex and Citizenship*. Durham, NC: Duke University Press.

Bhabha, Homi, ed. (1990) *Nation and Narration*. London: Routledge.

Bradshaw, Peter (2004) *The Guardian*, http://film.guardian.co.uk/print/0,3858, 4966304-3718,00.html, July 9.

Brockes, Emma (2004) "The lie that killed my son," *The Guardian*, http:// film. guardian.co.uk/print/0,3858,4965990-101730,00.html, July 8.

Bush, George W. (2001a) "Statement by the President in his address to the nation," http://www.whitehouse.gov/news/releases/2001/09/11-16.html, September 11.

Bush, George W. (2001b) "Address to a joint session of Congress and the American people," http://www.whitehouse.gov/news/releases/2001/09/ 20010920-8.html, September 20.

Bush, George W. (2002a) "President delivers State of the Union Address", http://www. whitehouse.gov/news/releases/2002/01/20020129-11.htlm, January 29.

Bush, George W. (2002b) "President Bush delivers graduate speech at West Point," http://www.whitehouse.gov/news/releases/2002/06/2002061-3.html, June 1.

Bush, George W. (2003) "President Bush addresses the nation," http://www.whitehouse.gov/news/release/2003/03/20030219-17.html, March 19.

Bush, Laura (2001) "Radio address by Mrs. Bush," http://www.whitehouse.gov/news/releases/2001/11/print/20011117.html, November 17.

Bush, Laura (2004) "Remarks by First Lady Laura Bush to the Republican National Convention," http://www.whitehouse.gov/news/releases/2004/08/print/20040831-15.html, August 31.

Caro, Mark (2002) "*Collateral Damage*," http://www.metromix.com, February 8.

Cassells, Manuel (1998) *The Rise of the Network Society*. Oxford: Blackwell.

Chazan, Alana (2003) "Reinventing Republican motherhood: The role of the family in the war on terror(ism). An analysis of David Fincher's *Panic Room*," unpublished essay.

Chomsky, Noam (1965) *Aspects of the Theory of Syntax*. Cambridge, MA: MIT Press.

Clark, Mary Marshall (2002) "The September 11, 2001, Oral History Narrative and Memory Project: A First Report," *The Journal of American History* September: 569–79.

Coontz, Stephanie (2000) *The Way We Never Were: American Families and the Nostalgia Trap*. New York: Basic Books.

Crepeau, Dick (2001) "Lost and found," http://www.poppolitics.com/articles/printerfriendly/2001-10-01-innocence.shtml.

Der Derian, James (2001) "9.11: Before, after, and in between," http://www.ssrc.org/sept11/essays/der_derian.htm.

Dick, Philip K. (2002) *Selected Stories*. New York: Pantheon.

Doherty, Thomas (2001) speaking on "Four Corners," BBC Radio 4, November 5.

Dubus, Andre (1996) *Selected Stories*. New York: Vintage.

Duffield, Mark (2001) *Global Governance and the New Wars*. London: Zed Books.

Ebert, Roger (2002) "*Collateral Damage*," *Chicago Sun-Times*, http://www.suntimes.com/output/ebert1/wkp-news-damage08f.html, February 8.

Ebert, Roger (2004) "Fahrenheit 9/11," *Chicago Sun-Times*, http://www.suntimes.com/cgi-bin/print.cgi, June 24.

Edelstein, David (2002a) "Blame Runner: *Minority Report* is a fabulous, witty totalitarian nightmare," http://slate.msn.com/toolbar.aspx?action=print&id=2067225, June 21.

Edelstein, David (2002b) "Before the Boondoggle: *We Were Soldiers* is a bloody, harrowing look at the early days of the Vietnam War," http://state.msn.com/toolbar.aspx?action=print&id=2062661, March 1.

Edelstein, David (2004) "Proper propaganda," *Slate*, http://slate.msn.com/toolbar.aspx?action=print&id=2102859, June 24.

Edemarian, Aida (2001) "The film Bush asked to see," *The Guardian*, October 26.

Edkins, Jenny (2001) "The absence of meaning: trauma and the events of September 11," http://www.watsoninstitute.org/infopeace/911/index.cfm?id=4#.

Edkins, Jenny (2003) *Trauma and the Memory of Politics*. Cambridge: Cambridge University Press.

Elshtain, Jeane Bethke (1995) *Woman and War*. Chicago, IL: University of Chicago Press.

Englehardt, Tom (1995) *The End of Victory Culture: Cold War America and the Disillusioning of a Generation*. New York: Basic Books.

Falk, Richard (2001a) "A just response," *The Nation*, http://www.thenation.com/doc.mhtml?i=20011008&s=falk, October 8.

Falk, Richard (2001b) "Defining a just war," *The Nation*, http://www.thenation.com/doc.mhtml?i=20011029&s=falk, October 29.

Falk, Richard (2001c) "Falk replies," *The Nation*, http://www.thenation.com/doc.mhtml?i=20011126&s=exchange, November 26.

Ferguson, Kathy and Phyllis Turnbull (1999) *Oh Say Can You See?*. Minneapolis, MN: University of Minnesota Press.

Fraser, Graham (2001) "Journalist's life quickly changed by *Kandahar*," http://www.thestar.ca, October 26.

French, Philip (2001) "An emotional journey through the shadow of the veil," *The Observer*, http://www.guardian.co.uk/review/story/0,,596435,00.html, November 18.

French, Philip (2002) "*About a Boy*," *The Observer*, http://film.guardian.co.uk/News_Story/Crier_Film_of_the_week/0,4267,640685,00.html, January 27.

Fuchs, Cynthia (2002) "*We Were Soldiers*," *PopMatters*, http://popmatters.com/film/reviews/w/we-were-soldiers.htm.

Fukuyama, Francis (1993) *The End of History and the Last Man*. New York: Perennial.

Gibson-Graham, J.K. (1998) "Queer(y)ing globalization," in H.J. Nast and S. Pile (eds) *Places Through the Body*. London: Routledge, pp. 23–4.

Gitlin, Todd (2004) "Michael Moore, alas," *Open Democracy*, July 1.

Griggers, Camilla (1997) *Becoming Woman*. Minneapolis, MN: University of Minnesota Press.

Grunwald, Michael (2002) "A tower of courage," *The Washington Post*, October 28.

Gubar, Susan (1985) " 'The blank page' and the issues of female creativity," in Elaine Showalter (ed.) *Feminist Literary Criticism*, New York: Pantheon, pp. 292–313.

Halliday, Fred (2002) *Two Hours that Shook the World*. London: Al Saqi.

Hardy, David T. and Jason Clarke (2004) *Michael Moore is a Big Fat Stupid White Man*. New York: Regan Books.

Hitchens, Christopher (2004) "Unfairenheit 9/11," *Slate,* http://slate.msn.com/toolbar.aspx?action=Print&id=2102723, June 21.

Hoberman, J. (2002) "Private eyes," *The Village Voice.* http://www. villagevoice. com/issues/0226/hoberman.php, June 20

Hoberman, J. (2004) "Eviction notice," *The Village Voice,* http://www. villagevoice.com/print/issues/0425/hoberman2.php, June 21.

Holden, Stephen (2001) "When grief becomes a member of the family," *The New York Times,* http://nytimes.com/gst/fullpage.html?res=9401EED 8143AF930A15752C1A9679C8B63, November 23.

Hunt, Lynn (1992) *The Family Romance of the French Revolution.* London: Routledge.

Huntington, Samuel P. (1998) *The Clash of Civilizations and the Remaking of World Order.* New York: Simon and Schuster.

Irigaray, Luce (1985) *Speculum of the Other Woman,* translated by Gillian C. Gill. Ithaca, NY: Cornell University Press.

Jeffords, Susan (1989) *The Remasculinization of America: Gender and the Vietnam War.* Bloomington, IN: Indiana University Press.

Karten, Harvey S. (2001) "Safar e Ghandehar," http://us.imdb.com/Reviews/303/30320, October 26.

Kelly, John D. (2003) "U.S. Power, after 9/11 and before it: If not an empire, then what?" *Public Culture* 15(2): 347–69.

Kermode, Mark (2004) "All blunderbuss and bile," *The Observer,* http://film.guardian.co.uk/News_Story/Critic_Review/Observer_Film_of_the_week/, July 11.

Khan, Shahnaz (2001) "Between here and there: feminist solidarity and Afghan women." *Genders 33,* http://www.genders.org/g33/g33_khan.html

Kuhn, Annette, ed. (1990) *Alien Zone: Cultural theory and contemporary science fiction cinema.* London: Verso.

Lacan, Jacques (1982) *Feminine Sexuality,* edited by Juliet Mitchell and Jacqueline Rose. London: Palgrave Macmillian.

Lacy, Mark (2003) "War, cinema, and moral anxiety," *Alternatives* 28: 611–36.

Lacy, Mark (2004) "War is Beautiful: Reflections on Popular Culture since 9/11," unpublished manuscript

Ling, L.H.M. (2001) *Postcolonial International Relations.* Basingstoke: Palgrave.

Lithwick, Dahlia (2002) "Hiding the dirty bomber from the US Constitution: The Bush administration establishes a Department of Precrime," http://slate.msn.com/toolbar.aspx? action=print&id=2066866, June 11.

Lodge, David (2002) "Why the academy fell for *In the Bedroom,*" http://books.guardian.co.uk/Print/0,3858,4364866,00.html, March 1.

Lott, Jeremy (2002) "Prophecy and paranoia," http://reason.com/hod/j1061702.shtml, June 17.

Lowenstein, Adam (2001) comments made on radio program "How do movies respond to social trauma?" *Odyssey* WBEZ Talk, Chicago, http://www.wbez.org/services/od-rasep01.htm, September 21.

Macnab, Geoffrey and Mohsen Makhmalbaf (2001) "The land without a face," *The Guardian* http://freeserve.filmsunlimited.co.uk/Print/0,3858,4236872, 00.html, August 11.

Makhmalbaf, Mohsen (2001) "Afghans are deserted, desolate and famished people," http://www.Screenindia.com.

McAlister, Melani (2001) *Epic Encounters: Culture, Media, and U.S. Interests in the Middle East, 1945–2000.* Berkeley, CA: University of California Press.

McClintock, Anne (1995) *Imperial Leather.* London: Routledge.

Michel, Sonya (1989) "American women and the discourse of the Democratic family in World War II," in Margaret Randolph Higonnet, Jane Jenson, Sonya Michel, and Margaret Collins Weitz (eds) *Behind The Lines: Gender and the Two World Wars.* New Haven, CT: Yale University Press, pp. 154–67.

Mirzoeff, Nicholas (1999) *An Introduction to Visual Culture.* London: Routledge.

Mitchell, Elvis (2002) "Fed up and going after the terrorist himself," *The New York Times*, http://www.nytimes.com/2002/02/08/movies/08COLL.html. pagewanted=print, February 8.

Mohanty, Chandra Talpade (1991) *"Under Western Eyes: Feminist scholarship and colonial discourses,"* in Chandra Talpade Mohanty, Ann Russo, and Lourdes Torres (eds) *Third World Women and the Politics of Feminism*, Bloomington, IN: Indiana University Press, pp. 51–80.

Molloy, Patricia (2002) "Redesigning women, refashioning the nation: Mohsen Makhmalbaf's *Kandahar* and Afghanistan as a 'nation without an image,'" unpublished manuscript under review at *Feminist Media Studies.*

Moore, Harold G. and Joseph L. Galloway (1992) *We Were Soldiers Once and Young.* New York: Random House.

Moore, Michael (2002) *Stupid White Men.* New York: Regan.

Moore, Michael (2003) *Dude, Where's my country?* New York: Warner Books.

Morrow, Lance (2001) "The case for rage and retribution," *Time*, September 11, no page number.

O'Brian, Geoffrey (2004) "Is it all just a dream?" *The New York Review of Books* vo. 51, no. 13, http://www.nybooks.com/articles/17315, August 12.

Onstad, Katrina (2001) "Afghan Exile Turned Reluctant Star," *The New York Times*, http://www.nytimes.com/2001/11/05/movies/05PAZI.html? pagewanted=print, November 5.

Palladino, Paulo (2004) "On the political animal and the return of 'just war'," under review at *Theory and Event.*

Puig, Claudia (2002) *"Collateral Damage* is damaged goods," http:// www.usatoday.com/li...2002-02-collateral-damage-review.htm, February 8.

Rosenberg, Emily S. (2002) "Rescuing women and children," *The Journal of American History*, September, pp. 456–65.

Roseneil, Sasha (2001) "A moment of moral remaking: the death of Diana, Princess of Wales," in Frank Webster, ed. *Culture and Politics in the Information Age: A New Politics?* London: Routledge, pp. 96–114.

Ryan, Michael and Douglas Kellner (1990) *Camera Politica: The Politics and Ideology of Contemporary Hollywood Film.* Bloomington, IN: Indiana University Press.

Said, Edward (1979) *Orientalism: Western Conceptions of the Orient*. New York: Vintage.

Sardar, Ziauddin and Merryl Wyn Davies (2002) *Why do People Hate America?* London: Icon.

Scott, A.O. (2004) "Unruly scorn leaves room for restraint, but not a lot," *The New York Times*, http://nytimes.com/search/article-printpage.html?res+9C0DE5DE1039F30A1..., June 23.

Shapiro, Michael J. (1997) *Violent Cartographies: Mapping Cultures of War*. Minneapolis, MN: University of Minnesota Press.

Singer, Peter (2004) *The President of Good and Evil: Taking George W. Bush Seriously*. London: Granta

Sommer, Doris (1991) *Foundational Fictions: The National Romance in Latin America*. Berkeley, CA: University of California Press.

Spivak, Gayatri Chakravorty (1999) *A Critique of Postcolonial Reason: Toward a History of the Vanishing Present*. Cambridge, MA: Harvard University Press.

Stewart, James B. (2002) "The real heroes are dead," *The New Yorker*, http://www.newyorker.com/printable/?fact/0201fa_FACT1, November 2.

Taylor, Charles (2002) "Modern social imaginaries," *Public Culture* 14 (Winter): 91–124.

Thomson, David (2002) "Their man in Saigon," *The Guardian*, G2, pp. 18–19, November 2.

Tin Man-5 (2001) "An insult and a travesty," http://us.imdb.com/CommentsShow?213149/20, September 11, 2001.

Tolkin, Michael (2001) "The movie I didn't know how to write," *New York Times*, wysiwyg://4/http://www.nytimes.com/2001/09/23/magazine/23tolkin.html, September 23.

Travers, Peter (2004) "Fahrenheit 9/11," *RollingStone*, http://www.rollingstone.com/reviews/movie?id=6184937&pageid=rs.ReviewsMovie, no date. Downloaded August 5, 2004.

US Department of State (2001) "Report on the Taliban's war against women," http://www.state.gov/g/drs/6185.htm, November 17.

Walker, R.B.J. (1993) *Inside/Outside: International Relations as Political Theory*. Cambridge: Cambridge University Press.

Waxman, Sharon (2004) "*Three Kings* director plans documentary on Iraq war," *New York Times*, http://www.nytimes.com/2004/08/16/movies/16warn.html?pagedwanted=print&position, August 16.

Weber, Cynthia (1999) *Faking It: US Hegemony in a "Post-Phallic" Era*. Minneapolis, MN: University of Minnesota Press.

Weber, Cynthia (2003) "Epilogue: Romantic mediations of September 11," in Francois Debrix and Cynthia Weber (eds) *Rituals of Mediation*. Minneapolis, MN: University of Minnesota Press, pp. 173–88.

Weber, Cynthia and Mark Lacy (2004) *Orange Alert*. Lancaster: Pato Productions (short film).

Weber, Cynthia (2005) *International Relations Theory: A Critical Introduction*, second edition. London: Routledge.

Wiener, Jon (2002) "*Quiet* in Hollywood," *The Nation*, http://www.thenation. com/doc.mhtml?i=20021216&s=wiener, December 16.

Wisdom Fund (2002) "Poll: Bush 'biggest threat to justice and peace'," http:// www.twf.org/News/Y2002/1109-Poll.html, November 9.

Woodward, Bob (2002) *Bush at War*. New York: Simon and Schuster.

Woodward, Bob (2004) *Plan of Attack*. New York: Simon and Schuster.

Wright, Elizabeth (1999) *Speaking Desires can be Dangerous*. Cambridge: Polity.

Yahoo Movies Box Office Charts (2004) http://movies.yahoo.com/boxoffice/ latest/rank.html.

Younge, Gary (2004) "Fahrenheit 9/11 sets US alight," *The Guardian*, http:// film.guardian.co.uk/print/0,3858,4956033-3156,00.html, June 25.

Zakaria, Fareed (2001) "The real world of foreign policy," *Newsweek*, October 8, p. 15.

Žižek, Slavoj (2002) *Welcome to the Desert of the Real*. London: Verso.

# Index